Minority Education and Ethnic Survival:
Case Study of a German School in Denmark

Multilingual Matters

1. "Bilingualism: Basic Principles"
   HUGO BAETENS BEARDSMORE
2. "Evaluating Bilingual Education: A Canadian Case Study"
   MERRILL SWAIN AND SHARON LAPKIN
3. "Bilingual Children: Guidance for the Family"
   GEORGE SAUNDERS
4. "Language Attitudes Among Arabic-French Bilinguals in Morocco"
   ABDÊLÂLI BENTAHILA
5. "Conflict and Language Planning in Quebec"
   RICHARD Y. BOURHIS (ed.)
6. "Bilingualism and Special Education"
   JIM CUMMINS
7. "Bilingualism or Not: The Education of Minorities"
   TOVE SKUTNABB-KANGAS
8. "An Ethnographic/Sociolinguistic Approach to Language Proficiency Assessment"
   CHARLENE RIVERA (ed.)
9. "Communicative Competence Approaches to Language Proficiency Assessment:
   Research and Application"
   CHARLENE RIVERA (ed.)
10. "Language Proficiency and Academic Achievement"
    CHARLENE RIVERA (ed.)
11. "Pluralism: Cultural Maintenance and Evolution"
    BRIAN BULLIVANT
12. "Placement Procedures in Bilingual Education: Education and Policy Issues"
    CHARLENE RIVERA (ed.)
13. "The Education of Linguistic and Cultural Minorities in the OECD Countries"
    STACY CHURCHILL
14. "Learner Language and Language Learning"
    CLAUS FAERCH, KIRSTEN HAASTRUP AND ROBERT PHILLIPSON
15. "Bilingual and Multicultural Education: Canadian Perspectives"
    STAN SHAPSON AND VINCENT D'OYLEY (eds.)
16. "Multiculturalism: The Changing Paradigm"
    LOIS FOSTER AND DAVID STOCKLEY
17. "Language Acquisition of a Bilingual Child"
    ALVINO FANTINI
18. "Modelling and Assessing Second Language Acquisition"
    KENNETH HYLTENSTAM AND MANFRED PIENEMANN (eds.)
19. "Aspects of Bilingualism in Wales"
    COLIN BAKER
20. "Minority Education and Ethnic Survival"
    MICHAEL BYRAM
21. "Family Immersion"
    MARRIANNE CELCE-MURCIA
22. "Age in Second Language Acquisition"
    BIRGIT HARLEY
23. "Pluralism and Schooling in Canada"
    JOHN R. MALLEA
24. "Language in a Black Community"
    VIV EDWARDS

Please contact us for the latest information on recent and forthcoming books in the series.

**Derrick Sharp, General Editor, Multilingual Matters,
Bank House, 8a Hill Road, Clevedon, Avon BS21 7HH, England.**

MULTILINGUAL MATTERS 20

Minority Education and Ethnic Survival: Case Study of a German School in Denmark

Michael S. Byram

MULTILINGUAL MATTERS LTD

British Library Cataloguing in Publication Data

Byram, Michael
  Minority education and ethnic survival :
  case study of a German school in Denmark.—
  (Multilingual matters; 20)
  1. Minorities—Education—Denmark—Case studies
  I. Title   II. Series
  371.97   LC3736.D4

ISBN 0-905028-55-4
ISBN 0-905028-54-6 Pbk

Multilingual Matters Ltd,
Bank House, 8a Hill Road,
Clevedon, Avon BS21 7HH
England.

Typeset by Photo Graphics, Honiton, Devon.
Printed and bound in Great Britain
by Colourways Press Ltd, Clevedon BS21 6RR.

For Marie Thérèse, Alice, Ian

Contents

PREFACE ix

INTRODUCTION xi

1 NORDSCHLESWIG AND THE GERMAN MINORITY 1

   A farming family 1

   Others in the minority 7

   Three generations of history 10

   A little geography 13

   The "official" minority 14

2 THE MINORITY'S SCHOOL SYSTEM 21

   The relationship to Denmark and Germany 21

   Reconciling the differences 27

3 DESCRIPTION OF A SCHOOL 29

   Introduction 29

   Tinglev/Tingleff 30

   Die deutsche Schule Tingleff 32

   Pupils – where they come from and go to 34

   Teachers 43

   "A day in the life of . . ." 45

   "Unsere Schule ist eine deutsche Schule . . ." 48

4 "LANGUAGE AND CULTURE" IN THE SCHOOL 66

   Spoken language: Pupils 66

   Spoken language: Teachers 71

   Written language 72

   The language component in the subjects German and Danish 73

The literature component in the subjects Danish and German 77
The school as a mediator of Danish and German culture 80
Pupils' perception of their language 82

5 ON LEAVING SCHOOL 89
   Introduction 89
   The former pupils 89
   Pupils in the 10 Klasse – before leaving school 94
   Post-school experience 103

6 "LANGUAGE AND CULTURE" IN THE MINORITY 112
   The "basis" of the minority 112
   Concepts of culture 113
   Culture and language policy 117
   A sociolinguistic view 120
   Policies in Minority school and society 128

7 ETHNICITY, LANGUAGE AND SCHOOLING 132
   Membership of the Minority 132
   The Minority as an ethnic group 138
   Language as a symbol of ethnicity 149
   The school and ethnic identity 154
   Bilingualism and biculturalism 158
   Conclusion 161

   APPENDICES 164
   BIBLIOGRAPHY 187
   INDEX 191

   ILLUSTRATIONS .... facing pages 16 & 48

Preface

A book like this comes to fruition only in a propitious environment. There are many facets, academic, social, financial, and many debts.

The study could not have even begun without the co-operation of school and education authorities in the German minority. Schulrat Peter J. Sönnichsen and Realschuldirektor Harald Kracht have always done their best to smoothe the way, even when they did not know in detail what my needs and intentions were. The school's teachers and pupils always gave freely of their time and patience too. What began as a working relationship became friendship and it is due to my friends in the Deutsche Schule Tingleff that my and my family's stay in Denmark was not only intellectually rewarding but also a pleasant and memorable experience. I would like to thank them here on behalf of all of us.

Of all the pupils I came into contact with my largest debt is of course to those in the tenth class. They are the ones who helped me most towards an interpretation which I hope they recognize. Yet there are many others — pupils, parents, teachers, they cannot all be named — who talked to me freely and at length. Though they remain anonymous, my thanks to them are nonetheless heartfelt.

My academic debts are first to the teachers who read my manuscript, but also to colleagues in the Department of Anthropology of the University of Durham. A special thanks must go to Bent Søndergaard of the Pädagogische Hochschule Flensburg and Karen Margrethe Pedersen of the Institut for Grænseregionsforskning Aabenraa both of whom read and commented in detail on my manuscript at various stages. Many of their suggestions have been incorporated and I am grateful for their friendship as well as their help.

To type a manuscript with a mixture of languages is not easy and I am grateful to a number of typists but especially to Frau Ch. Köhler, Flensburg and Ms K. Gordon, Durham for their efficiency. Petra Pfisterer and Waltraud Coles improved my German summary, for which I thank them. I would also like to thank the staff of the Dansk Centralbibliotek for Sydslesvig in Flensburg, who packed and sent me many books. The research was made possible by financial support from the Nuffield Foundation, London and from the Ministry of Education, Copenhagen.

It has become customary for authors to comment on their use of third person pronouns. I have decided to use he/him for simplicity's sake and also as a means of protecting informants' anonymity. The school might appear to be an all male establishment. It is not, of course, but the sex of informants has no bearing on their views.

Need it be said that the final responsibility for the following pages is entirely mine?

Michael Byram
University of Durham, 1984

Introduction

Few people in Germany are aware of the existence of a German minority in Denmark, despite a general political consciousness that European history in the twentieth century has created and been influenced by German-speaking minorities beyond the border of present-day West or East Germany. For an Englishman brought up in a country which, at that time, perceived itself as monolingual and monocultural, chance acquaintance with the border area between Germany and Denmark was a fascinating experience — all the more so because of the lack of general awareness amongst the Germans themselves.

In the area to the north of the German-Danish frontier, known in Danish as Sønderjylland and in German as Nordschleswig, there live some 20,000 members of the German minority. The names of the area, the number of members and even the adjective "German" are concepts whose contentious nature will become clear in the following pages. For the superficial observer who might easily come across statements to the effect that the legal and educational position of the German minority might serve as a model for other European minorities, the situation in Nordschleswig is non-problematic. Indeed, in contrast with the Catalans, the Basques, the Sami or the many other groups in Europe who in some cases are fighting openly and in other cases have suffered in silence, the position in Sønderjylland/Nordschleswig seems very favourable.

At this point it is important to note that south of the border, in the area known in German as the Landesteil Schleswig and in Danish as Sydslesvig there is a Danish minority. For the purposes of negotiations between Denmark and the Federal Republic of Germany, the existence of in some respects comparable minorities is a crucial factor. Although care is taken by the governments to make clear that treatment of one minority is not dependent on reciprocal treatment of the other, it is nonetheless a political reality that arrangements for the two minorities are linked. Therefore the Danish minority in Germany, whose existence is a result of

the same historical events which created the German minority, is undeni-
ably a factor in the contemporary affairs of the Germany minority.
However, it would be wrong to see the minorities as mirror-images of each
other and the following pages will be concerned only with the German
minority.

The purpose of the following pages is above all to describe the
German minority as I saw and experienced it during six months' fieldwork,
preceded by visits over more than a decade. There already exist several
descriptions of the minority, some written by its members (Henningsen,
n.d.; Kardel, 1971), others written by academic outsiders (Svalastoga &
Wolf, 1963; Sievers, 1975; Salomon, 1980; Zeh, 1982; Elklit & Tønsgaard,
1979). The pesonal experience of the first is lacking in the statistics and
"objectivity" of the second — Svalastoga & Wolf (1963) is an exception —
and this is not untypical of the vast and growing literature on European and
American minorities, be they "ethnic", "linguistic", "immigrant" or whatever. In my attempt to close the gap, I do not claim to provide a complete
description, nor do I claim to be "subjective" or "objective". My intention
is to provide some insight into the life and existence of the minority. I hope
that insight will be of interest in itself, for every minority is of course
unique, and yet also of generalizable interest because this minority has
already acquired a position which others might wish to use as a model, (cf.
Krejci & Velimsky, 1981).

One aspect of that position will be at the focal point of the study: the
school. Although at first sight the minority is "German" because of the
language and culture it possesses, more careful observation suggests that
the existence of the minority depends on its schools. This aspect too has its
specific and general interest. The schools are the result of their unique
situation in the historical and geographic development of the area (Brandt,
1975; Rerup, 1982), but a cursory glance at the position of other minorities
will reveal that the issue of the education of their children is crucial, and
understood as such both by minority members and by external observers
and researchers. Here again the comparatively favourable position of the
German schools in Sønderjylland/Nordschleswig might be taken as a
model for other minorities and some insight into the reality of the schools
will be of general interest.

The school in Nordschleswig is perceived as the most influential force
in the socialization of the individual as a member of the minority. The
school pupil lives his membership of the minority in his daily life more
vividly than anyone else — with the possible exceptions of his teachers and
a small number of other officials employed by the minority. In this way,

school life is the area of experience where being a member of the minority is so natural as to pass almost unnoticed. Through attendance at a German school, the pupils' minority membership is the dominant influence in their life, and activities which link them to the majority society are deviations from the normative influence, although the majority society's influence is not insubstantial. On the other hand, the adult members of the minority live much more within the majority society and it is their membership of the minority which creates deviations from the normal course of daily life. In very rough and unrefined terms, then, the life of school pupils is the reverse of the life of their parents.

In one particular respect, this reversal is very obvious: in formal situations the language of school life is German whereas the language of adult life is Danish. At school the pupil speaks "German", at home and at work the adult speaks "Danish". At some period there is transition from the norms of school life to the norms of adult life. At all points in people's lives the existence of the contrast between norms and deviations of this kind make them conscious of the influences on their daily life, and the use of two languages is the factor of which they are particularly aware. Yet the degree of awareness is complicated by the fact that children's social awareness is developing as part of the process of education and cannot be compared with the awareness of the adult. Therefore there is one period when the individual is likely to experience the norms and deviations most consciously: during the period of transition from compulsory school to post-school life, whether at work or in further education. This is also the period when the young person's social awareness is comparable with the adult's. Again language maintenance or shift is a very obvious issue in this period of transition.

It is on the basis of these considerations that part of my study is devoted to a description of the transition period. Like the rest of the study, the description is founded on observations, discussions, interviews, documents and whatever else might provide insight. The difficulty of capturing the situation as described above will be obvious. This is all the more the case because the above sketch is a much simplified version. The simplification is both in the terminology — for example in saying people speak "German" or "Danish" — and in the divisions into life periods. Furthermore the experience of any individual is unique and there are exceptions to every generalization.

The following pages contain seven chapters. The first chapter is a description of what being a member of the minority involves. It is an introduction to the whole minority but concentrates on the people and area which are traditionally considered to be the heart of the minority (*die Hochburg des Deutschtums*) and where the school at the focus of the study is situated. It will become clear in the first chapter that the minority's schools are a *sine qua non* for its existence and the second and third chapters describe the schools, first the web of institutions and beliefs within which they function and second as one school is experienced by its pupils. The fourth chapter isolates the one factor in the school which pupils are most conscious of: the use of German and Danish.

The fifth chapter concentrates on the transition period and tries to capture the experience of a small group of young people as they emerge from compulsory schooling and, in some cases, take their first steps into majority social institutions.

Chapter 6 widens the sphere of interest to a discussion of "Language and Culture" — a key phrase in the life of the minority — as it is realized in the minority as a whole. This chapter puts the preceding description of the school system into a fuller context.

The final chapter reviews and summarizes key issues which have arisen in preceding pages. I comment here on the identity of the minority and on the interplay between ethnic identity, school and language policy. The relationship with the majority language and culture is also discussed as the final context within which the minority has to be understood.

————

It will be evident from the following pages that, not unlike many other minority situations, there are considerable emotional forces at work in the relationships between majority and minority. The situation is now much improved in comparison to earlier decades, but there is a latent antagonism which occasionally surfaces, even though at an official, governmental level the problems of the past have been largely resolved. An outsider, such as I, who has the privilege of working in the minority, has in such an emotion-laden situation a peculiar position. On the one hand my work acquired recognition for its impartiality and was accepted because I had worked with people over a considerable period. This is a very pleasant experience and I am grateful that the pupils and teachers with whom I have worked have been prepared to accept and give consideration to my work, even where it has suggested weaknesses.

On the other hand, there are those within and outside the minority who might seize on the weaknesses revealed by an outsider, or read into my text support for their own point of view, for their own criticisms and antagonism. Such people will be misusing my text and will have misunderstood the spirit in which it is written. I am acutely aware that, for example, my discussion of the curriculum might be used against the school system or my comments on language use in the school turned against its pupils and teachers. My text is potentially a political document as well as an academic research report. There is nothing new in that. Yet there is little point in attempting to reduce the potential danger by referring to the school anonymously. For those for whom it matters the school would be all too easily recognizable, whatever attempt at anonymity were made.

I consider it very important therefore to record my position. I have dealt with only one aspect of the school's life, and even though it is a significant one the impact of the total ethos of the school is more important than its separate parts. The fact that I had free access to all lessons, that I was welcomed as a colleague by teachers and as a teacher by pupils is more significant than any carping criticisms which may be read into my text by others. The openness and self-awareness of teachers and pupils which dominated my experience of the school should set the tone for the reader who peruses the pages which follow.

There are no more serious and certainly no better informed critics of the minority and its schools than the minority itself. They have welcomed outsiders and listened to their comments but are rightly apprehensive about dogmatic criticism from the majority. If my study is helpful, I shall be pleased, but in the final analysis it is the members of the minority who must make changes, if there are to be any.

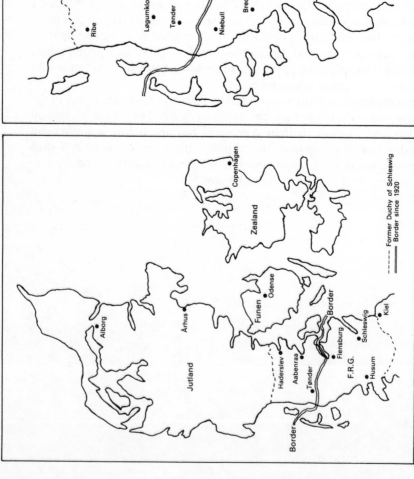

MAP 1 The Border Area in Relation to the Rest of MAP 2 The Danish–German Border Area
Denmark

1 Nordschleswig and the German Minority

A farming family

Imagine a long, wide, flat landscape with straight, lonely roads. On the horizon, a short distance away in this flat perspective, there are clumps of trees and smaller and larger woods. Some of those trees hide hamlets of two or three farms, which are reached down narrow roads, winding as they become less important. The long, straight main roads pass often in a curve through the villages to which those hamlets belong, designated as, for example, Uge Mark (Uge Field) or Vester Højst (Western Højst) to show their relationship to the villages Uge or Øster Højst.

At first sight, there is nothing to distinguish one of those farms from the others in a hamlet. Indeed the inhabitants themselves do not notice any differences in the material surroundings and equipment from one home to another. They have the same style of furniture, wear the same kind of clothes, eat the same kinds of food. There may be a flag-pole for the Dannebrog (Danish flag) in the garden of one house. There may be a copy of the German-language newspaper *Der Nordschleswiger* in another. The television is less often tuned to one of the German stations in the first and scarcely ever tuned to the Danish station in the second. The second will definitely not have a flag-pole, but otherwise there is nothing inevitable or decisive in these characteristics; it is a matter of degree.

Yet one of those families belongs to the German minority and the others do not. They are like their Danish neighbours not only in the details of daily life, but also in their relationship to the land they own, to the socio-economic conditions in which they have to earn a living and in their sense of belonging where they are because the farm has been in the family for generations. Their historical justifications for belonging where they are and their contemporary political convictions as an outcome of their version of history will differ markedly from those of their neighbours. However, they will hardly ever discuss these issues, for as a mark of difference they

1

are considered — due to events of German history during and after two world wars — to be too provocative and liable to upset the good day-to-day relations between neighbours. The parents of this family were young in the years "after 1945" and have lasting memories of ill-treatment by the Danish authorities and by their fellow-villagers. Even today they are likely to interpret any slight or social snub as resulting from their minority identity, but this may be as much a result of their heightened sensitivity as of any intention on the part of "a Dane". Here we have one of the markers of difference expressed in the language. The members of the family will speak of themselves as "Deutsche" (Germans) in contrast to "die Dänen" (the Danes) even though they all possess Danish citizenship, and have no desire to have citizenship of the Federal Republic of Germany. Yet when they expand the designation "Deutsche", the difference between generations becomes apparent. For the grandfather, who went to school before 1920 when the area was part of the German empire, "Deutsch" means "belonging to Germany", in particular Schleswig-Holstein and a sense of being an exile from his country. For, although he could have opted to go to Germany instead of accepting Danish citizenship in 1920, his ties with the land were too important to make this a genuine choice.

For his daughter, "Deutsch" means almost the same, tempered by a realistic knowledge that she will never in fact belong to Germany. For his son-in-law "Deutsch" means being "a Dane who speaks German", even though he seldom does. For one of the grandchildren, "Deutsch" means "belonging to Nordschleswig", feeling at home there with his Danish neighbours, belonging to a German hand-ball club but also a Danish shooting club — because there is no German one nearby — and attending a German school. For another grandchild the whole issue is without interest; she is tired of being different and feels much happier as a Dane, although this too has a special meaning, as it does for her neighbours. For "being a Dane" is really "being a Sønderjyde", belonging to this area and speaking the dialect which people from other parts of Denmark scarcely understand. However, she too attended the German school until she was seventeen, before going to a Danish vocational school to start her career as a shop-assistant.

These nuances of marking the boundary between minority and majority are, however, largely internal to the minority. They are accompanied by a sensitivity to other people's language. Although all three families speak Sønderjysk — a Danish dialect which has borrowed widely from Low German — the Germans feel that their dialect is influenced by their knowledge and use of German. They hear, when they meet someone for the first time, that he is German because he uses more German words; that

is sometimes because he then corrects those words with a Danish expression and sometimes because there is a higher proportion of "German"
words in his language. This perception may be a result of the fact that the
speaker has less standard Danish influence in his language and uses a purer
form of Sønderjysk, where the relationship to German is particularly
evident. It may also be a result of the speaker's attending a German school
and being accustomed to mixing and code-switching between the two
languages. Whatever the causes, this perception when reinforced by other
indications, is one way in which members of the minority know each other
and may more or less consciously and deliberately differentiate themselves
from the Danes around them.

The strongest reinforcing indicator would be the knowledge that the
other went to a German school.[1] The frequency with which people of any
European society talk about their school life in ordinary conversation is
perhaps higher in this area, where it is known to be so crucial. The
exchange of school stories and experiences can be the basis for further
friendship due to the sense of sharing an identity partially created by
school. Thus in the early morning, when the children from our three farms
leave home, some of them get on the regular school bus which takes them
to the school in a larger village or to the main town of the municipality in
which they live. The child from the Germany family has to get up earlier
and wait for the private bus which will take him in the opposite direction,
across the municipal boundary, to the German school. Doing this every
morning, he is declaring in the most public and frequent fashion for all his
family, that they are German. This may, however, be a misinterpretation
of the facts, particularly in more recent times, and if the family is young.
The fact that the children go to the German school may indicate that in a
"mixed marriage" one of the partners has persuaded the other. People
believe that the mother will usually insist on her children going to the same
kind of school as she did, but this perception is not always justified by the
facts; the father may have made his intentions clear on this point before the
marriage and the mother was aware that she was marrying into a German
farm.

For the child of school age, German is part of everyday life. He went
to the German Kindergarten in the village two kilometres away, from the
age of three. Until that age he spoke only the dialect Sønderjysk, because
that is the language of the home. At Christmas, he learnt a few German
songs and sometimes there was a visit from a distant relative from
Germany. Then his parents and older sister would speak German, but he
would already be used to hearing the language because he regularly
watched German television programmes for children. Indeed, before he

went to bed he would see his father switch to Danish television only at 7.30 in the evening, to watch the news — especially if the government was debating agricultural matters at the moment — and then switch back at 8.00 p.m. to watch the German version of the news.

When he started Kindergarten, therefore, it was no surprise that the teacher spoke German to him, although sometimes she had to explain things in Sønderjysk too. In his village there were two Kindergärten, a German one and a Danish one. Yet his friends from the Danish farms in the hamlet did not all go to the Danish Kindergarten. One went with him to the German one, because there were more places than in the hard-pressed Danish Kindergarten, and furthermore it did not cost as much. So they both began to speak as well as hear German. His friend had often watched German television at home too, and after a few months the teacher was able to speak to them entirely in German. When they reached school age, however, their ways parted, one going on to the German school, the other to the Danish school. For the first five years, however, they went into the same village, where there are two schools. The most striking difference between them is that the German school has far fewer pupils, in some years less than ten, but with an average of about thirteen. This means much closer contact with the teacher, but it also means that pupils of different ages are taught by the one teacher in the same classroom, and that a child might be the only one in his or her year-group.

When the boy started school it was a further step into the minority community and it also brought his father back into contact with the school system which he himself attended, in the difficult years after the war. (In this, he was exceptional, as there were few German schools at the time.) It was natural that he should be drawn into membership of the school's steering committee, which the school needs, as a private, self-owning institution, to decide as much on financial matters as on educational and pedagogical issues. Thus together with other parents he really feels that the school belongs to the small German community in the village, that it serves as a focal point for the dozen or so families spread throughout the village and its hamlets not only because of the schoolwork which goes on during the day but also as a meeting place for other events. There are one or two evening classes in the winter months held there, and when there is a local meeting of the minority's general organization, "der Bund deutscher Nordschleswiger", it is in the school. In some villages there is a community building for the Germans and another for the Danes, but here the school serves as a community centre. So the threat which appears from time to time to close the school, because of the small number of pupils, is more than a threat to the education of the children; it endangers the community life of the minority.

After five years, it was time to move on to another school, slightly larger, in the next village. The boy spent only one year there before spending the last three years in one of the five German town schools in Sønderjylland/Nordschleswig, which have classes and facilities up to school-leaving age. Here for the first time he came in contact with large numbers of pupils, up to 200. But even this does not compare with the experience of his Danish friend, who by now is in a school with more than 500 pupils. They sometimes talk of their different experiences at school, for although the German children living in the town can spend all their time among friends from the same school, in the village there are more mixed friendships, and the two children have never lost contact with each other. The main difference which the German boy hears in his friend's talk of school is that the teacher-pupil relationship seems to be less formal; the Danish pupils say "du" to their teachers — standard practice in Danish these days but in stark contrast with the formal German "Sie" — and often call them by their first names. This is not unknown in the German schools, but is very much the exception.

When the boy leaves school, after ten years, one more than the compulsory nine which his Danish friend did — in this they are representative of the trends in their two schools[2] — he will probably work on a farm in another village for a few months before doing a basic vocational agricultural course in the winter months. He will most probably do this course in the one German "Continuation School", whereas most of his contemporaries from the German school will begin their vocational training in one of the standard Danish schools. A few of them will go on to the German Gymnasium, which represents the pinnacle of German education in Sønderjylland/Nordschleswig. After that, they will have to choose between Higher Education in Denmark or in the Federal Republic.

Thus as long as he goes to school, the child is in daily contact with one of the most central institutions of the minority. This is in striking contrast with his parents, whose daily life is much less involved with minority institutions and who may give little thought in their daily routine to the differences which mark the boundaries between minority and majority. Apart from watching German television, there is, however, one more direct link to the minority institutions: they read *Der Nordschleswiger*, their German-language newspaper, where there is coverage of F.R.G. news, major news at regional and national level in Denmark, and a large section devoted to Sønderjylland/Nordschleswig from the minority viewpoint. Here they can read the newspaper's editorial which offers comment on national and international events, but just as often takes up issues relating to the well-being of the minority. They can keep in touch with cultural and political events in the minority as a whole, often reading the complete texts of speeches made at various meetings. Finally they will find a section devoted to their own area within Sønderjylland/Nordschleswig, with local news covering both general, Danish, events — be they on the industrial or agricultural front, or in the world of sport — and the particular news of members of the minority in their area. They often read the regional Danish paper too, sharing the expense of two newspapers with the grandparents. In this way it is possible to keep in contact with the core of events and people which maintain a sense of activity and life in the minority, even if they scarcely ever take part in the meetings, lectures, musical evenings and so on which usually happen 20 or 30 kilometres away. For one of the problems of belonging to the minority is that except in a few villages and small towns where there is a relatively high concentration, its members are spread over a wide area. Though they know many people by sight and even by name, individuals frequently meet only a small number of fellow-members in their local area.

In other respects the parents of our farming family are engaged only infrequently in activities which are peculiar to the minority. The father goes to the school committee meetings three or four times a year. His wife is still in the steering committee for the Kindergarten from the time when her children attended, and also has a few meetings. Recently the father had a telephone call to ask him if he was willing to be elected to a committee of the "Bund deutscher Nordschleswiger" and, out of a sense of duty, he agreed. He has been a member of the organization almost all his life, indirectly through his sports club when a boy and then directly through a modest yearly subscription. However, he has had little to do with the organization in recent years. He occasionally goes to the local group's meetings or the social evenings they organize and he usually votes in the regional elections for the candidate put up by the German party, which is an off-shoot of the organization. He is also a member of the agricultural society, whose consultants he sometimes calls in and whose organized visits to other farms in Germany and Denmark are part of his professional and social calendar in the summer months. Thus there are some weeks in the year when mother and father have several contacts with the social institutions of the minority, sometimes bringing them in contact with familiar faces and old acquaintances. On these occasions, there is a sense of belonging, of mutual support, of the security from being among like-minded people and of sharing a common identity, of being "Deutsch" — even if individuals would understand that identity in widely differing ways. Yet at other periods of the year they have no such contact, and simply meet a few German friends in their village.

As for the grandparents, who are now retired, the picture is slightly different. They make more effort to go to the functions — the lectures, the occasional operetta of a company touring from Germany, a school play — even if this means a car journey. They go partly from a sense of duty, a feeling they have to support the functions all the more as the numbers in the minority gradually fall.[3] There are few of their generation left, those who have experienced all the minority's ups and downs since the separation in 1920. They sometimes join the excursions for retired people organized by the Social Service of the minority. On the whole they are resigned to the fact that the minority has changed in character in recent decades, perhaps due to the greater mutual tolerance of majority and minority. The grandfather is not happy with this and hopes the minority will continue to flourish even if there is a different character. The grandmother tends to be more pleased that the general atmosphere of tolerance has replaced the bitterness she can remember from years ago.

Others in the minority

The above account of a farming family somewhere in Sønderjylland/ Nordschleswig is not intended to be "typical". The family does not exist, but is rather a construction from a number of sources. My intention is to offer some insight into the structure of the minority as a particular family might experience it. However, this kind of family is only one among the many which form the minority. There are combinations of experience, opinion and participation which are unique to individuals and to families. There are also many kinds of individuals and families, in socio-economic terms, apart from the farming community. However, the farming family is a good point of departure because its sense of tradition and its professional immobility were fundamental forces in the maintenance of a German minority after the referendum of 1920: farmers felt that they had to assert their minority identity in order to keep ownership of the land[4], and for other people too the sense of pressure on them created a need to resist. One of the sayings in the minority sums this up: "Druck zeugt Gegendruck, tryk avler modtryk" (*Pressure creates counter-pressure*).

The minority also includes, however, people living in the towns, working as employees in trades and light industry, being shop-keepers, owners of small industries and companies, working as teachers and other officials within the minority's institutions and so on. In a survey of the parents of children in minority schools, Weigand (1966) found 38.2% farmers, 33.4% wage-earners, 4% minority officials, 2.4% retired and 22% in self-employed or liberal professions. Toft (1982: 13–16) compares two unpublished surveys from 1961 and 1978, similarly based on questionnaires to school-children:

Socio-economic groups	1961	1978
Landwirte (farmers)	35.9	27.6
Selbstständige Handwerker (self-employed artisans)	10.2	17.0
Fach- und Spezialarbeiter (skilled and semi-skilled workers)	24.9	13.5
Selbstständige (Handel u. Dienstleistungen) (self-employed – commerce and services)	9.3	7.0
Akademiker, Pädagogen u.a.. (academics, teachers et al.)	7.6	14.8
Angestellte (unskilled workers)	8.2	11.6
Rentner (retired)	3.4	1.9
Sonstige (others)	0.5	6.6
	100	100
	N = 977 couples	N = 1150 couples

It is, however, difficult to know who belongs to the minority and who does not. There are two reasons for this. First, the agreements between Denmark and Germany protecting the minorities north and south of the border define membership according to the individual's own assertion that he is a member, rather than on "objective" grounds. This is made all the more intangible by the prohibition which prevents any official requiring an individual to state whether he is a member or not. It is thus possible for there to be degrees of membership of a more or less public nature. The family described above are relatively highly committed and openly adherent members. Some members would be even more so, having as many of their cultural and socio-economic contacts within the minority as their life in a Danish state permits. The paradigm case could be a teacher family, who may not even have Danish citizenship but are more or less permanent immigrants, with professional ties still with the West German education system. On the other hand, there are people who are not even passive members of the "Bund deutscher Nordschleswiger", may have apparently given up their ties with the minority's organizations and functions, but still vote for the German candidate through the secrecy of the ballot box. Whether this can be properly called membership of a minority and how theoretical accounts of minorities would categorize the German minority with such diverse membership are questions which will be left for later chapters.

Because of these extremes of membership, because of the geographical spread and isolation of the members and because of the officially subjective nature of the identity and membership, it is difficult to describe the minority as a whole. There are undoubtedly objective behavioural traits which many, if not all, of the minority members share even though there is no single distinctive feature (Svalastoga & Wolf, 1963:63). However, only a small number of members embody all the traits, most share only some of them. Briefly a list of such traits, some of which were introduced in the opening description, includes:

- ability to speak German
- attendance at a minority school
- membership of the "Bund deutscher Nordschleswiger"
- membership of sub-organizations of the BdN, and possibly of their committees
- support of the functions organized by the BdN and its off-shoots
- voting for the German candidate in local, regional and, until recently, national elections
- reading *Der Nordschleswiger*
- watching almost exclusively West German television and listening to West German radio
- visiting West Germany under the aegis of organizations from the BdN.

No one of these behavioural traits is a *sine qua non* of membership of the minority nor does, say, attendance at a minority school inevitably lead to lasting membership. However, in the perception of members themselves, attendance at a minority school is usually the means to an ability to speak German, and these two are usually the pre-conditions for a full sense of belonging and feeling at ease in the other behavioural traits of membership. Thus attendance at the minority school — in contemporary times when there are no adverse conditions, and no lack of facilities, in most of Sønderjylland/Nordschleswig — is a crucial decision in the life of a child and its family. The school is perceived as the purveyor of German language and culture in a way which the family cannot compete with, even though school teachers themselves would contest this. In how far this perception corresponds to observed reality is one of the issues to be explored in later chapters.

Three generations of history

The history of debate over the status of the Duchy of Schleswig, and military and political action to resolve the debate, is a long one. With it are closely interconnected the histories of linguistic development, contact and conflict, and of the schools and school systems. Various arbitrary starting points are possible, from the period of the Völkerwanderung, through the effect of the reformation, the awakening of national identity in the nineteenth century, the imperial fortunes of Bismark's Germany, to the referendum and consequent shift of the frontier in 1920 (Brandt, 1975; Rerup, 1982; Fink, 1955; Rohweder, 1976). If one makes a distinction, however, between the history acquired from teaching and the history learned through direct personal experience, then the starting point is at the beginning of the twentieth century, when the oldest of those alive today were at school.

The reason for making this distinction here is that our perspective is firmly from the point of view of contemporary experience. There are broadly three generations alive today who have experienced the history of the minority in different ways, and it is the differences in experience which determine the present shape of the minority and its probable future. The oldest generation went to school in the German Empire and then, after the Treaty of Versailles and the referendum of 1920, they suddenly found themselves in Denmark, where they completed their schooling in a Danish school, or at best in a special German branch of the Danish public school (Biehl, 1960). The German language was, however, firmly established through school and in many cases in the home. Sønderjysk was acquired in play with other children and in contact with Danish-speaking families, for even under the German Empire Sønderjysk was widely spoken (Søndergaard, 1980). The Reformation and the instructions to clergy about the use of German and Danish as church languages left Danish with official status north of a line corresponding closely to today's frontier (Fink, 1964).

The referendum in 1920 created a German minority in the state of Denmark by moving the frontier south to its present position. The fanaticism, particularly with respect to the enforcement of the official language by means of the school system, which had coloured the cultural policies first of the Danish government (from the linguistic ordinances of 1852) (Bracker, 1972–73; Hjelholt, 1923), then of the Prussian government (after 1864) (Schütt & Vaagt, 1975; Hauser, 1959) had left a legacy of mutual intolerance which determined the experiences in school and adult life of today's oldest generation. Throughout the 1920s and early 1930s, the economic difficulties of the Danish state added fuel to the intolerance, particularly by creating difficulties for the landowners in the minority. These are still remembered today.

The advent of National Socialism was perceived as a means of support in adversity (Lenzing, 1973) and during the occupation of Denmark, members of the minority were, to varying degrees, active supporters of the occupiers. During this period a second generation was born. Some went to German private schools which had state financial support. Others began to go to the German branch of public schools during the war years, when the situation lessened the pressure on those who thus declared their German identity but on the other hand created teaching problems for all branches of the school system. The situation became much worse for them, however, at the liberation of Denmark when all the German schools and school branches were immediately closed and many teachers were put in prison accused of collaboration as were many other members of the minority. This was as a result of a retrospective law of the Danish government which was perceived by many as an act of revenge. This perception reversed a potential change in the minority among those members who were prone to turn away from Germany and give up their German identity as a consequence of the defeat. Again, as in the 1920s, there arose a need to resist pressure by holding together. The foundation of the "Bund deutscher Nordschleswiger" by a group who expressly said that they wished to be a part of Denmark, loyal Danish citizens, and yet maintain a German cultural identity, met with favour and support. Nonetheless, the closure of the German schools and school branches, which were only gradually reopened as state-financed private institutions, created difficult educational conditions for today's middle generation, the parents, and left permanent memories. Thus both generations share a past, in particular an educational experience, which was turbulent and in some respects unhappy. Unlike the oldest generation, who had a firm German-language upbringing, the closure of the schools in 1945, and in many cases the imprisonment of the father of the family[5], led to minimal use of German in the formative years and, in some families, a permanent change to Sønderjysk as the home language. There are members of that generation for whom the behavioural trait of ability to speak German with confidence and in a manner up to the normal standards of the minority cannot serve as a criterion of membership. Both these generations experienced vividly the post-war decade when feelings on both sides ran high, and for the older generation this was a renewal of the feelings of the 1920s and 1930s. That sense of being beleaguered and the accompanying sense of holding together is no longer appropriate to contemporary attitudes. But it is not far below the surface, and sometimes regretted by older people in view of the decreasing degree of commitment to the minority among the younger generation.

TABLE 1   *Overview of events since 1800*

Early 19th Century	– Schleswig/Slesvig (from Konge Å to Eider) and Holstein (from Eider to Elbe) were ruled by Danish kings, but had special status and a degree of independence within the state.
1830	– Uwe Jens Lornsen voiced growing national feeling by demanding independence for Schleswig and Holstein together.
1848–51	– Rebellion/war between Schleswig-Holsteiner claiming independence and Denmark
1852	– Introduction of language laws which were intended to make Schleswig Danish.
1864	– After a declaration which was to make Schleswig an integral part of Denmark, Prussia and Austria attacked and defeated the Danish army. Schleswig and Holstein became part of the sphere of influence of Otto von Bismarck.
1866	– Austria abandons all claims to Schleswig-Holstein which became a Prussian province.
1888	– Introduction of German as the language of schooling in North Schleswig.
1920	– Referendum and moving of the frontier to its present position.
1935	– Creation of a National Socialist party in the minority.
1940	– Occupation of Denmark.
1945	– Closure of all German schools. – Founding of "Bund deutscher Nordschleswiger".
1955	– Bonn–Copenhagen Declaration: recognition of rights and privileges for the German minority in Denmark and the Danish minority in the Federal Republic of Germany.

That younger generation, finally, has a quite different historical experience. Although it too experienced some of the hostile attitudes and was obliged by the parents to maintain a distance from their Danish contemporaries, the experience was in their earliest years. Because they had no personal involvement and responsibility in the events of the more turbulent decades, they are less sensitive and more able to shrug off the insults and hostility they were exposed to. Clearly this was no pleasant experience and may be more easily forgotten in some cases than others and sometimes even now their contact with Danish contemporaries is very limited, but in general they do not experience the same need to resist, for the pressures now and in their past have been much less. This generation has benefited from the agreements drawn up in 1955 between the Bonn and

Copenhagen governments (Deutscher Schul- und Sprachverein, 1976: 133–7) which put the minority on a much firmer footing. It was particularly important that the right to hold public examinations was accorded to the minority schools, thus giving them a better status and sense of security.

This account of the experienced history of the minority is schematic in the sense that not everybody falls neatly into the particular generational divisions that I have drawn. In another sense, too, it cannot represent the whole experience of the members of the minority, for the precise way in which individuals experience, interpret and recall their experience is in every case unique. Nonetheless it is clear to anyone who listens to people in the minority that there is a shared folk history, a recognizable difference from one generation to another and a feeling that the past experience of those still alive today colours quite distinctly people's sense of belonging to the minority, whatever their age.

A little geography

After a sketch of the historical context, we turn to the geographical. The farming family described at the beginning of this chapter were living in a part of Sønderjylland/Nordschleswig which is often described as part of the backbone of Schleswig-Holstein and Southern Jutland. The second ice age left a rolling, hilly eastern Baltic edge running up from Lübeck and beyond the area of Southern Jutland. There are islands and arms of the sea cutting into the coast, and the heavy soil is fertile and leads the farmers to concentrate on arable culture. To the west of this narrow, perhaps 10–20 kilometre wide strip, begins the Geest, the sandy-soiled backbone running down the middle of the Schleswig-Holstein and Jutland peninsula. This flat landscape is the home of many of the members of the minority. It is often windswept, it is less fertile than the eastern moraine and the dominant culture is dairy-farming. The Geest gives way on the western North Sea coast to the marshlands, to the reclaimed, dyke-protected stretches of low-lying fertile land which is a mixture of arable and grazing land.

In this landscape, there are many villages and hamlets ranging from a few farms in a cluster to long-streeted, narrow and thinly spread villages along the roads which cut North–South and East–West through the land. Some few of these villages have grown into transportation and market centres until they are almost but not quite small towns. Then there are several towns, mainly on the Eastern side, the most important of which, Aabenraa, is the regional administrative centre; it is here that the minority's only Gymnasium (Sixth Form College) is situated. Here, too, are the central offices of the "Bund deutscher Nordschleswiger", of the newspaper *Der Nordschleswiger*, and of the "Deutscher Schul- und Sprach-verein", which co-ordinates the work of all the Kindergarten and schools of the minority. None of the towns are very large (Aabenraa has a population of some 21,000 for the town and municipality) and indeed the whole area is thinly populated like others in Denmark. The towns still give the impression of being unhurried, quiet and walkable, and even its position as a port of some significance does not bring any noticeable international bustle to Aabenraa. Of course, there are many German visitors in the area, some are true tourists here to pass a few holiday weeks, others are regular visitors from just across the border who come to do some shopping and reap the advantages of being borderland inhabitants. Yet the empty countryside easily swallows them up and it is possible to drive from one coast to the other without meeting more than a dozen cars, whether German or Danish.

The distribution of the whole population over this area is uneven, and the distribution of membership of the minority — as far as such membership is assessable — is disproportionate to that of the population as a whole (Toft, 1982:18). In part this reflects the large proportion of farming families among the minority, but it is also a result of historical phenomena too complex to describe here. Not surprisingly, the distribution of the schools reflects the general picture, and in turn helps to maintain it, for where schools are lacking there is little chance of maintenance of the minority's membership, as the members themselves realize and as sociological studies have indicated (Schulte-Umberg, 1975; Svalastoga & Wolf, 1963; Toft, 1982).

The "official" minority

Thus far my account has concentrated on the "grass-roots" of the minority. One of the reasons for this is that, as I pointed out above, membership of the minority is not limited to membership of its institutions and organizations. The sociological studies cited above which have attempted to use sociometric methods have all had to begin by saying that they have been unable to establish the total population from which to draw their samples for questionnaires. However, it remains true that the "Bund deutscher Nordschleswiger" (BdN) is the official representative organization. It may not represent at all accurately the views and feelings of those people who are "sleeping members" of the minority, who do not belong to the BdN or support its functions, yet still have emotional ties to the minority. It may not represent the youngest generation who are members indirectly through sports and cultural clubs. Finally, like any organization, it may only partially represent the views of its committed members; the younger members of the middle generation and the older members of the third generation may in particular feel under-represented. Like any such organization, the BdN is aware of a possible gap between itself and the "grass roots" and yet is also conscious that it has to create as well as listen to opinion.[6] Therefore any analyis of the BdN has to be seen within the context that it is partially representative both in the sense that it is not always in tune with its members and in the sense that it is deliberately ahead of its members.

The BdN is described by its members as the "Dachorganisation" (umbrella organization) of the minority, and describes itself as having "völklich-politische, kulturelle, soziale und wirtschaftliche Arbeitsricht-ung" (popular-political, cultural, social and economic concerns) and as being the "Trägerorganisation der Schleswigschen Partei" (i.e. the organiz-er of the party which puts up candidates in local and general elections). As well as a central committee, elected from representatives of 13 Bezirks- und 27 Ortsvereine (area and district associations), it has an adminis-trative office and two main sub-committees, one political and one cultural. The BdN provides administrative support for many of the organizations under its umbrella and creates the policies and ideology of the minority. As the official organization, it represents the minority in political and cultural affairs in negotiations with government in Copenhagen and the F.R.G. Its position as an umbrella organization is clearly represented in the diagram (Table 2). It remains, however, unclear who belongs to the BdN, as both Toft (1982:25) and Sievers (1975:17) discovered, and thus the whole issue of representation is confused. In the otherwise detailed annual publication of the BdN, 1982 edition, *Grenzland "82"*, no mention is made of membership, but a map with statistics of all European minorities is reproduced, where the German minority is said to have 23,000 members (Source: *Nationale Minderheiten in Europa*, Opladen, 1975). In the BdN's yearbook for 1982, it is stated that there are 4,416 members. The election committee has a list of approximately 7,000 family addresses (Kracht, 1984). Toft obtained a list of 6,066 addresses, which cover individuals and whole families, but like Sievers met an unwillingness to reveal lists of members of societies. Sievers attributes this attitude not to the officials of the minority's organizations but to its members' inheritance of fears from the post-war years that any list might lead to black-listing. These are then further factors in the issue of the representativeness of the statements and policies of the BdN. On the other hand, there are many people who are quite open in their commitment to the BdN and to the minority, who

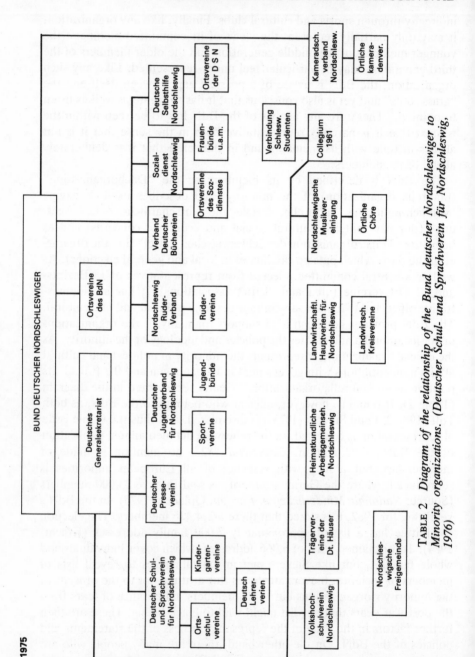

TABLE 2 *Diagram of the relationship of the Bund deutscher Nordschlesiger to Minority organizations. (Deutscher Schul- und Sprachverein für Nordschleswig, 1976)*

a long, wide, flat landscape with straight, lonely roads ...

some of the trees hide hamlets of two or three farms ...

the roads pass often in a curve through the villages ...

there is nothing to distinguish one farm from the others ...

regularly read *Der Nordschleswiger* and who thus at least pay attention to the ideas and policies which leading members of the BdN propound.

In the following chapters I shall examine how the school system in policy and in practice mediates the ideology of the minority as represented by officials and in documents. It is thus necessary at this point to consider the policy of the "Dachorganisation" here in the light of the problems of representation just discussed. Let it be said already at this point, however, that the relationship of the BdN to schools is unclear. The umbrella organization for the schools, "der deutsche Schul- und Sprachverein", has no official ties with the BdN. The two were described by the retiring chairman of the schools' organization as "two arms of one body". However, the many committees of the two organizations have frequently a number of members in common and the thinking of one organization cannot go unheeded by the other. Furthermore, as we saw in the diagram above, the BdN appears to claim the Schul- und Sprachverein as part of its whole.

I suggested above that the different historical experience of the youngest generation — roughly those who attended school in the atmosphere created by the 1955 agreements — has created different attitudes to membership of the minority: from a commitment to a sense of community additional to an identity as a Dane, through a feeling that there are certain general benefits to be gained from attending a German school, to a complete lack of interest. An awareness among older people of these new attitudes — and a feeling that some of the middle generation themselves no longer feel a need to "hold together" — is evident in the debates of the last few years in the *Nordschleswiger* and elsewhere. One consequence of that awareness appears in the BdN's *Grenzland "82"*. A closed seminar was held in the spring of 1982 for "leading members of the minority" during which a number of position statements "crystallized" (BdN, 1982:5).

The first two statements contain the paradox on which the minority is founded: on the one hand a profession of German values, language and culture; on the other hand loyalty to the Danish state.

"1. Die geistige Grundlage der deutschen Volksgruppe ist das Bekenntnis zum Deutschtum. In diesem Sinne gilt es, die in der nordschleswigschen Heimat und in den nord-	*(1. The spiritual basis of the German minority is the profession of Germanness. It is, in this spirit, necessary to nourish and maintain the values of German tradition and of German*

schleswigschen Familien geschichtlich gewachsenen Werte deutscher Tradition und deutscher Sprache und Kultur zu pflegen und zu erhalten. Das Bekenntnis muss deutlich und selbstbewusst der Umgebung gegenüber sichtbar gemacht werden.

2. Die deutschen Nordschleswiger legen Wert darauf, als Bürger des Staates Dänemark an den gesellschaftspolitischen Aufgaben im lande loyal und gleichberechtigt mitzuwirken."

language and culture which have grown up historically in the Nordschleswig homeland and in Nordschleswig families. The profession must be clearly and self-confidently made visible vis à vis surrounding society.

2. *German Nordschleswigers attach importance to playing their part, loyally and equally as citizens of the state of Denmark, in socio-political tasks.")*

This remains a paradox as long as, in common sense perceptions, the state is equated with a nation and a nation is defined by its cultural values and its language. As the states of Europe, including Denmark, come to recognize their pluri-national character, this paradox will grow less. The first statement describes the language and cultural values as belonging to and arising within Nordschleswig; "German" does not, in this conception, mean belonging to the state of Germany, however that state may be defined politically. In a later chapter I shall consider how far this implied independence of culture and language reflects the actual situation. Furthermore, with a relatively new emphasis, the first statement requires that these German values be professed publicly. This is in contrast to the tendency since and as a consequence of the war to keep a low profile in cultural and linguistic affairs, to avoid what might be thought of as provocation of the majority by frequent public declarations of values and beliefs. The thrust of this new emphasis was taken up in a slogan propagated during 1982, that all members of the minority should have "Mut zum Bekenntnis" (*Courage to declare one's beliefs*). The second statement develops this new sense of self-assertion by juxtaposing a wish for equality with the older declaration of loyality in socio-political affairs. In this different formulation the paradox arises from being culturally German and politically Danish and the attempt to resolve the paradox is described in the third statement as a matter of finding "eine angemessene

Balance zwischen dem Bekenntnis zum Deutschtum und der Integration in die dänische Umgebung" (*an appropriate balance between the profession of Germanness and integration into Danish surroundings*).

In psychological terms, this is undoubtedly demanding — a demand to which schools might help pupils to respond, as later chapters will reveal. The last three statements reveal a certain unease among those who formulated them. There is a suggestion that there must be a limit to tolerance and liberality in order to protect the identity of the minority internally. This is first of all a shift in focus from the individual to the group, and secondly a clear indication of the fear that the paradox for the individual may be resolved by abandoning the group identity. The fifth and sixth statements suggest on the one hand that the leaders want more help from the ordinary members in realizing their aims, and on the other hand that they recognize that more consultation with ordinary members is needed than has hitherto been the case.

The two aspects of the dichotomy evident in these statements are reflected in the sub-committees of the BdN, one for culture and one for elections. It is worth noting that there is some internal debate about the relationship between politics and culture. The question is whether there should be a clear separation in order to give greater emphasis to a wider range of cultural affairs and to make the preparation for elections — which have seen significant losses of German representation recently — more continuous and effective. The debate as to whether cultural life can flourish independently of political power has to be considered in the context of the financial subsidies acquired from Danish and German governments. These support many aspects of cultural affairs, not least the schools. The BdN thus seeks to sustain the values, culture and language which are at the heart of the identity of the minority and to keep the political foothold which will guarantee the conditions in which that identity can flourish. The political position is, however, made difficult by the fact that socio-economic issues dominate politics, to the detriment of purely cultural matters. Therefore its candidates have to define their position in the political spectrum with respect to social and economic policy. Yet in doing so they cannot hope to represent a unity of belief within the minority as they can with respect to cultural matters. As the minority, and especially its younger members, become increasingly diverse in their political convictions, the position of the minority's candidates becomes weaker. Thus in recent times there has been an attempt to re-think the nature of the party and to appeal to voters as a party wishing to represent the region as a whole, not just the interests of the minority.

While noting that the BdN is not the minority, but only a part of it, that its representativeness is not clear-cut, I have sketched its position and its system of beliefs because it is an important element in the whole picture. The linguistic, cultural and general educational policies of the official organs of the minority are essentially in harmony with each other, and the BdN's statements are a useful summary. My purpose now is to consider how individuals experience and respond to those policies and to the reality which they attempt to shape.

Notes to Chapter 1

1. Svalastoga & Wolf (1963:78) consider the school to be "of decisive significance" and hypothesize that school attendance not only strengthens commitment but can also be an important factor in change of identity. They claim that their hypothesis is partially supported by their survey. The evidence of the present monograph is also supportive.
2. In the whole of Sønderjylland, 60.6% of the age group stay on into the tenth class, whereas 76.5% of the age group stay on in German schools (Sønderjyllands amtskommune, 1983; Deutscher Schul- und Sprachverein für Nordschleswig, 1983). The high proportion of country schools in the German system may be a factor in this comparison.
3. The question of numbers is one which cannot be dealt with in a satisfactory way. Because of fear of reprisals after 1945, no membership lists have been kept until the present. There are mailing lists but they do not necessarily give an accurate picture. It is nonetheless widely agreed that numbers have gradually fallen since the second war. For a discussion of sampling of the minority's membership, see Toft (1982:25).
4. In the depression years special action was taken to help minority farmers avoid bankruptcy by supporting them with money from Germany.
5. A total of 2,958 members of the minority were condemned to up to 10 years or more. 1,292 were to serve between one and two years (Deutscher Schul- und Sprachverein, 1976:124).
6. An indication of this attitude is to be found in an editorial of *Der Nordschleswiger* (8 January 1982) which comments on the results of a small survey carried out by students in one of the commercial colleges. The editorial calls for recognition of "democracy-deficits", of lack of contact between the General Secretariat and ordinary members and delegates.

2 The Minority's School System

The relationship to Denmark and Germany

The role of the school in the cultural and ethnic history of the Duchy of Schleswig has been cónsiderable from the beginnings of education for the majority of the population (Japsen, 1968). It was at first subordinate to the influence of the church, but has in the twentieth century replaced the church as a central socializing force in the life of the young. There is plenty of evidence to attest the key position of the school in the maintenance of the German minority. Schulte-Umberg's (1975:113) analysis of a question-naire to parents suggests that the decision to send children to a German Kindergarten or school is "in erster Linie Ausdruck einer ethnischen Identität" (*in the first instance an expression of ethnic identity*). Evidence of a different kind can be obtained by asking a person how he knows who in his village or general environment is "German". The degree to which he can provide a confident answer will depend on how much belonging to the minority is an important aspect of his life, but where an answer is forthcoming it will include the criterion that people send their children to the German school. Even where a person has little or no contact with the functions of the minority after leaving school, the fact of having attended a German school is the key to discovering other like-minded people in a new environment. Although the sense of shared memories and mutual under-standing is a feeling that can arise in any group of people reminiscing about their school life, nonetheless the shared experience of the German school is something more. For it involves memories of being different from the majority — and sometimes being mocked for it — and of a relatively small and close-knit community with an education oriented southwards, often involving visits to Germany. Even those people who have little interest in the minority as such will nonetheless intend to send their children to the German school. This means that a possibility of continuity exists in the children even if there is no immediate interest among parents, and that

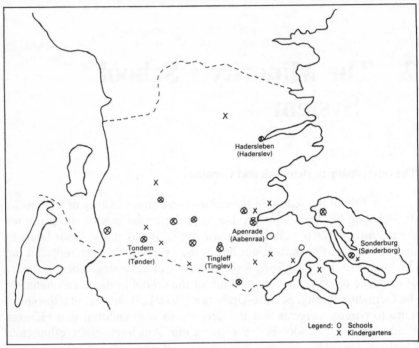

MAP 3   *The Minority Education System*

continuity is a direct result of the school system. Of course, if there were nothing else, then the minority would be highly artificial, an educational minority, but this kind of case demonstrates the significance of the school. The importance of the school for other minorities too is almost self-evident and widely attested. Edwards (1977) argues that there can often be a mismatch between leaders and ordinary members of a minority where the former see the school as a force for maintenance of the minority and their own position in it, where the latter would prefer a school which promotes mobility out of the minority and increased prosperity. In Nordschleswig, parents who want to opt out of the minority system can do so easily. Those who remain are therefore in considerable harmony with the leadership. This gives all the more significance to the school.

It is important, therefore, to consider the relationship of the school system to the other organizations of the minority. Each school and Kindergarten is in essence a self-owning independent institution. In many, but not all, cases the institution qualifies for financial aid under the Danish law (*Lov om friskoler og private grundskoler*) which allows any group of people to establish a school provided certain minimal conditions are fulfilled. Despite this apparent independence of the individual schools, they are formed into a system through the "Deutscher Schul- und Sprachverein für Nordschleswig". This organization co-ordinates the work of the schools through an elected committee and an executive led by a Schulrat (Education Officer). The co-ordination consists both in the detail of bringing together groups of pupils and groups of teachers for a variety of activities, but also in the establishment of curricular policy, resulting most importantly in detailed curriculum documents outlining the work in each subject year by year. These documents ensure that the work of the schools is similar throughout the region.

To a large degree then the existence of the schools depends on ordinary Danish law and in this sense they are not exceptional to the Danish education system, which has included both public and private schools since the mid-nineteenth century. The schools work to the same ends as all other Danish schools in so far as they prepare pupils for the ordinary Danish school-leaving examinations, after nine or ten years education. Yet the relationship to the Danish school system is not the same as that of other private schools. Essentially it is a question of orientation. Although we saw above (pp. 14–20) that a recent statement has attempted to define the culture of the minority as one which is indigenous to and centred on the traditions and values of the minority itself, the aims of the schools point to a cultural focus elsewhere:

"1. Unsere Schule ist eine deutsche Schule. Sie will ihre Schüler in deutscher Sprache in die deutsche Kulturwelt hineinführen und die deutsche Gemeinschaft festigen.

2. Unsere Schule ist eine deutsche Schule im dänischen Staat. Sie will daher ihre Schüler in die dänische Kultur- und Sprachwelt einführen und auf das Leben als Bürger dieses Staates vorbereiten."

("1. Our school is a German school. It intends to introduce its pupils in the German language to the German cultural world and reinforce the German sense of community.

2. Our school is a German school in the Danish state. It intends therefore to introduce its pupils to the Danish cultural and language world and to prepare them for life as citizens of this state.")

Although the phrases "the German cultural world" and "the German community" could be interpreted as "Nordschleswig German", the introduction to the curricular documents states that they have been revised in the light of reforms in Denmark and in Schleswig-Holstein. Thus the reference point for an interpretation of "the German cultural world" and "the German community" is south of the border; whereas the reference to reforms in Denmark does justice to the second of the aims. It will become clear in the following pages that the orientation to a reference point south of the border is strong in the schools and the minority as a whole and that the notion of an indigenous culture and values is scarcely justified by reality.

It could be argued, therefore, that this underlying orientation is somewhat at odds with the first paragraph of the law under which the schools operate. The requirement there is that the schools should "giver en undervisning inden for 1–9 Klassetrin, som står mål med, hvad der almindeligvis kræves i folkeskolen" (Ministry of Education, 1977) (*schools should give instruction within the first to ninth classes which is equal to what is normally required in the (public) folkeskole*). It might be argued on a broad interpretation that the spirit of this is broken by the German orientation of the schools, although on a narrower interpretation, the German schools doubtless make the same intellectual demands and require the same standards as the "folkeskole" (primary and lower secondary school). On the other hand the second aim of the schools is very much in harmony with the aims of the "folkeskole" and the practical issue is whether the first and second aims are complementary or mutually contradictory. Clearly it is the opinion of those who are responsible for them that they are neither philosophically and conceptually nor in pedagogical practice contradictory. An indication of this in recent years has been the decision to "open" the schools, to attempt to attract parents who are not members of the minority (Søndergaard, 1983). The priorities are, however, put in a different order for these purposes. For example, one school in its town's directory (Løgumkloster Vejviseren) lists the two aims of the schools in third place after mentioning the advantages of being a small school, and of pupils growing up bilingual. And in fact the order of the aims themselves is reversed, so that the education to be a "responsible citizen of the Danish state" is mentioned first. There is then at first sight a certain ambivalence in the position of the schools *vis à vis* the Danish school system, which will become clearer after consideration of their relationship to the school system of the Federal Republic.

There is one very significant respect in which the schools are linked into the F.R.G., or more precisely the Schleswig–Holstein, education system: through the teachers. The overwhelming majority of the teachers have the same status (Beamter – civil servant) as their colleagues in

Schleswig–Holstein. They trained in the F.R.G. Higher Education system, entered the teaching profession in the normal way and obtained the security of civil servant status. In order to work in Nordschleswig they are seconded without pay from the Schleswig–Holstein education service, but remain within the service with respect to such matters as pension rights and also as far as their duties and rights as civil servants are concerned. Under normal circumstances their professional life would be determined by the Schleswig–Holstein regulations for civil servants in general and for the education system in particular and they would be under the supervision of a Schulrat (Education Officer) as well as the Head of the school. This is also the case in Nordschleswig, for which there is one Schulrat, even though the regulations which the teachers work with are Danish and German. Although in principle the teachers could be of any geographical origin — with training in any of the states of the F.R.G. or indeed with Danish qualifications — in practice about half of the teachers are from Schleswig–Holstein, often from the northern half, with about half from Sønderjylland/Nordschleswig itself. This clearly has an effect on the character of the minority education system, which as far as staffing is concerned functions largely as an extension of the Schleswig–Holstein system. It is significant first with respect to the conditions of employment for the individual teacher. He is not geographically distant from his place of origin and ultimate professional responsibility, and need not therefore feel exiled or cut off from his homeland. Hence there are many teachers who have spent their whole careers in minority schools. This creates the stability and continuity which a teaching force taking secondment for a few years only would not provide. A second significant effect of the close link with Schleswig–Holstein is less tangible: the educational philosophy is heavily influenced by the education and teacher-training system of Schleswig–Holstein. This has effect on the teaching methods, on the attitudes to teacher–pupil relationships and on beliefs about the aims and responsibilities of the school. On the other hand, the stability and long service of the teaching force means that they are often exposed to Danish educational philosophy and methodology which may modify their basic philosophy. The result in practice can be an interesting blend, which creates the special nature of the schools, spanning the gap between two education systems.

The second major area of contact with the Schleswig–Holstein system is in curriculum. The simple legal requirement that the schools "measure up to" the demands of the ordinary Danish folkeskole, with scarcely any further detailed determination of the curriculum, allows the schools considerable freedom. It allows them, working together under the aegis of the "Schul- und Sprachverein", to shape a curriculum to fit their own peculiar nature and their attempts to span two cultures. Reference is made to the curricular documents of both Denmark and Schleswig–Holstein; the special character of the resulting documents is, however, more evident in, say, history than in the less culture-bound subjects such as mathematics. Nonetheless the practical application of these documents has to be seen in the light of the training of the teachers who are more familiar with the German origins than with Danish curriculum theory. This may result in a bias which brings out the German more than the Danish element. We shall return to the details of this later.

The financial position of the schools is determined by Danish laws pertaining to all private schools. Subsidies are payable up to 85% of running costs. The actual percentage is determined by the Minister of Education. Subsidies for the minority's schools are approximately 70% of costs. In some other private schools, parents are requested to cover the difference through fees and other means. The minority schools do not require parents to pay fees — as the advertisements opening the schools to the majority emphasize. The necessary financial support for the schools has to come partly from local initiatives to raise money and partly from sponsors in West Germany. Major sponsors are the state of Schleswig–Holstein and the Federal Government, especially where major building projects are concerned. The budget for the minority as a whole in 1981 was made up as: 46% grant from Danish state and municipal funds, 39% from the F.R.G. and 15% income directly from the minority. 45% of the grant from the F.R.G. was given over to the schools sector (*Der Nordschleswiger*, 27 October 1982). There are also many individual arrangements between schools and organizations and municipalities in Germany, again largely in Schleswig–Holstein. These arrangements (Patenschaften) (sponsorships) are not only financial but are also the basis of much personal contact between pupils and parents of the minority's schools and the people of the towns and villages they are sponsored by. Similar arrangements sometimes exist to encourage visits from other organizations of the minority, for example, the sporting and cultural societies. Although the visits are often reciprocated, the relationship is a dependent one — as the word "Patenschaft" indicates — and the image which springs to mind is of members of the minority acquiring cultural nourishment from south of the border, of acquiring an infusion of new blood from the reference culture, without which the indigenous culture would not flourish. This is another element in the orientation of the schools and the minority to Schleswig–Holstein. In the routine of the schools the relationship to the sponsoring bodies works out in terms of school journeys, which are almost exclusively south of the border, with destinations both in the sponsoring municipalities and elsewhere in the Federal Republic. This is one of the contributing factors to pupils' feeling that they are more familiar with Germany than with Denmark, a factor which separates them from their majority contemporaries.

Reconciling the differences

Danish educational philosophy emphasizes that the responsibility for schooling is shared between parents and state. Parental choice should therefore be as open as possible. In this sense, the decision of parents, whether members of the minority in some degree or not at all, to send their children to a German school is fully consonant with the normal situation in Denmark. Indeed, the "Deutscher Schul- und Sprachverein" is a member of the "Frie Grundskolers Fællesråd" (Private Schools Joint Council), the umbrella organization for private schools, and is thus integrated into the private system. Although in essence the law which regulates the private sector implies that each school is an independent institution not only in financial terms but also as the realization of an educational philosophy, there have since the origins been groups of schools created with a common philosophy — not least the Grundtvigian schools. In this respect too, therefore, the notion of a group or system of schools is not an alien concept. The point where the minority's schools begin to diverge is in their purpose of serving an ethnic minority within Denmark. However, it is not so much the ethnic character of the minority which is the major factor, for Danish educational philosophy could at least in theory find ample room for this, just as it does for religious or political minorities who wish to create their own schools. It is rather the fact that the German minority relies to a large extent on a cultural reference point outside the state boundaries which makes its schools a special case. One of the practical consequences of this, as we have seen, is the importation of teachers from the Federal Republic who bring with them a different educational philosophy. A similar situation might arise if any of the new, immigrant minorities in Denmark were to create their own schools under Danish law, but the contrast between Danish and Muslim philosophy would be so great as to be immediately noticeable, and would more quickly provoke debate as to whether they were reconcilable. The differences between Danish and German philosophies are, however, much less crass.

The issue of reconciling aspects of German and Danish philosophy is not, therefore, much debated, any more than the issue of whether pupils can be successfully educated both in German culture and in preparation for Danish citizenship. It is a difficult factor to grasp and document, but it is nonetheless evident that Danish and German society are radically different, and that the differences are reflected in the schools and their philosophies. The popular perception that German schools are "more strict" is symptomatic of this difference but is too unrefined a judgement to be of great value. Thus the question as to how the German schools can successfully prepare pupils for Danish society and social philosophy requires consideration. An answer which is part of the rhetoric of the minority's official organs is to say that the minority adds a further, enriching dimension to Danish life in the region by providing people with an understanding of two cultures. Yet to add a new element is not necessarily to see it absorbed into the compound of elements in a society; the result may be no more than a mixture. How far the schools and other organizations realize this rhetoric successfully remains a moot point. The following pages will throw some light, without pretending to offer a definitive answer.

3 Description of a School

Introduction

The decision of parents to send their children to a German school is realized at a definite point in time, and is then scarcely ever reversed. That crucial point comes at the latest at the age of seven, when the child is required by Danish law to begin school, but the creation of a "Kindergarten class" attached to the folkeskole has in practice lowered the age of entry for many children throughout Denmark to six. It may also be the case that the decision to send a child to a German Kindergarten at age 3 is simultaneously the decision to keep him in the German system throughout his school career. This need not be so however, as many parents who are essentially Danish use the German Kindergarten, before changing to the Danish school system. Wherever the point of decision falls, it is followed by a process which lasts at least nine years, the minimum of compulsory schooling in Denmark. It is that process, as we have argued in earlier chapters, which is largely responsible for the sense of membership of the minority which graduates from the schools have. It is nonetheless worth emphasizing again that the school is not exclusively responsible, that it is an experience which may be developed by other social institutions and forces, and that without the support of the home in particular, it may well be of minimal significance.

To understand the process of schooling in all its complexity is a mammoth task, wherever it is and whatever the focus of the research. My approach was through participating and observing in one school over a substantial period of time with the primary aim of understanding the process from the point of view of those involved, while keeping the perspective of the outsider who notices things which insiders take for granted (Agar, 1980; Spradley, 1980). Some of the results of such observation are presented here. The school in question was not selected for its "typicality"; it does not represent some norm of experience in the minority's schools. It was chosen rather because of the homogeneity of its pupils: they are mainly from the kind of family described above (pp. 1–7) which have always been the heart of the minority. Few pupils are sent to the school for reasons other than membership of the minority. The school

29

has not yet become involved in "opening" to non-minority pupils (cf. pp. 21–26). It is also the case that the families involved are usually strongly committed in their membership. The area is known as "*die Hochburg des Deutschtums*" (the stronghold of Germanness) and was one of the few areas which in 1920 had a majority of German votes and yet became part of Denmark because it belonged to a "zone" with a Danish majority. The school has two kinds of pupils: those who live in the town where it is situated and spend all their school years in it, and those who live in the surrounding countryside and come to the school after spending up to six years in one or two smaller village schools.

Even a six-month period of study is clearly not enough to grasp the whole educative process of the school. A focus is, however, provided by the considerations of Chapter 2, where it was argued that the special nature of the school is more evident in some aspects than in others — the most salient one being the use of the German language as the teaching medium. A second method of concentrating observation was the decision to work with the pupils who were about to leave the school; this will be the subject of a later chapter. This chapter will be a description of those aspects of the school which characterize it as a minority school.

Tinglev/Tingleff

The town, with approximately ten and a half thousand inhabitants in and around it, is situated some 20 kilometres from the Baltic coast, therefore in the eastern half of Sønderjylland/Nordschleswig but already on the central Geest area. The town itself is relatively small, with some two and a half thousand inhabitants. As a municipality it jumped to its present size through an amalgamation of villages and communities in 1970. It lies on an important east-west road linking the two main arteries which run north–south on both coasts. It is not one of the main towns, which are situated on the north–south axes, but it has a certain significance as a result of the nineteenth century decision to run the railway line northwards through Tinglev/Tingleff rather than along the undulating Baltic coast. From being just another village, Tinglev/Tingleff grew to the status of a "railway town" (Danish: stationsby) and to being a small industrial, business and cultural centre, with a population partly developing from the agricultural base, providing craftsmen and tradesmen, and partly growing through the arrival of new people connected with the railway and other services. There are today some light industries and the railway is still significant, but the town is still scarcely more than a large village.

The results of the referendum of 1920 are still evident in the strong German proportion of the population of Tinglev/Tingleff as a town and municipality. The German majority of 1920 has however gradually fallen away although the absolute number has changed little. Bearing in mind the problems of establishing statistics discussed above (pp. 14–20), it is nonetheless indicative that Toft (1982:18) establishes that 14.1% of the minority live in Tinglev/Tingleff, whilst only 4.1% of the total population of the Amt Sønderjylland live there. He cites the absolute number of 858 addresses for Tingleff supplied by the "Bund deutscher Nordschleswiger". These figures are surpassed only in Aabenraa/Apenrade (with 17.9% of the minority but 8.5% of the total population) and in Tønder/Tondern (with 17.9% and 5% of the total, thus very similar proportions to Tinglev/Tingleff). Two other places, Sønderborg/Sonderburg (13.6% of the minority and 11.4% of the total) and Haderslev/Hadersleben (12.0% of the minority and 12.1% of the total) have significant proportions of the minority but because they are large municipalities, the minority members are a relatively insignificant proportion of their populations. The rest of the minority are scattered throughout Nordschleswig and Toft cites no figure above 5% for any of the other municipalities. Tinglev/Tingleff is thus one of three places where, according to Toft's figures, there is a minority population which is numerically strong *vis à vis* the surrounding population and which can therefore feel culturally secure. This impression is strengthened by the more reliable figures from local elections, when in 1981 Tinglev/Tingleff was one of only three places where the vote for the German party (die Schleswigsche Partei) increased. Although other municipalities have elected German representatives, Tinglev/Tingleff has four whereas others (Højer/Hoyer, Løgumkloster/Lügumkloster, Tønder/Tondern) have two and Aabenraa/Apenrade only one. Although these are only four of 17 places in the municipal council two others have four and the rest are divided in ones and twos among four other parties.

The relative strength of the minority in Tinglev/Tingleff is evident in the number and size of its institutions. The school in the town itself is, on the numbers in 1982, the largest in the minority school system, though closely followed by Apenrade. There is a Kindergarten, a "Continuation School" (Danish: efterskole; German: Nachschule, for people aged 14–18) the only one of its kind in the minority, and a sports hall, which serves both schools and general community purposes. In the villages belonging to the municipality there are other German schools and Kindergarten. Furthermore there is a very successful youth club, closely connected to the school — run by one of the teachers and using school rooms — and there is strong sporting activity, in which again teachers from the school are heavily involved. There is also a German priest, who shares the use of the local church with his Danish colleague.

To the casual observer there is nothing in the town which advertises the presence of the minority. The vast majority of the members speak the local Danish dialect, Sønderjysk — the main exception being the teachers from Germany. The buildings which belong to the minority are anonymously without signs or labels although this is soon to be remedied. The town's presentation of itself in its directory has only brief mention of the minority and does not mention the German or other private schools in the account of the local education system. It does, however, list the Kindergärten, an indication of the way in which these are used by the majority before sending their children to Danish schools.

Despite this superficial anonymity the members of the minority, depending on their degree of commitment, can live a full cultural life within their own social institutions. For most of them, their economic activity is part of the majority system, for example the farmers are quite clearly part of the Danish agricultural industry. For a small number, principally the teachers, even their economic activity is bound up with the minority, although their rates of pay and taxation are determined by the Danish education system. It is natural therefore that the degree of commitment to and activity for the minority is high among teachers, and their consequent influence on the official institutions and policies are considerable. The one area where they have little or no influence is on the minority's agricultural society and its branches. The pupils of the school, who are in a sense economically independent of the majority, can also live their lives largely within the social institutions of the minority. Both their school time and their free time is catered for, particularly for those who live in the town rather than villages. The degree of separation from the majority in this way varies from one person to another. In short, as Svalastoga & Wolf (1963:142) showed for Tønder/Tondern — where the proportions are similar — the network of relationships can be relatively closed. One of the original causes for the closedness was undoubtedly the hostility and mutual lack of regard between minority and majority which has been part of the way of life since 1920, part of the experienced history of the minority described above (pp. 10–13). Although this has undoubtedly decreased in recent years, it has far from disappeared. The older and middle generations have experienced it, but so have many of the young and some members of the majority will confess to their dislike of the minority.

Die deutsche Schule Tingleff

A red-brick building standing fifty yards from the main street along a road leading to the station, the school is large but easily overlooked. There is no sign or indication that this is the school, except when children are playing in the yard, visible from the street. When I first arrived I asked an old gentleman passing by if this was the school. He in fact directed me to the building next to it where there is a large front entrance, which proved to be locked; as I later discovered, it is the "Continuation School". Across the road is the Kindergarten, and on the other side of the two schools lies the sports hall. This group of buildings forms a cultural centre for the minority in the middle of the town, two minutes walk from the town hall. When I eventually saw a young child in the yard and asked him to take me to the Headteacher's office, he was pleasant and eager to do so, with a friendliness which is common in the school. In fact I discovered there was no main entrance proper, perhaps a result of the way the buildings have been enlarged over the years.

The image which the school presents is found most directly in its yearbook, published for the first time in 1982. The yearbook, in German like all documents issued by the school, is addressed in the first instance to the initiate, to pupils, parents, former pupils and the rest of the German community. It is noticeable that, apart from a small number of pupil contributions, there is considerable emphasis on life after leaving school. There is a description of the work of the Guidance and Counselling teacher (Berufsberater) and two articles about former pupils who have had successful careers. Both of them, it is emphasized, found their bilingualism helpful in their careers. Another article describes a visit from the Danish radio company, when pupils from the seventh year were asked to write an answer to the question why they attend a German school. Nine said it was a tradition in their family, two thought they learnt more because of the small classes, two gave the reason that they were of German nationality and one with Danish parentage had attended a German Kindergarten and then wanted to attend a German school. Furthermore, nine of the children said they were pleased with their parents' choice, two particularly mentioned the advantage of being bilingual. Three pupils mentioned the disadvantages: that they had had to suffer insults and that their best friends were at a Danish school. Although there is no particular significance in these figures, the article is clearly considered to give a fair impression of the school and corresponds with my own observations.

There are, however, signs of a paradox in this publication which can also be found elsewhere. In an advertisement attempting to attract non-minority pupils to the schools, another school states that "a bilingual education gives (the pupils) more and greater opportunities in a modern bilingual society". Yet the Head of that same school has publicly stated that his school will never become a language school. On the one hand the career benefits of bilingualism are stressed — and pupils asked about advantages and disadvantages always reply in this vein, yet seldom let it influence their own career-choice — on the other hand the schools are expressly minority, not bilingual institutions. They do not ignore the fact that pupils are bilingual but treat it more as a problem than as an advantage. This is an issue which will be taken up in more detail later (pp. 47–64), but it is significant that it appears already at this point.

Another striking aspect of the yearbook is the emphasis on links with the Federal Republic. There is a report of a visit by a group of adults from the sponsoring town in Schleswig–Holstein, which involved the parents and friends of the school rather than the pupils, an indication of how the school is a focus for the whole community. There is also a list of school journeys, most of which were to destinations in Germany, and finally a page describing the sponsorship aid, in monies and in kind, which the school received in the previous year.

A few figures will complete this first sketch of the school. There are (in 1982–83) some 200 pupils and approximately 20 teachers. The pupils are in ten year-groups and one Kindergarten class. The first six year-groups have normally between 12 and 16 pupils, although the second year has only six. The size of the year-groups from the seventh year on is larger, as children join the school from the village schools in the areas which do not go beyond the sixth year. However, the eighth to tenth years are divided into two classes or, for certain subjects, into two courses, and there is scarcely in the whole school a teaching group of more than 20. Even in Denmark, which has one of the best teacher-pupil ratios in Europe, these figures are very favourable and are one of the attractions of the school for many parents, and doubtless teachers too. Furthermore there are arrangements for individual pupils to be withdrawn for extra help if they are weak, especially in German, Danish and mathematics.

Pupils – where they come from and go to

Towards 7.30 a.m. the main street of Tinglev/Tingleff is busy. Children arrive on foot, by bicycle and by bus for the start of school. There are four older children at the pedestrian crossings wearing armbands who direct the younger ones across the road. Many of the children are going to the Danish school, some are on their way to the nearby German school. There is no apparent difference. They all look a little tired, they all carry large bags; the younger ones have them strapped on their backs, with bright strips of orange to protect them from the traffic, the older ones tend to carry large sports bags. Many of the German pupils have travelled in from the villages on the same school buses which bring their Danish contemporaries; both groups are provided with free transport by law. Some pupils will spend the journey, which can last half an hour because of the many pick-up points, in the company of friends who go to the Danish school. Some will know Danish pupils only by sight.

There is, however, one noticeable difference in the transport system. At 7.25 a.m. a small, red bus arrives with the legend "Deutsche Schule Tingleff" in small letters on the side. This is the private transport which the school provides for a special group of pupils. The Danish school takes its pupils only from the municipality Tingleff, but the catchment area of the German school crosses municipal boundaries. Public transport is provided mainly from west to east, as Tingleff town lies at the eastern extremity of the municipality. Thus the German school has to provide its own transport for those coming from the east. Every day the school driver fetches in the early morning and returns about midday some thirty pupils. One of the morning circuits is described below.

To school by bus

5.55 a.m. Looking a brighter red than usual in the morning light the bus leaves from the driver's house a few yards from the school. It is a sharp, sunny morning with mist lying in the hollows.

Some fifteen minutes later it arrives in a small village, a few minutes earlier than the timetable says, and the driver switches off the engine. Soon the first of two sisters arrives, school bag on her back, slowly walking down the road. As she gets in, the driver jokes: "Könnt Ihr Euch nicht vertragen heute morgen?" ("*Can't you get on together this morning?*"), "Næe" — and she sits in her place behind the driver. Her sister appears round the corner, slowly, like the proverbial schoolboy. This morning and all this month, it is their turn to be picked up first; next month they will be the last to be picked up and will be able to sleep a little longer.

By the end of the round, on a normal day, the bus will be full, with the small pupils squeezed up in the corners. Today, however, the ninth and tenth classes are free, preparing for their oral examinations next week.

Now it is time to set off to the next village; the timetable must be followed. But as we arrive, there is nobody waiting. The first boy arrives in a hurry, puffing and panting, saying that his brother will soon be there, and sure enough he too comes hurrying round the corner. "Was macht Hans denn noch?" ("*What's Hans doing then?*") says the driver. The answer, in

Sønderjysk, is that he has overslept. Soon the third arrives, apparently still finishing breakfast and the bus can go on, but later than usual. It makes a difference all the way round, and the last group to be picked up, an hour from now, will complain that they have been waiting longer than usual.

As we drive along a narrow road, through the typically flat, green meadows with trees along the sides, a blue anorak appears in the distance. As we approach, the girl moves forward from the entrance to the road leading up to her farm and the bus slows. This is a girl I know; she is in a class I have taught and observed. In one piece of writing in a Danish lesson she said she wished she did not attend the German school, but her parents insist. Is the early rising and the long journey one of the reasons for her dislike? As she climbs in, however, she does not look quite as sleepy as the others and manages a quiet "Moin". She sits near the front of the bus, the driver pulls on a strap he has rigged to allow him to close the door from his seat and the Mercedes diesel engine noise increases as we move off again. That noise, louder at the front, is surely sufficient to keep us all awake.

The next stop is at the end of a farm road, hard in this weather but untarmaced. The bus reverses and turns beneath the trees, but there is nobody there. The girl we might have found has been ill for a week, but it is necessary to drive up, the driver tells me, in order to check if she is ready for school again. One of the boys at the back complains at this, driving up here every morning for nothing — but it is part of the procedure.

It is now 6.30 a.m., and we are travelling further south. Two more boys from a farm on the roadside are the only people in the landscape; the mist has cleared and from the high seats of the bus one can see a long way. We approach some open land with bushes and trees becoming a small wood. Beside the road there is a large orange car. We all look to the right and the driver calls out that they have shot a roe-buck. Then, as we drive through the sudden darkness of the wood we see a buck standing in the middle of the road, looking away from us. Strange, that he has not heard, and the bus slows. It is only at the noise of changing gear that the buck suddenly looks around, startled, and shoots off into the wood, turning at a sharp angle and leaning sideways with the speed of his reaction. The bus picks up speed, we arrive in a two or three farm hamlet and pick up another passenger, returning the way we came.

As we pass the orange car again, the two hunters are clearly visible walking slowly towards the road, a fine roe-buck hanging between them. "Synd" ("Shame!") say the children behind me, but the hunters raise their arms cheerily, clearly pleased with their morning's kill.

Soon we arrive at one of the main north-south roads and, turning north, travel a little more quickly; but throughout the journey we scarcely go more than 80 km per hour. On the left, a kilometre or so along the road, there stands a now familiar figure, waiting in the sunshine. There is no apparent reason for him to be at just that point, but the bus turns in left towards him, into the beginning of a farm track, and I can now see a few hundred metres away the farm from which he must have walked. The bus reverses out onto the main road — there is little traffic and the open countryside and long, straight road allow the driver to see a long way. We set off south again.

We are now approaching the frontier and a number of larger villages which flourish on the tourist and general frontier trade. It is 6.40 a.m. and the increasing number of children in the bus together with the gradual awakening of those who got on first produces a rising sound of conversation: Who do you have first period, what lesson is the last lesson? — the usual talk of pupils going to school — but in Sønderjysk.

Turning eastwards, we drive parallel to the frontier and out towards the Flensburger Förde. This is a main road. We see more cars and people walking or cycling to work; on the longest stretch without a stop, we head out to Kollund. Kollund is one of the destinations of the steamers from Flensburg which thrive on the fact that an hour's sailing across a frontier allows a lot of people to consume a lot of food and alcohol and then go straight back to Flensburg.

It is 6.50 a.m. when we arrive in Kollund and pick up the three small pupils who live farthest from the school. They look far more awake as they get on the bus than the first one did, 40 minutes or so ago.

We head back westwards, but as we approach one of the main frontier crossings we turn towards it. Going past the shops, the banks, the petrol stations, the bus almost reaches the passport office but then swings round and faces back into Denmark. The boy standing on the pavement has come across from Germany. He climbs in, the driver pulls on his strap to close the door and we move back into Denmark, but then, turning left, find ourselves heading south, still parallel to the frontier. The bus stops two or three times in the next village and another five pupils get on. There is more German being spoken in the bus, particularly since we picked up the boy at the frontier crossing and the bus is gradually filling. Another village yields two more passengers and there is some argument as the bus sets off: the girls near the front don't want to move farther back among the boys, but there is not enough room for the new arrivals; the seats which unfold down the centre close the gangway and stop the new arrivals from moving through to the middle of the bus. A few words from the bus driver, a little pushing and squeezing — particularly of the smaller pupils — solves the problem.

For the last 20 minutes we have been travelling through the more heavily populated belt near the frontier. As we now turn north again we pass the large customs centre for commercial vehicles and head out into the countryside again. Through a wooded area, we pick up the last passenger at 7.10, and go off to school. We see other children now more frequently, waiting patiently for their school bus, provided by this municipality and going in the opposite direction.

At 7.22 a.m., the bus pulls into the school yard, the chatter-level has been increasing steadily in the last ten minutes and as they hurry off the bus there is considerable shouting and chatter and banter with the driver. We are finally there, with a few minutes to spare before lessons begin at 7.30 a.m. Some pupils have been on the bus for more than an hour. The last passenger to get on has had a ten-minute ride. The sun is shining, the countryside is blossoming and, by the end of the journey, everyone seems bright and happy — but are they as happy every day? Are they looking forward to another hour's journey at the end of the day's school? What is it like to spend an hour in the cold and darkness of a winter morning?

Going to school by bus is a part of life in the thinly populated area around Tinglev/Tingleff, and even those who live nearer school and can use public transport have to get up early and sometimes arrive earlier than they need. Yet this group from the south east have a different start to their school day, a winding journey through the countryside which takes them away from school before moving in the direction of the school, in a bus which clearly marks their particularity and for these 30 pupils — from a total of 200 — going to a German school is different from the moment they get on the bus.

Leaving the first load in the school yard, the bus sets off again. For not all pupils start at 7.30 a.m. The first class does not start until 8.15 a.m. and so a second tour, shorter this time, is needed to pick up the smallest members of the school. Some of them were among the first load already, because they live too far away to be able to fetch them on the second tour. In fact this morning, only one child gets on the bus, weighed down by her rucksack-like school-bag, and travels in solitary splendour to school.

And that is the first part of the day's work done for the driver. He can go home, a few yards from the school and have breakfast. Later in the morning, he will come into school to check on arrangements for other journeys, for he works full-time for the school and is kept busy. Within the next week or so, he will take one group to a village in Schleswig–Holstein, which sponsors the school. He will take the school brass orchestra to two Ringreiten (horse-riding) festivals — and then, especially in winter, there are the sports fixtures on Saturdays. During the coming summer holidays he will be driving a tenth year group to England, and he often has to fetch and take people home in the evenings after class parties. In this way the bus helps to overcome the difficulties of any rural school, which are, however, all the more acute for a school whose catchment area is determined not by local municipality boundaries, but by the desire of parents to send their children there.

Origins

The proportion of pupils from the countryside is roughly two-thirds of the school's total, one-third living in the town itself. The teachers, however, live almost without exception in Tinglev/Tingleff itself, as their conditions of service require. Over the last decade or so, the number of pupils from the countryside has dropped. Large families are not so frequent in the farming population. The decrease has been compensated in some degree by the development of housing in the town. The issue of falling rolls is a crucial one. In the village schools it may mean a loss of revenue as they approach the minimal number required for state subsidy, with a consequent threat of closure. For the town school, it is a threat to the number of teachers on the staff. This is a common problem of course, but here it sharpens awareness of additions and losses, for a loss is not only a loss to the school but quite probably a loss of a future member of the minority. Therefore, when a family moves to another district, there is particular interest in whether they continue to send their children to a German school.

Destinations

Having considered some aspects of the pupils' origins, let us turn to their destinations. Statistics are published each year of the career choices of pupils leaving the minority schools. The numbers involved in the five schools in question are small; ranging over a four year period 1979–82, the totals for all five schools were between 137 and 224. These figures can, however, confirm impressions of trends gained by teachers concerned with career advice. Pupils leaving Tingleff school are, in a majority of cases, hoping to pursue a career in commerce by taking a commercial vocational course. Between a quarter and a third of them enter a course, usually at the German Gymnasium ("Sixth Form College"), which is primarily intended to prepare them for Higher Education. Another small group of fluctuating size intends to work in agriculture and a few want a career in the trades and crafts. This general pattern is more marked than in the other four schools, but certain basic similarities can be seen in three of them, particularly Tondern which has a similar catchment area and history to that of Tingleff.

The fifth school, Apenrade, is clearly exceptional in that the proportion of pupils going to prepare for Higher Education is much higher and is usually greater than the total of all the other options. This contrast reflects not only the common phenomenon that town children are more likely to have higher educational aspirations but also the special fact that the educational and administrative centre of the minority is in Aabenraa/ Apenrade. One teacher said that in Aabenraa/Apenrade the teachers provide their own pupils. Martensen (1975:58) found in his analysis of the social structure of the minority that employees and civil servants are under-represented in comparison with the norm of the total population of Nordschleswig, even though they had increased in proportionate size since Svalastoga & Wolf's (1963) investigation. Toft's (1982:13) figures are not directly comparable but tend in the same direction. Within the group of civil servants and others with Higher Education, the teachers are probably a large percentage, since except for a handful of posts in the administration of the minority, teaching is the only profession within the minority open to those with a Higher Education qualification. Willkommen (1975:138) was told that there were no Danish civil servants among members of the "Bund deutscher Nordschleswiger" and Svalastoga & Wolf (1963:84) found 7 among a list of 1167 who were employed in some capacity by the local authority. Add the factor that teachers are expected to send their own children to the minority's schools, and it is not surprising that the school and the Gymnasium in Aabenraa/Apenrade are perceived as having a large number of children from teaching families. Indeed the word "Lehrerkind" (child of a teacher) is frequently used to designate individuals of whom there are higher expectations, in the first instance linguistic: they are assumed to be better speakers of German, because German is their home language, and are the only ones to whom pupils expect to use German in private conversation. Willkommen (1975:139) finds a correlation between the amount of formal education and the percentage of German-speakers, meaning those having German as the dominant home language: "mit steigender Schulbildung zeigt sich ein deutlich zunehmender Prozentsatz an Deutschsprachigen" ("*with increasing education there is a clearly increasing percentage of German speakers*"). He makes the mistake of interpreting this causally: "Die Schulbildung hat offentsichtlich Einfluss auf das Sprach-verhalten" ("*education evidently has an influence on language behaviour*"), whereas the causation, if there is any, could just as well be in the opposite direction: school success being dependent on being German-speaking. There is indeed a vast amount of pedagogical literature which argues for this interpretation in that ability in the code of instruction is argued to be *a sine qua non* of educational success (e.g. Stubbs, 1983 and Donaldson, 1978). It is, however, clearly the case that linguistic ability correlates with other social factors which may contribute to educational success, and in the minority Willkommen found that the German speaker is "z.B. eher in der Stadt geboren, hat eine weitergehende Schulbildung, ist etwas jünger, ist eher Angestellter oder Beamter und bei den Selbstständigen eher Kauf-mann oder in einem freien Beruf tätig" (1975:138) ("*for example, tends to be born in town, has a further education, is rather young, tends to be an employee or civil servant and, among the self-employed, tends to be a shopkeeper or in a liberal profession*"). There are no conclusions to be drawn from the preceding considerations — not least because the statistical evidence is weak — but a careful observer notices that children whose home language code coincides with the school's code — in the minority the children of teachers are a large proportion of such a group — are likely to do well in the educational system.

It might appear appropriate to investigate some of the preceding speculations by statistical analysis of children's careers rather than based on the somewhat doubtful samples obtained for the adult population. Since, however, the declarations of the Bonn and Copenhagen govern-ments in 1955 expressly state that people should not be asked by majority officials about their minority loyalty, questions about home language and other private matters are not normally asked within the minority either. Nonetheless some statistics for Tingleff school are available and show that, in 1982:

14.8% had German as their home language; about half this figure could be accounted for by "Lehrerkinder";

62.2% spoke Sønderjysk at home;

1.6% spoke standard Danish (Rigsdansk), which meant one child;

17.5% said they spoke a mixture of Sønderjysk and German, which could mean that they speak German with some family members, Sønderjysk with others; or it could mean that they speak sometimes German, sometimes Sønderjysk; or it could mean that they mix the two languages within one utterance; or it could mean that they speak German to relatives visiting from Germany; or . . .

4.4% spoke some other language, in fact accounted for by one family where the mother is from Greenland.

Again, I would emphasize that these figures are to be approached with caution, for as I have indicated under the "mixed" category, pupils' awareness of their own language use is far from straightforward (cf. pp. 94–103).

The thrust of the preceding paragraphs shall be made explicit. There is no conclusive statistical evidence, but the statistics available, the perceptions of members of the minority, pedagogical reasoning and observation can be combined to support the argument that a pupil with German as the home language will, other things being equal, be more successful in minority education than one with Sønderjysk. It is therefore not surprising to find that the majority of school leavers from Tingleff do not go on to Gymnasium or equivalent and that the majority of pupils have Sønderjysk as their home language; individual exceptions to this, perhaps causal, correlation are easy to find.

Turning now to the large group of Tingleff school leavers who choose a commercial course, we find linguistic issues are prominent here too. Perceptions among career teachers differ, but there is clearly a debate to be considered as to whether pupils' bilingualism is an advantage or not in this kind of career. The proximity of the frontier and the consequent heavy trade opens up opportunities for young people with a good command of the two languages. When asked about the advantages of bilingualism pupils inevitably mention this as one of the first things to come to mind, even though few of them let it influence their own choice of career. Although teachers can cite instances of German pupils being preferred for work in banks or transport agencies, the path to such positions passes through a further education commercial course. It is here that the quality of the individual's mastery of standard Danish is in question, a question which occupies the educationists of the minority in a general manner, not only with respect to this particular application. Former pupils do have difficulty with their Danish. On the other hand they are well ahead of their contemporaries in German, and as far as English is concerned can hold their own. These are the purely academic aspects and the degree to which they affect an individual's performance will vary in part with other aspects of his accommodation to the new surroundings, an issue we shall meet later (pp. 103–11). It is not simply a question of weighing one against the other as if they were physical objects and though one teacher might wish that fewer pupils would choose this kind of career, they are more likely to be influenced by the lack of jobs in this sector than by such linguistic matters.

Teachers

We saw in Chapter 2 that the minority's schools system is closely connected to the Schleswig–Holstein school system through arrangements for staffing. Tingleff is no exception. The character of the whole staff is overwhelmingly "German" and yet different from a German school south of the border. Thirteen of the 21 are German nationals, seven are Danish but from Sønderjylland/Nordschleswig and the minority, and the one who is from elsewhere in Denmark is married to a German and, with German as the home language, identifies strongly with the minority. Twenty of the 21 were trained in the Federal Republic, all but three at the Pädagogische Hochschule in Flensburg, half-an-hour's drive away. The one exception with a Danish education was nonetheless trained in a a local teachers' college, in Tønder/Tondern, a few miles away. Of the 14 German nationals, eight are from the Schleswig part of Schleswig–Holstein. Most of the staff have been in the school for a long time, some for more than 20 years, and appear to be committed to a career in the school, creating a sense of stability. More than 90% of them are "Beamten des Landes Schleswig–Holstein beurlaubt für den Dienst im Nordschleswig" (*"civil servants of the state of Schleswig–Holstein granted leave for service in Nordschleswig"*).

In linguistic terms, this composition means that the staff are predominantly native-speaker German. Though the German spoken is Hochdeutsch, the accent is that of Landesteil Schleswig and, in a few cases, of Sønderjylland/Nordschleswig. Those born in Sønderjylland/Nordschleswig also speak Sønderjysk, although when teaching Danish they of course speak the standard language. Those born in Germany are offered the opportunity to take Danish lessons when they first arrive and the degree of proficiency in Danish, especially comprehension of Sønderjysk, depends partly on the length of stay but also partly on the interest of the individual in his degree of integration in Danish society. In the main, the language-model created in the school by the teachers is that of Hochdeutsch, spoken with a certain degree of formality in the classroom, with a Schleswig–area pronunciation. The ways in which this model is modified in practice and affects the pupil's language will be discussed in more detail later (pp. 71–72).

The influence of the teachers, linguistic and otherwise, goes beyond their immediate pedagogical work. There is a certain tacit expectation that they become involved in extra-curricular matters more than would normally be the case in Schleswig–Holstein. This means above all organizing and training sports clubs, but may also include organizational responsibility for other kinds of youth work. There is an important youth club connected with the school which other schools are encouraged to emulate; and there is a regional umbrella organization which brings together the youth activities once a year at the minority's youth college, as well as providing courses and other activities. Usually the official language of the organizations is German whereas the language used by the children among themselves is Sønderjysk. There has been an attempt to encourage more use of German, especially by those young people who take on responsibilities within the sports and other clubs. In other words, the area of application of the norm was to be extended from committee meetings, speech-making and announcements on festive occasions, and correspondence or other uses of the written language, to all discourse which was directly linked to the purpose of the club or society; sports training, for example, was to be in German. However, where the people involved share Sønderjysk as their home and colloquial language, it is difficult to extend the domains of German. The model of the German nationals is difficult to follow.

I suggested in general terms in Chapter 2 that the origins and training of staff influence the philosophy of education, within an organizational and legal framework that is largely Danish. Some aspects of this philosophy and the hidden curriculum it helps create are evident in the teacher–pupil relationships. Walking through the corridors of the school — one decorated with a pictorial map of the catchment area, another lined with sports trophies — a stranger is greeted by older and younger pupils with a polite "Guten Morgen". A more familiar face evokes a cheerful "Moin", which is the Sønderjysk greeting with more familiar and relaxed connotations, which is borrowed into German. This friendliness is typical of the relationships in the school, where the small number of pupils allows every teacher to know and have taught every pupil. Underneath, however, there is a clear sense of role-respect, and doubtless person-respect, for the teachers. The nature of the relationship is clearest in the use of Du (Tu) and Sie (Vous): unlike Schleswig–Holstein schools, here teachers address Du to pupils up to school–leaving age. On the other hand, pupils are expected to address Sie to teachers, whereas the popular pupil conception is that in Danish schools they use Du and first names. (In fact this is widespread practice though not exclusive.) Among staff themselves it is the norm to use Du and first names, even with the Headteacher, which is not often to be found in West German schools, even where teachers have known each other for many years.[1] On the other hand, the Danish outsider's perception of the minority schools is influenced by stereotypes of Prussian formality and discipline. This is a false perception, but the semi-formal relationships with pupils and the informality between colleagues put the school somewhere between the Danish and West German systems. In not many schools in West Germany would one see pupils freely walking into the staffroom, sent to fetch a book or simply in search of a teacher. Staffroom talk is peppered with discussions of problem children. They exist, but perhaps because of the size of the school and the nature of the catchment area, they are usually contained by a staff with many years of experience. Incidents, of say bullying, occur and are discussed but where everyone is known and where there is the close knowledge of families arising from frequent contact within the other aspects of the minority, the response can be moderate, even though the individual teacher here as in any school has to find a *modus vivendi* with classes.

The sense of harmony of a small staff is not absolute. There are disagreements on educational issues and occasional informal meetings on an evening to discuss school matters before they are put on the formal agenda of a staff meeting. The particular circumstance of living culturally, socially and economically within the bounds of the minority reinforces a common tendency among teachers to know each other socially, and this creates a harmonious atmosphere at work. This in turn is sustained by a tacit agreement about the role of the school within the minority, even though there may be differences on other educational issues.

"A day in the life of . . ."

It is 7.25 a.m. on a spring morning. The sun is high but invisible and a cool breeze fills the leaves of the chestnut trees at the end of the school yard which rise up to the roof of the two-storey building. Some children have been in the yard or in the classroom for half an hour or more, travelling from the villages by ordinary bus. Those who came by the regular school bus arrive nearer the starting time and the private bus is just turning into the yard. Teachers start arriving about 7.20 a.m., on foot, by bicycle or by car, although the Headteacher was already there by 7.00. In a private school, his adminstrative duties are increased by responsibility for the finance as well as educational matters, and the early morning and late afternoon offer opportunity to do paper-work.

At 7.30 the master-clock in the staffroom chimes and sets the bells ringing in the school. The same will happen again after each 45 minute lesson, but sometimes there are breaks to be signalled too. This morning lessons start immediately but on Monday morning there is an assembly, with singing led by the Headteacher or a presentation from one of the classes. A small group of final year pupils, 10. Klasse, move off to join some from the 9. Klasse to do Latin, a subject which is extra and voluntary. They use Danish books and so all the commentaries and grammatical explanations are in Danish; however, they translate into German for the teacher, even if the whispering among them is in Sønderjysk. In another wing of the school the 7. Klasse have started their Danish lesson. Here they are expected to speak as well as write standard Danish. Sometimes the teacher takes extracts from their essays to bring to their attention mistakes they have made because of interference from German, but when they speak or read aloud it is Sønderjysk pronunciation which has to be corrected, but gently so as not to undermine their confidence or denigrate their dialect. The balance is a difficult one, which the teacher is acutely aware of. Today's lesson is a continuation of a project where they are making a display in words and pictures to portray themselves and their interests. The words are Danish but the magazines they can cut pictures from are both Danish and German — an indication of an undogmatic attitude to the issue of keeping the languages separate. On another occasion, the pupils decided that they wanted to do something with the topic of experiments on animals. The ideal of pupils being responsible for decisions about the content of their work, laid down in the law of the Danish *folkeskole*, has had greater influence on the teachers of Danish than others in the school.[2] The pupils were given tape-recorders and sent out to interview people inside and outside the school. Thus social issues are taken into the subject in a way not uncommon in the ordinary Danish *folkeskole*. In the last three years, the pupils have a subject which is officially called by the German term "Gegenwartskunde", but is often referred to as Danish, "Samtidsorientering", for it is in essence a subject in which social issues are discussed (Social Education) and which is a creation of the Danish education system.

In fact in the third lesson this morning, 9.15–10.00, the 10. Klasse will be having a lesson of "Samtids" and will be discussing, in German, the Danish taxation system. This means that the Danish terminology has to be introduced, for the teacher cannot be sure that if he uses a German translation, the pupils will connect it back to the correct term in Danish. At the moment, though, the first lesson is drawing to a close, and as the pupils look out of the window, they see the little ones from the Kindergarten class and the first year class arriving at school, for they never start before 8.15.

The second lesson goes straight on without a pause. The 9. Klasse have a German lesson. They are beginning to revise and prepare for the examinations. In German they will have the oral examination prescribed by the Danish education system, where they will, however, have read and prepared far more texts than their contemporaries in the *folkeskole*. They will in addition have a written examination — a dictation and an essay — set by a committee from the minority's "Schul- und Sprachverein" and which will give them the equivalent of a leaving certificate ·from a Schleswig–Holstein Hauptschule (the least academic of German secondary schools). This is one of the arrangements for recognition of the minority pupils' qualifications in Germany. So today they are practising for the oral examination. The teacher names one of the books they have read and picks a pupil at random. The pupil has to recount the story and comment. Although there are two courses in the ninth year, "basic" and "extended", most of the year group are in this "extended" course, with the result that the range of performance in the language, as well as recall of the texts, is very wide. At the one extreme is the daughter of a teacher who speaks easily and with grammatical correctness, albeit with the Nordschleswig accent. At the other extreme are the hesitant and awkward accounts, where the teacher sometimes corrects a definite article, a past participle or a wrong noun, but also lets other mistakes pass without comment so as not to destroy the flow. It is impossible to know how much this hesitancy is due to linguistic incertitude and how much to lack of familiarity with the texts, but in this situation of sustained speech, the strengths and weaknesses show.

After the second lesson there is 15 minutes break. Back in the staffroom, someone has been putting out the coffee cups and has brought in a basket of bread rolls, some cheese and cold meats. It is her birthday today and this is one of the staffroom traditions. Birthday occasions are not the only ones, however, for if someone has been on a course, he might provide something in appreciation of the other teachers supervising his classes. We might even be treated to the unfinished food from a weekend party, or simply the extra baking someone did yesterday. When the chime and bell go again 15 minutes later, the lucky two or three who are free this lesson can continue to enjoy the food, which will gradually disappear during the morning.

In the third lesson the first and second classes, a total of 19 seven- and eight-year-olds, are to have a swimming lesson. They have already crossed the sports field and are waiting outside the sports hall for the teacher to arrive with the key. There is great excitement. The first lesson was German and the next lesson will be mathematics, so they mean to make the most of it. The lessons follow a fixed timetable, partly because they have more than one teacher, even though their class teacher takes them for most of their subjects. Nonetheless there is room for flexibility and at the end of the year they will prepare in lesson time, and produce for their parents in the evening, a circus performance, where they play both animals and trainers, as well as acrobats and clowns.

And so the morning passes. During the ten or twenty minute breaks pupils bring out their sandwiches and drinks. It is a long time since breakfast and for many there is a bus journey before they arrive home to eat. After four lessons the first two years go home. The third and fourth usually have five lessons, but the older ones scarcely get away before 12.55, the end of the sixth lesson. On two or three days a week they have a seventh lesson and so it is at least 14.30 before some of them get home, having left at 6.30 in the morning.

The above account is not of one actual day, but a selection and combination of observations over a period of several weeks. It describes only a time slice of the school's life and could be expanded almost indefinitely. Even that slice cannot pretend to be "typical", but encapsulates some of the experience of the school.

"Unsere Schule ist eine deutsche Schule . . ."

In my introduction to the minority's school system (pp. 21–26), I pointed to the basic paradox of the aims of the schools: on the one hand to introduce pupils to German language and culture, on the other hand to introduce them to Danish language and culture and prepare them for life in the Danish state. I suggested there that the orientation of the schools is southwards, that "German" means "West German" with an emphasis on Schleswig–Holstein. It is possible to define "German" in other ways and I quoted a document from the minority's central organization which implies a different reading. (pp. 17–19). The question of what is "German culture" in the minority is one which will be treated separately (pp. 113–17) but an initial approach to it will be made here through the school, one of the main mediators of culture. The tendency to separate and yet link "language" and "culture" which is evident in the quoted aims of the school system (pp. 21–26) and frequent in other contexts is also an interesting phenomenon which lends itself to semantic and philosophical analysis. I propose to treat it, however, in a more pragmatic way.

Pupil views

If pupils are asked what, apart from the language, makes their school German, the replies vary from "die Schule ist deutsch in der ganzen Aufmachung" (*"the school is German in its whole make-up"*) to complete silence and then a statement to the effect that one cannot ignore the language when talking about the school, or that the language is the only

Tinglev/Tingleff ... lies on an important east–west road ...

Die deutsche Schule Tingleff

The school band at a riding festival

The teachers have a day out

thing about the school which is German. The question is a difficult one for most pupils because they usually have no direct experience of any other school — or at best a brief visit, when they see the school buildings and physical environment. It is also difficult because for them everything which they experience in school even in a sense their Danish lessons, is associated with the word "German". Therefore to ask them to separate out traits which might be called "German", and others which might be "Danish" is for most to ask them to think for the first time in those terms. The response "everything" is therefore similar to the response "nothing". Paradoxically then, the school is indeed German in "everything" and yet, if the language could be ignored, it is German in "nothing". The first response is from someone who recognizes the German nature of the school; the second from someone who cannot see anything particularly German (except the language) because it is *all* German. "Deutsch", as a substantive, means "die deutsche Sprache" ("*the German language*") and "eine deutsche Schule" (*a German school*") means at a first level of connotation "eine Schule deutscher Sprache" ("*a German language school*"). However, it is not as simple as this and sometimes with a little insistence, sometimes spontaneously, pupils begin to pick out features which make the school German.

Consider the following comments:

"die Schule ist deutsch in der ganzen Aufmachung, finde ich, die Dänen, die sind da ..., das ist alles viel grösser, viel gelockerter also (...) ich glaube diese Schule geht doch mehr nach dem deutschen Muster (in der Stimmung), ja das glaube ich, auch die Art wie die Lehrer hier so noch gehen, einige immer noch im Schlips und so, während die Dänen ja nun wirklich mit langen Haaren und ... wir sind ja begonnen jetzt dänische Bücher zu kriegen und so eigentlich ist der nicht mehr der grosse Unterschied, früher ist der bestimmt schon mehr gewesen (...) diese

(the school is German in its whole make-up, I think, the Danes, they are ... it is much bigger, much looser there (...) I believe this school follows much more the German pattern (in its atmosphere), yes I believe that also the way in which the teachers are here, some still wearing a tie and such like, whilst the Danes, well really with long hair ... we have begun to get Danish books now and so really there is not the same difference as before; before it was definitely more (...) the whole atmosphere and mood, it's getting more and more Danish, but we still speak more about German

ganze Stimmung und Atmosphäre, die wird immer mehr dänisch aber wir sprechen immer noch mehr über deutsche Politik und Samtids (orientering) als wir dänisch, obwohl das wird auch schon oft durchgesprochen, (die Politik) in Dänemark, auch der Unterricht, also irgendwie macht das doch was aus, dass man im Unterricht Deutsch spricht, denn die Bücher sind ja zum Teil dänisch und trotzdem wird immer wieder übersetzt."

politics and social issues than we do Danish, although it is often discussed, (politics) in Denmark; the lessons too, it does really make a difference somehow, that we speak German in the lessons, because the books are partly Danish and still it is frequently translated.")

"Das ist sehr schwer zu sagen also, da ist eigentlich nur die Sprache, die wirklich auffällt, beim Benehmen sieht man ja nicht ob der deutsch oder dänisch ist, also die Gewohnheiten sind vielleicht ein bisschen anders, ich meine, wir haben vielleicht, ja ich war ja nicht so bei dänischen Veranstaltungen, aber wenn wir zum Beispiel Kinderkarneval haben, zu mich ist dann eine grosse Gemeinschaft da, ich glaube, das pflegen die Dänen nicht so doll."

(It's difficult to say, there is really only the language, which is really noticeable; you can't see from the behaviour whether someone is German or Danish; perhaps the customs are a bit different, I mean, we have perhaps — well I wasn't at Danish functions, — but when we have the children's festival, for me there is a great community there, I don't think the Danes do that as much.")

Both these statements find it impossible to ignore the language, and both use the comparison with Danish schools, even though they have little personal experience of them. The first refers particularly to the teachers and their difference from Danish teachers; the issue of using Du and first names is mentioned later, a point which almost all the pupils interviewed fixed on, even if there was nothing else they could isolate. The reference in the second to "a great community" includes implicitly both pupils and teachers and thus gives a counter-balance to the formality mentioned in the first.

The reference to the emphasis on German politics in the first statement is one of the few direct references to the subject "Samtids-orientering" (Social Education) — here the use of the Danish word is typical — but many pupils said that in History there is emphasis on Germany.

"... uber dänische Geschich-te, das haben wir eigentlich nie (gelernt), wir haben im-mer deutsche Geschichte"	*(Danish history, we have never really learnt that, we have always had Germany history.")*

This is one of the most extreme statements, but it is not the only one which is so categorical. History is the subject which evokes an immediate and definite response. (This may change with the recent purchase of sets of Danish history books.) Other aspects of the curriculum are not mentioned spontaneously, although when music is mentioned, it is said that only German songs are learnt. When asked how much they learn in school about the minority — the internal word is "Volksgruppe" rather than "Minderheit" — pupils agree that they learn a little, if time allows, but it is not a topic which is allocated much importance and in general they don't seem to mind. One said "das Thema interessiert mich nun auch gar nicht" (*"that topic doesn't interest me at all"*). It must be clear, however, that there may be a difference between the perceptions of pupils and those of teachers, between perceptions of both and what an observer might see. It is at the least unlikely that Danish history is "never" taught, particularly as it is expressly part of the syllabus, as we shall see. There is in fact a significant distinction between "never" and "never really", a distinction between experience and perception of the experience. In the final analysis, however, it is the latter which matters in the question of discovering the nature of the school. It is worth noting that for the pupils the basis of comparison in thinking about their school is the Danish state education system. Though they have little direct experience of it, they have even less of schools in the Federal Republic. Their orientation is essentially towards Denmark or more precisely towards Sønderjylland/Nordschleswig, and when this clashes openly with the orientation of the school — in history and contemporary affairs — the experience is remembered. Some are quite openly dissatisfied with this. In other respects the clash is not so evident, and their lack of basis for comparison, the position which makes them say "all" and "nothing" is specifically German, prevents them from seeing and analysing their school experience.

"Hidden" curriculum

Let us consider some of these less evident matters, the not-so-hidden German curriculum, some of which have been described before. The intention here is to consider the cumulative effect.

Second only to the language as an obvious German characteristic of the school come the teachers, both in the perceptions of the pupils and of the teachers. A small but significant indication of the effect of German educational philosophy is the use of the German system of evaluation of work for the first seven years, after which the Danish system is used. An official equivalence is established between the two systems so that pupils' qualifications can be recognized in Germany:

From best to worst the equivalences are:

Denmark	13 11	10 9	8 7	6	5	0 3	0 0
F.R.G.	1	2	3	4	5	6	

The use of the German system in the first seven years is facilitated by the fact that Danish state schools do not give marks during this period but verbal reports. The law requires marks for the last years and it is at this point that the German school begins to use the Danish equivalences. Normal procedure in Schleswig–Holstein is to give marks from the first year — pupils beginning school a year earlier than in Denmark — and it is "because the parents wanted it", said the Headteacher, that the procedure was introduced into this school. Whether this was the only reason or not, it allows the teachers to evaluate the pupils' work in a familiar way. On the other hand, the fairly rigidly regulated Schleswig–Holstein system of making pupils without satisfactory grades repeat the year is not transferred to the minority school.

The recognition of pupils' school-leaving qualifications in Germany is obviously a peculiar trait of their situation, but it is only rarely important to them. They take an additional written examination in the ninth year, described earlier, and if they go on to take the "extended" course examination (folkeskolens udvidede afgangsprøve) at the end of the tenth year they are recognized as having the equivalent of Hauptschulabschluss (basic secondary leaving certificate) and Realschulabschluss (extended secondary leaving certificate) in West Germany. The fact that the "extended" examination in German as a foreign language is equated with a qualification in German as mother tongue is one of the difficulties the minority school has to live with. It is a small compensation for the pupils who might not do so well in Danish as mother tongue but have an advantage in German as a foreign language. All this is of little importance, however, because of the difficulty of having the trade examinations, which they might want to work for in Germany, recognized in Denmark. The leaving qualification is only the first step and therefore, except for the few who know at this stage that they wish to make a career in Germany, they are advised to stay in Denmark.

When it comes to materials, the teachers can capitalize on their pupils' bilingualism and use sources in Germany and Denmark. There is in fact a policy to use Danish text books in mathematics from the sixth year, in natural sciences from the eighth year and in history to have an additional book in Danish. In the subject "Samtidsorientering", taught according to Danish syllabus recommendations, a mixture of materials is used in both Danish and German. It is as a result of Danish regulations too that one of the teachers has a joint post as school librarian, providing books and audio-visual materials from school stock but also to a large extent borrowed from the regional Danish resource centre. There is also the possibility of borrowing from Schleswig–Holstein's educational system, but this is not used as much, perhaps because German materials are available from the Danish centre. In this way there is a mixture of German and Danish teaching materials, where differences in presentation may be marked and where science teachers, for example, find the Danish books more palatable for pupils. Yet the pupil quoted above still found that the use of the German language and the translation of texts meant that the lessons remain firmly "German".

Links with Germany of another kind have already been mentioned: the sponsorships which the school has at administrative area level (Kreis Schleswig), at town level (Stadt Schleswig) and at village level (Gemeinde Westerrönfeld). It is the latter which, of a comparable size, has a personal as well as financial dimension, and it is as a result of these sponsorships that many school journeys are made to Germany, and personal contacts created by return visits. In some cases, these kinds of visit are the nearest personal contact that pupils have with German people and even those who have relatives in Germany do not visit them often and have little direct experience of daily life in Germany. They are, however, aware that these journeys make them different from their Danish contemporaries.

Sport provides a similar link. Sports clubs often have such sponsorship partners, but school sport is even more closely linked to Germany. At one level school teams and representatives have competitions with other schools in the minority, but at a higher level, they compete in the West German system in Schleswig–Holstein and beyond. The badges and qualifications they receive are German, even though they are Danish citizens. Both tacitly and openly, the role of sport as a means of keeping pupils in the minority is evident. Tacitly, teachers with sporting interests are expected to give of their free time — more than would usually be the case in Germany — and they in turn expect pupils to work for the school and indirectly for the minority. The links between school sport and club sport are close in both personal and organizational terms. It is at the level of the umbrella organization ("der deutsche Jugendverband für Nordschleswig" — *the German Youth Association for North Schleswig*) that the connection between sport and the ideological purpose of maintaining the minority is open:

"Die Verantwortlichen der ausserschulischen Jugendarbeit werden immer bestrebt sein müssen, im Rahmen deutscher Sprache Sport und Kultur zu fördern. Diese Aufgabe muss erfüllt werden, wenn die deutsche Volksgruppe in Dänemark weiterhin den Wunsch hat, auch in den nächsten Generationen deutsche Volkszugehörigkeit als dänische Staatsbürger zu bewahren ... Die Frage, die am Schluss offenbleibt, lautet: Kommt beim Mannschaftssport volksgruppen-politisch das nötige Zusammengehörigkeitsgefühl zustande?"
(Nickelsen, *Der Nordschleswiger*, Nov. 1982).

("Those responsible for non-school youth work will always have to strive to promote sport and culture in the framework of the German language. This task must be fulfilled if the German minority in Denmark still has the desire to maintain their belonging to the German people as Danish citizens into the next generation ... The question which in the final analysis remains open is as follows: Is the necessary feeling of belonging, with respect to the politics of the minority, achieved through team sport?")

Thus although the "content" is not culture-bound — the same sports are played north and south of the border with handball being as popular among Danes as among Germans — the structure within which the pupils and young people play is German in tone and orientation.

In all these matters the German language is central, although the exact nature of its position will be considered later. The cumulative effect is to give the school a strong German character, especially if viewed through pupils' eyes. For, in addition to the fact that they know little else, it is also noteworthy that many of the matters which impinge directly on the pupils in their daily school routine are German, whereas the Danish influence —

chiefly in matters of regulations — are rather the concern of the teachers. Nonetheless, the cumulative force of the factors discussed here on the nature of the hidden curriculum is combined with the influence of Danish regulations, examinations, norms of teacher-pupil relationships and so on in a whole which cannot be neatly disentangled into German and Danish.

Official curriculum

We turn now to the official curriculum. This is determined for all the minority schools by a series of subject committees drawn from the staff of the schools and working under the auspices of the "Schul- und Sprachverein". In its yearly report for 1981/82, the "Schul- und Sprachverein" published for the general public a document summarizing the curriculum. The chairman of each subject committee was asked to write an introduction to the subject. These introductions do not contain much detail, but they do make explicit some of the assumptions with which the committees worked, and therefore some of the framework within which teaching is done. The following analysis will use both this popular document and the full official syllabuses (Lehrpläne).

In the introduction to the official documents, the Lehrpläne are said to be based on the "Lehrplanwerk für Schleswig–Holstein" (Syllabus compendium for Schleswig–Holstein) and "det vejledende forslag til læseplaner i Folkeskolen" (guideline proposals for syllabuses in the *folkeskole*.) In both popular and official documents the aims (Zielsetzungen) of the schools are printed as a further element in the work. It would be possible to do a detailed comparative analysis of the official documents and the German and Danish originals. This would not only be tedious but also add little to our understanding of the experience of the pupils. For in practice the teacher comes between the syllabus and the pupil to such an extent that the attitudes implicit in the syllabuses can be changed. We have already seen, for example, how history is perceived as German and how the minority as a topic in "Samtidsorientering" has low priority, despite the Lehrpläne. The official introduction stresses that the syllabuses should not limit the freedom of the teacher more "als es zeitgemässe Lehr- und Lernpläne von ihrer Konzeption her tun" (*than syllabuses appropriate to contemporary times do in their original conception*). However, the need for colleagues to work together is stressed, especially in the matter of pupil transfer from school to school. This kind of formulation, the role of the teacher in deciding on the content of examinations, and the absence of examinations in some subjects, allow considerable freedom of interpretation.

"Deutsch" is the first subject, "Dänisch" the second. The official papers emphasize the significance of the subject German:

"Als eine kulturprägende Kraft nimmt die deutsche Sprache in den deutschen Schulen Nordschleswigs eine zentrale Stellung ein.
Der Deutschunterricht hat daher im besonderen die Aufgabe, die Schüler so zu bilden, dass sie sich in der deutschen Sprache heimisch fühlen. Dieses kann nur erreicht werden, wenn der Unterricht darauf abzielt,
– in den Schülern ein sicheres Sprachgefühl anzulegen
– sie zur selbstständigen Festigung und Erweiterung ihres Sprachgutes zu befähigen
– ihnen durch Textbeispiele ein zunehmendes Einleben in den deutschen Kulturbereich zu ermöglichen."

("As a force which moulds the culture, the German language has a central place in the German schools of Nordschleswig. German teaching has therefore the special task of educating pupils so that they feel at home in the German language. This can only be achieved if the teaching aims,
– to form a secure feeling for the language in pupils
– to make them able to reinforce and expand their language competence independently
– to make possible for them an increasing familiarity with German culture through textual examples.")

The syllabus is then stated to have been worked out following the equivalent in Schleswig–Holstein, but with allowance made "in no small measure" for the linguistic factors in the area "so unter anderen Rechtschreibkonkurrenzen aufgrund der Zweisprachigkeit" (*"for example, inter alia, spelling interferences caused by bilingualism"*). However, in the almost 90 pages, the only significant reference to the problems posed by bilingualism is in the area of interferences in spelling. The tone, including the tendency to refer the reader for whole sections to Schleswig–Holstein documents, is that pupils should be taught as if German were their mother tongue, that learning processes and difficulties to be anticipated will be those of the native-speaker. Where bilingualism is mentioned it is considered to be a problem, a hindrance to mother-tongue abilities rather than a source of enrichment. Clearly this is in keeping with the aims quoted above. Although the term "Muttersprache" is linguistically vague, in popular use the majority of pupils claim that they have one mother tongue,

Sønderjysk, and as a reflection of their emotional attachment at least, this is an accurate account. The syllabus uses the phrase "to feel at home in the German language"; teachers claim to teach German "muttersprachlich" — in one description there is the following: teachers "haben den Auftrag muttersprachlich zu unterrichten" (*have the duty to teach as mother tongue*) (Jahresbericht 1979–80), and the justification for special examinations in the ninth class is that pupils may obtain a qualification equivalent to German in Germany. The phrase "feel at home" is an attempt to span the difference between pupil perception — and in many cases their actual German capacities — and the desire of the schools to teach them as if they were native-speakers. The popular account ends rather optimistically:

> "Bisherige Ergebnisse zeigen, dass diese Forderungen weitgehend in Wirklichkeit umgesetzt werden können."
>
> (*"Results so far show that these demands can to a large extent be realized."*)

It may be that the reality for many pupils would be best described as a "second language situation", but this would have so many consequences of an educational and ideological nature that I shall discuss it in detail later. Suffice it for the moment to say that the syllabus scarcely attempts to come to terms with the complexities of the situation.

The position for Danish is different and for the writer of the popular introduction, rather easier. The basis for the subject is quoted in translation directly from "Vejledende forslag til læseplan for faget dansk" (*"Guideline proposal for a syllabus for the subject Danish"*), a document issued by the Ministry of Education. Furthermore, the writer can claim with confidence:

> "Der Dänischunterricht an den deutschen Schulen Nordschleswigs muss als muttersprachlicher Unterricht angesehen werden, da die Schüler wie fast alle Schüler in Dänemark nach dem 9. bzw. 10. Schuljahr die gleichen staatskontrollierten Prüfungen ablegen."
>
> (*"Danish teaching in the German schools of Nordschleswig must be viewed as mother tongue teaching, since the pupils like almost all pupils in Denmark must take the same state-controlled examinations in the ninth or tenth year."*)

As far as possible, then, the Lehrplan follows the official proposals. However, the teaching of Danish in a "systematic" way starts not in the first year as in Danish schools, but in the third year, preceded by teaching through a Spielstunde (play lesson) in the first and second years, where only oral work is done (Søndergaard, 1981). It is therefore necessary to distribute the work differently, but by the ninth and tenth classes, the syllabus is in phase with the guideline proposals. The official status of Danish in the German schools appears therefore to be unproblematic: it is treated as the mother tongue. There are nonetheless several problems. The fact that many pupils have Sønderjysk as their mother tongue is not exclusive to the German schools, but affects all the schools in the region to some extent (Pedersen, 1977; Nyberg, 1981). In the Danish schools, however, the presence of standard Danish as the norm for the language of the school means that the pupils receive and are required to produce standard Danish much more than in the German schools. Another factor is that the process of learning to read is carried out in German in the first two years of school, and assumed to be completed for most children as they enter the third year. The process of transfer of reading ability to Danish has to be done during the third year. The special nature of this process is not considered in the syllabus. Thirdly, the fact that the pupils are bilingual is not mentioned at all, neither as a problem, nor as an enrichment of their linguistic experience, even though the aims of the subject include giving pupils the prerequisites "sich in einer vielschichtigen sprachlichen Gemeinschaft behaupten zu konnen" ("*to be able to assert themselves in a multi-layered linguistic community*"). This could, with a little stretching, be interpreted to include the special linguistic situation of the pupils themselves. A fourth and final problem arises when the syllabuses for German and Danish are juxtaposed, as they are in the popular document but were presumably not in the process of working them out. Juxtaposition brings out the implication that both subjects are to be treated as if they were the mother tongue. As before I would point out that this is a vague term and that some pupils will claim to have two Muttersprachen, even if most would not. Yet even if the pupils were balanced bilinguals, in German and Sønderjysk, there is little chance in this linguistic environment of them being balanced trilinguals, adding standard Danish. There would have to be some consideration of precisely what that involved for pedagogical purposes. Such considerations are almost entirely absent.

If we look for traits in the other subjects which give the school its particular German character, we find them most explicitly in History and "Gegenwartskunde" (Social Education) (Danish: "Samtidsorientering"). These are the areas which pupils also notice, as we saw above, which is an indication of the strength of influence of the syllabuses. However, the pupils' perceptions that they learn almost exclusively German history — even though they are probably thinking only of the last period of their school careers — are not in harmony with the claims of the syllabus:

"Für die Ausbildung von Jugendlichen an Schulen in einem Grenzland kommt dem Geschichtsunterricht besondere Bedeutung zu, die gleichzeitig Verpflichtung und Verantwortung beinhaltet. Verpflichtung insofern, als in einem Grenzland Geschichte wissenschaftlich so korrekt und in der Auswahl so tendenzfrei wie möglich unterrichtet werden muss.

Verantwortung insofern, als das Fach Geschichte an den deutschen Schulen in Nordschleswig integriert sein muss in die Existenz der Volksgruppe zur Vergangenheit und zur Zukunft hin.

Beides muss berücksichtigt werden auf dem Hintergrund, dass die Abgänger der deutschen Schulen sich sowohl in Dänemark als auch in der Bundesrepublik Deutschland zurechtfinden sollen."

("In the education of young people in schools in a border region, history teaching has a particular significance which includes simultaneously duties and responsibilities. Duties in so far as history in a border region must be taught as scientifically correctly and, in the selection, as free of tendentiousness as possible.

Responsibilities in so far as the subject history in the German schools of Nordschleswig must be integrated into the existence of the minority in the past and in the future.

Both must be taken into account against the background that pupils leaving German schools must be able to cope both in Denmark and in the Federal Republic of Germany.")

In the light of this very explicit statement, it is interesting to speculate on pupils' perceptions (cf. pp. 48–51). I did not ask them to develop their impressions as this might have led to unethical discussion of the teaching and teachers involved, nor did they volunteer any further comment. Since History is an obligatory subject only until the ninth year and because the procedure is to develop chronologically from the fifth year, the last two years cover the period from the French Revolution until the present. Let us suppose that pupils' general impression is most influenced by these two years.

The syllabus has ten topics for the eighth year and five for the ninth:

8th Year

1. Die Entstehung der U.S.A.

(1. The Emergence of the U.S.A.

2. Die Französische Revolution
3. Napoleon
4. Technische und Soziale Veränderungen im 19. Jahrhundert
5. Erwachen des Nationalgefühls
6. Vom Deutschen Bund zum Deutschen Reich
7. Dänemarks Weg zur Demokratie
8. Das Zeitalter des Imperialismus
9. Der Erste Weltkrieg und die Revolutionen
10. Nordschleswig als Teil des Deutschen Reiches

2. *The French Revolution*
3. *Napoleon*
4. *Technical and Social Changes in the 19th Century*
5. *The Awakening of National Feeling*
6. *From the German Federation to the German Empire*
7. *Denmark's Path to Democracy*
8. *The Age of Imperialism*
9. *The First World War and the Revolutions*
10. *Nordschleswig as a part of the German Empire)*

9th Year

1. Die Minderheiten im deutschdänischen Grenzland
2. Deutschland und Dänemark und die Welt zwischen den Weltkriegen
3. Der Nationalsozialismus in Deutschland
4. Der Zweite Weltkrieg
5. Deutschland und der Norden nach dem Zweiten Weltkrieg

1. *The Minorities in the German–Danish Borderland*
2. *Germany and Denmark and the World between the Wars*
3. *National Socialism in Germany*
4. *The Second World War*
5. *Germany and Scandinavia after the Second World War*

In the first half of the eighth year only the fifth topic has specific mention of Germany or Denmark, but is entirely devoted to the Schleswig question. The issue of nationalism is clearly much wider than this and could have included at least Norway, in order to give a Danish perspective on loss of land through nationalism. In the second half of the list, there is evidence of parallelism in topics 6 and 7. In topic 8 there is first analysis of the concept of imperialism, then comparison of imperial powers, and third, analysis of the tension created between world powers through imperialism; in this third part the issue is German imperialism. Denmark's relationship to imperialism is not discussed. The ninth topic obviously involves German history, but there is no mention of Danish policy during the First World War nor of the effects of revolutionary thought in Denmark — the so-called "Påskekrise" (*Easter Crisis*) — but only of the November Revolution in Germany. The last topic, despite the title, involves both Germany and Denmark. There is discernible in the eighth year an attempt to look at history in Denmark and Germany in parallel, yet there is limited but clear evidence of bias. The bias need not be ideological in the sense of putting only a German point of view, but rather an emphasis on German events.

In the ninth year, the balance is deliberate and evident, and because this period is so much part of the pupils' life, through their parents and grandparents, teachers are presumably at pains to work with the sense of "duties" and "responsibilities" emphasized above. Yet pupils come away with a sense that they have learnt German history. The reasons need not be sinister: there is no need to infer ideological bias. The causes may be partly in the historical training of the teachers, partly in the use of German textbooks — with Danish texts used as supplements — partly in the fact that German is the language of instruction. Whatever the causes, however, the effects give pause for thought.

It will be evident that the history of Schleswig is given attention in the eighth and ninth years. This is supplemented in the subject "Gegenwartskunde", which was originally proposed as part of the *folkeskole* reform in 1976 to treat in an interdisciplinary way contemporary affairs, social studies, political education and so on. The syllabus is largely based on the suggestions in Danish documents but deliberately offers flexibility. In addition, however, to three general areas of study (Problemfelder), a fourth one concentrates on the minority in Nordschleswig:

"Daraus ergibt sich die besondere Bedeutung dieses Faches für die deutschen Schulen und die deutsche Volksgruppe in Nordschleswig."

(*"Hence there is a special significance of this subject for the German schools and the German minority in Nordschleswig."*)

Four themes are suggested:

- Neubeginn der Arbeit der deutschen Volksgruppe nach 1945
- Normalisierung der politischen Verhältnisse

(– *New beginning of the work of the German minority after 1945*
– *Normalization of political relationships*

– Struktur der Volksgruppe und Arbeitsweise der Organisationen	– *Structure of the minority and operations of the organizations*
– Die deutsche Volksgruppe innerhalb der Minderheiten Europas	– *The German minority within the minorities of Europe)*

There is then considerable implication that the topic is important, an implication which contrasts with pupils' perceptions and with the priority allocated by teachers. The inference is that the school is not an active agent deliberately and openly attempting to create a sense of identity with the minority. Indeed the fear of slipping into some kind of indoctrination may be one of the reasons why teachers give the topic low priority. One further factor gives the subject a different character to that in Danish schools. It is taught in German, using both German and Danish materials, even though there is a necessity to use Danish terminology. This means, according to the syllabus, that teachers must have sufficient knowledge of the Danish language; obviously they must have adequate knowledge of Danish society too. One consequence of teaching in German is that it is not possible to combine the subject with the subject Danish as can happen in Danish schools. Given the nature of the subject Danish, which will be discussed later (pp. 73–80), this would be a natural combination with respect to both content and language.

Another subject has similar consequences. The subject "Heimat und Sachkunde" has been transposed from Schleswig-Holstein. It covers, according to the popular explanation, subject matter which in Danish schools is part of the subject Danish in the first two years and then split into Geography, History and Biology in years three and four. Here, too, the bilingualism of the pupils is seen as a problem: the number of specific terminological concepts is a problem for pupils speaking Sønderjysk. It would therefore be advisable that teachers possess "eine möglichst grosse Sicherheit in den Sprachen Deutsch und Dänisch" ("*as great a confidence as possible in the German and Danish languages*"). It is unfortunate that the initial clarity which stresses the importance of Sønderjysk is lost in the cover-term "Dänisch".

In one other subject, Music, there is explicit reference to the German influence on the curriculum. Although Music is not limited to singing, "die Pflege und Erhaltung des deutschen Volksliedes ist gerade hier in Nordschleswig ein besonderes Anliegen" ("*promotion and maintenance of the German folksong is precisely here in Nordschleswig of special importance*").

The introduction to Music also mentions the question of allocation of curricular time. A close comparison with Danish and German school timetables would reveal discrepancies in the allocation of time to subjects. Apart from the late introduction of Danish, perhaps the most important one is with respect to English. Because of the early establishment of both German and Danish, English does not start until the seventh year, whereas in state schools it begins in the fifth year, with German following in the seventh. Danish schools have English for six years of three lessons per week; German schools four years of four lessons per week. Both foreign languages have the same kind of leaving examination which includes written tests in the "extended" examination in the tenth year. Thus although German for pupils from the minority offers no problems at this stage, English has to be prepared in a reduced time-span.

Bilingualism and curriculum

In summary of the analysis so far of the character of the hidden and official curriculum of the school, I would like to develop the references to bilingualism. At several points in the syllabuses the linguistic competences of the pupils are mentioned, and in particular the fact that they speak Sønderjysk is treated as a problem. From the point of view of teachers who wish to use German as if it were the mother tongue, this is understandable. One of the purposes of such teaching is to develop in pupils knowledge and use of at least one variety of German, Hochdeutsch (standard German), to such an extent that they will be linguistically equipped to enter those domains of social life where Hochdeutsch is expected. Teachers might also want to equip pupils with other varieties for other domains, but in practice their main concern is with Hochdeutsch. From this point of view any deviation from the Hochdeutsch norm is a problem, and deviation caused by interference from another language is problematic. It is, however, possible to argue that knowing another language and being made conscious of how languages function (Lambert, 1977) is a way of becoming more aware of how a language variety relates to particular social domains. In this sense, the pupils' bilingualism could be useful to the teacher.

There is another aspect to the question. The purpose of German mother tongue teaching described above applies to minority pupils in only a very limited degree. For most of them, there will be at best only one social domain they will wish to enter where Hochdeutsch is expected: the formal occasions of the organizations of the minority. Their contact with such domains in West German society will be very limited and perhaps non-existent. School is, of course, another such domain; but school cannot be its own justification.

The same arguments apply to standard Danish, Rigsdansk. Here, however, the probability of pupils wanting to enter Rigsdansk domains is much higher. Even though Sønderjysk is the variety appropriate in many domains in Sønderjylland/Nordschleswig, it does not cover the whole spectrum, and is inappropriate in other parts of Denmark, where some at least of the pupils will wish to live. Yet in the school the opportunities for developing a command of Rigsdansk are limited, and the consequent minimal proficiency can be a factor in an individual's decision about living elsewhere in Denmark, even if he will develop proficiency should he move.

The conclusions from such an analysis would be as follows. There is a lack of fit between mother-tongue teaching and the potential social aspirations of many pupils. Furthermore, it is clear that the actual attainment of many pupils is not likely to be comparable to mother tongue competence, as pupils themselves recognize. The real situation is that German is taught in order to facilitate adherence to the minority and the productive and receptive competence required and attainable is more like that of Second Language speakers. Native-speaker competence is not, however, required for the domains of minority membership, not even for familiarity with German culture, as we shall see later (p. 117–20). With respect to Rigsdansk on the other hand, pupils do need native-speaker competence, and the implication might be that more opportunity for developing especially productive competence is needed. Such opportunity in the school can only come from introducing more Rigsdansk into the curriculum in some way.

A different analysis runs roughly as follows. The school is not a bilingual school, it is a minority school (cf. Sönnichsen in *Der Nordschleswiger*, 16 March 1983). The fact that pupils are or become bilingual is simply one of their common traits — "like the nose on their face", as one Headteacher once put it to me. The schools are the institutions of the minority to which parents choose to send their children because they are members of the minority. The school must therefore foster minority membership as its principal purpose, in response to society's demands.

Yet the responsibility of teachers to whom parents entrust their children requires of them professional interpretation of parental and societal needs. The aims of the school are explicit, and in accordance with parental wishes. The teachers are concerned with how those aims are implemented. My analysis of the curriculum shows that the interpretation of the concept of minority school, in the linguistic and to some extent in the historical aspects, is that pupils should be treated as if they were native-speakers of German, living in Germany. For the few — often the children of teachers and other academically educated people — who are native-speakers and who quite probably will live in Germany, this is fine; but not for the majority. Yet the conclusions drawn from the analysis are not a threat to the character of the school as a minority institution, and do not imply that the school needs to become an institution primarily concerned with producing bilingual pupils. For it is evident from preceding pages that there are many factors besides language which make the school German. If there were any one factor which gave a German character to the school it would be the teachers, with their training and philosophy clearly deter-mined by the German tradition in education. This is largely intangible and inter-linked with all the other factors described. The school is German for a whole complex of reasons, and language is just one of them.

Notes to Chapter 3

1. Since the early 1970s, there has been a significant shift in Danish usage from De (Vous) to Du (Tu) throughout society. The speed of the change, which was largely complete within a decade, has left some people especially older generations, behind. Nonetheless it is popularly said that the only person to whom De is addressed is the Queen; the Prime Minister is addressed with Du. This is a linguistic phenomenon which has become symbolic of changed social attitudes and one of which everyone is aware. In standard German, there has been no corresponding change, but in Nordschleswig German the sociolinguistic norms of Danish have caused some transfer and the switch to Du from Sie is more frequent than it is in Schleswig-Holstein.
2. The "Lov om folkeskolen" contains the following paragrah: "16.4 The more detailed planning and organization of the educational activities, including the decision on teaching forms, methods and materials, shall to the widest possible extent, take place in co-operation between the teachers and the pupils."
   (Ministry of Education, 1978)

4 "Language and Culture" in the School

The main purpose of this chapter is to develop some points made in a general fashion earlier by describing language use in the school and then examining what kind of "culture" the school mediates to the pupils. There are a number of ways of analysing language distribution, e.g. by function, by interlocutor, by topic. The emphasis here will be on the distribution of languages and language varieties over different types of situation, and I shall use three broad categories: spoken, written and, third, both of these when language is being taught.

Spoken language: Pupils

The initial impression is that this is a school where German is spoken. The fact that it is a school makes it different from many other social institutions in that one group of people, the teachers, regulate the behaviour of another group, the pupils. Both groups expect and accept this, with a few exceptions. Linguistic behaviour is included and in one respect particularly — the use of *Sie* to teachers and *Du* to pupils — language makes the relationship explicit. (The exceptions are also linguistic; the only pupil to use *Du* to me in an interview was a "problem pupil".) One of the expectations is that teachers should be addressed in German, except when Danish is being taught. In the past, it was also an explicit rule that pupils should address each other in German and were censured for not doing so. That rule no longer exists and the notion of censure has been dropped, even with regard to addressing teachers. The expectation, however, remains and regulates teacher–pupil conversation. Furthermore, a model is provided by the dominant group of the variety of language to be used. The fact that the majority of the teachers are native-speaker German nationals and that both they and teachers from Nordschleswig were mainly educated in Schleswig-Holstein, in particular at the Pädagogische Hochschule Flensburg, has a bearing on the language of the school. The model which they provide is fairly uniform: formal Hochdeutsch spoken with a regional accent, sometimes with a Nordschleswig intonation breaking through. Although the degree of formality varies, from person to person — the teachers of the subject German tend to be more formal — and from situation to situation, the pupils are not exposed to the informalities of slang, or even the changing fashions of colloquialisms.

The impact of the model is dependent on how much pupils are made aware of it and encouraged to follow it. Do teachers correct pupils' language towards the norms of the model? Where attention is on the message to be conveyed — answering a question in a History lesson, asking where a book is in the library, for example — I observed no correction. Where attention is divided between form and content — in a pupil's prepared talk to the class about a given topic — or where the teacher's attention can be devoted entirely to aspects of form — a child reading aloud from a text the teacher knows well — then correction takes place. In the first kind of situation, correction tends to be at the level of syntax and morphology, with attention also to semantics. In the second kind, the teacher can correct at a phonemic level and at a segmental phonetic level, but does not correct at the level of intonation. At the semantic, syntactic and phonemic levels, teachers share a store of well-known problems, problems caused by interference, and are on the watch for them. The emphasis, however, is on semantics and syntax.

As a result of this tacit policy, the teachers have no influence on the accent of the vast majority of their pupils. Pupils speak German with a Nordschleswig accent, as do the majority of their parents. Some pupils — primarily those with parents who are German nationals — scarcely have this accent, and this may be one of the factors which helps their peers to identify them as "German-speaking" a category we shall examine shortly. In general, then, the teacher model serves as a norm at levels other than phonetic, and at the phonetic level a process of accommodation to the regional, Nordschleswig, norm takes place (Giles & Powesland, 1975).

Norms and expectations are not always fulfilled. We turn now to the question of actual behaviour and language distribution. Consider first pupils talking to each other. There is no longer any explicit teacher pressure on them to speak German. Therefore there is no difference in their behaviour according to place or time; what is important is that they are speaking to each other, whether in the classroom or the playground, in the presence or absence of a teacher. The topic is also of importance: discussion of a school subject will differ from discussion of private life and personal relations, for example. The identity of the interlocutor within the general category of "fellow-pupil" has to be further categorized as "deutschsprechend" ("German-speaking") or not. "Deutschsprechend" is to be interpreted in the following way: the pupil comes from a home where German is the dominant language, that is where both parents speak German and do so much of the time if not exclusively. This usually means the children of teachers and therefore the term "Lehrerkind" is largely interchangeable with "deutschsprechend". The process of identification does not happen in this essentially synchronic way, however; it is dependent on diachronic knowledge. The pupils have known each other at least since the age of starting school. At that age, and in the third class when Danish is introduced into the curriculum, it is easy for them to see who speaks predominantly or only German, who speaks little or no Sønderjysk and has difficulty with the Danish lessons. Therefore, although such pupils *may* acquire by the age of sixteen a sound, productive command of Sønderjysk — all acquire a receptive competence — they are still identified as "deutschsprechend", that is as preferring German even if they speak some Sønderjysk.

The effect of these two factors, interlocutor and topic, is to produce a dominance of Sønderjysk; pupils other than those who have not acquired Sønderjysk, perceive themselves as always speaking Sønderjysk to their fellow-pupils. Observation and their own more conscious analysis shows a different picture. Imagine a group of pupils sitting in the corridor, waiting to take their oral examinations. There are two German speakers among them. As they discuss their preparation for the exam, and ask those who have been in what they were asked about, the language is as follows. More Sønderjysk is spoken than German, as a result of the proportion of German speakers to Sønderjysk speakers present here and in the school as a whole. The Sønderjysk spoken is interspersed with German lexical items, some of which are terms from the school subject, others are simply German items replacing Sønderjysk items. When the two German speakers talk to each other it is in German; when the Sønderjysk speakers address one of the German speakers they do so in German, but not always when addressing the other. The difference is in the lack of proficiency in Sønderjysk of the first. The second German speaker addresses the Sønderjysk speakers in Sønderjysk, which is, however, nearer Rigsdansk than the others speak. When alone with one of the Sønderjysk speakers — a close friend — the second German-speaker normally speaks and is answered in German; it is not simply the presence of other Sønderjysk speakers which keeps them to Sønderjysk here; it is the fact that they are all involved in the same conversation.

One conclusion to be drawn from the stress on interlocutor and topic is that two Sønderjysk speakers sitting in a lesson talking about events

outside school, even while the teacher is teaching, would speak Sønderjysk. This is in fact the case. The classroom situation contains many
possible combinations of topic and interlocutor of which this is only one,
the most private. Let us start with the most public. When a pupil publicly
addresses a teacher in the role of learner, the expectation is that the pupil
speaks German and this happens in the overwhelming majority of cases; it
is possible to observe, however, pupil response in Sønderjysk usually as the
result of some emotion, excitement or sudden realization or recall. The
teacher who understands Sønderjysk accepts this response without comment. When a pupil interacts with a teacher in order to further their
relationship rather than directly as part of the learning process, the norm is
German, but again it is possible to observe Sønderjysk especially if the
teacher is known to be a Sønderjysk speaker, that is of Sønderjylland/
Nordschleswig origin. Moving to the situation where a pupil addresses
fellow pupils, three kinds of participation are identifiable. First, a pupil
refers to the "content" of the lesson — a comment that it is easy or difficult,
or an unsolicited contribution of relevant information — in a way which is
loud enough for all or most other pupils to hear and which allows the
teacher to respond or ignore it as he wishes. This can be in German or
Sønderjysk. Second, one pupil speaks to another about the structure of the
lesson — re-phrasing or repeating teacher instructions, for example — or
in order to explain content, again in a way which allows the teacher to hear
if he wishes. This kind of participation in learning, which can involve the
teacher, usually happens in Sønderjysk. Third, we return to the interaction
of two, or sometimes more, pupils where the teacher is not involved. This
may be on a private topic or about the lesson itself. In the latter case, the
interaction can be simply tolerated by the teacher as pupils work individually or encouraged as they work in groups. Here, where the teacher is
excluded, we have the same factors as were operating in the example from
the examination, interlocutor and topic, with the same consequence;
usually Sønderjysk. Here, as there, however, the significance of topic is
that it brings German lexical items into the Sønderjysk and the significance
of interlocutor is that a "German-speaker" can cause a switch to German.
This also applies to the first two kinds of event involving pupils only. In
fact, although most of the speech produced in the events described will be
perceived by the actors as Sønderjysk or German according to the identity
of the interlocutors, the role of topic can be so important that the outcome
from the forces of type of event, identity of interlocutors and topic can be a
"mixed" code, involving interference or combinations at semantic, syntactic and phonemic levels. It is impossible to quantify this in a natural
situation, but the perceptions of the participants remain fairly clear: they
perceive the identity of the interlocutors to be the dominant factor. This

applies both to pupils and to teachers: both groups consider that as a norm, people are Sønderjysk speakers, the exceptions being those with German as home-language. However, it is not always certain who the exceptions are, beyond the clearly identifiable "Lehrerkinder".

In summary of this description of pupils' response to the linguistic expectations of the school as an institution, I quote the comment of one pupil after he had recorded his own use of German and Sønderjysk over a week, a pupil with Sønderjysk as the home-language:

"ich habe also gedacht, dass ich hier in der Schule viel mehr Deutsch sprechen würde, aber das war gar nicht so viel, also Dänisch, Hoch-dänisch (Rigsdansk), das sprechen wir nur in den Stun-den (Dänischstunden), ah nicht mal so, zum Teil aber sonst viel Sønderjysk und dann auch ein bisschen Deutsch mit den Klassen-kameraden (und mit den Lehrern immer) Deutsch; und mit dem Dänischlehrer, das ist auch so verschieden, auch Deutsch und dann Hoch-dänisch, (und in den Stunden mit einem Nachbarn) Sønder-jysk immer. Wir reden Deutsch und Sønderjysk so miteinander, auch mit denen, die zu Hause Deutsch sprechen, gemischt, mit allen praktisch."

("I thought that I would speak much more German here in the school, but it was not much at all; Danish, standard Dan-ish, we only speak that in the Danish lessons, well not even then so much, partly but other-wise a lot of Sønderjysk and then a little German with friends; (and with the teachers always) German; and with the Danish teacher, it varies, Ger-man and also standard Dan-ish; (and in the lessons with a neighbour) always Sønder-jysk. We speak German and Sønderjysk with each other, also with those who speak Ger-man at home, mixed with almost everybody.")

In his account of Sønderjysk he is more perceptive and exact than many others; he is also at the age, 16–17, when the German speakers have acquired enough Sønderjysk receptively to allow one general category of interlocutor to be established for many situations.

Spoken language: Teachers

The official norms and expectations also apply to teachers talking to each other. Here the numerical pattern is reversed: the largest group has German as home language. Within this group there is a majority who are German nationals and native-speakers, and a minority brought up in Sønderjylland/Nordschleswig; a very small number speak German and Sønderjysk or Rigsdansk at home. German is therefore by far the dominant language among teachers though there are exceptions. Teachers of Danish sometimes discuss their subject in Rigsdansk, because one of them is from another part of Denmark; Sønderjysk speakers often discuss non-school matters in Sønderjysk; they also discuss pupils, especially problem pupils both present and formerly at the school, in Sønderjysk. The involvement of a German native-speaker usually means a switch to German. Sønderjysk for these speakers is associated with informality, either in topic or in interlocutor or in both. On one occasion I observed how influential this association can be. In the very relaxed atmosphere of the last day of school before the summer holidays, two Sønderjysk speakers and a German native-speaker with very limited competence in Rigsdansk or Sønderjysk were discussing a problem pupil and how he should be treated after the holidays. As the Sønderjysk speakers began to dominate the conversation because they had more knowledge of the pupil, they switched into Sønderjysk, excluding the German-speaker. There was no reason for them to want to exclude the German-speaker, but the factor of informality on this day combined with the factor of interlocutor. The fact that the German speaker did not protest but simply joined in again when the switch was made back to German — presumably as a result of the others realizing their "mistake" — is indicative of attitudes.

Both in teacher–pupil and in teacher–teacher interaction the norm set by the institution is that German be spoken. However, the norm is not applied rigorously — there is no censure for "wrong" behaviour — and the norm operates only at semantic, syntactic and phonemic levels and in a limited number of situations. This is surely a healthy attitude. Søndergaard (1981) also found an undogmatic and tolerant attitude in his much wider sample of teachers from the German schools born in Sønderjylland/ Nordschleswig. It might worry the minority's officials that the large amount of Sønderjysk spoken by pupils prevents them from improving their German. It is probable, however, that pupils learn little from each other but remain on a plane of mutual accommodation: change can only come from the model provided by the teacher. Thus the way to improve pupils'

German would be to improve the methods by which all teachers present the model and determine their criteria for normative action, for correcting their pupils' German. Furthermore, the affective benefit in pupils from a situation where attitudes are generous rather than aggressive is of enormous importance to the individual and to his relationship to the school as an institution. In rough, concrete terms, it is better to have pupils who enjoy school and make mistakes in their German, than to have perfect German speakers who reject school, and with it their attachment to the minority. The way to improve the German would perhaps be to recognize, as suggested above (pp. 63–64), that German is not the mother tongue of the majority of pupils and to change teaching methods accordingly.

Written language

The popular introduction to the syllabus for German claims that it has a special significance, "da Deutsch als Unterrichtssprache über den eigenen Fachbereich hinauswirkt und somit von grundsätzlicher Bedeutung für das Schulwesen ist" (*"since German as the language of teaching extends its influence beyond its own subject boundaries and thus is of fundamental significance for the school system"*). We have seen that not all spoken language through which teaching and learning occurs — which is what I take "Unterrichtssprache" to include — is in fact German. "Unterrichtssprache" also includes, no doubt, written language.

Again the institutional language is German, where the normative rules of Hochdeutsch are easy to apply with the help of standard dictionaries and grammars. All documents regulating the school and produced in the school are in German, including those sent to parents. Danish terms are usually translated but not always: on the timetable the tutorial period (Danish: Klassenstime), is translated as Klassenlehrerstunde and abbreviated to Kl.St. but the subject of Social Education, known in the Lehrplan as "Gegenwartskunde", is found on the timetable as Danish "Samtidsorientering", abbreviated as Samtids. Or.. In the spoken language the Danish terms for both are used almost exclusively. Another striking example of internal communication was to be seen on a blackboard. An exercise in Danish had been written up, which the teacher wanted to keep and the request to other teachers and pupils to leave the exercise was in German, "Bitte stehenlassen"; an indication that the informality of the spoken language is not extended to the written language, despite the Danish context.

How far does the institutional language extend into the written language of the classroom? The policy of using Danish text-books for certain subjects at certain stages has been mentioned (pp. 51–54). Pupils' receptive competence is thus developed in both German and Danish. This is often done through translation. The Danish text is translated orally into German as a check on understanding, with the usually justified assumption that terminology is acquired first in German and a receptive knowledge in Danish (Rigsdansk, of course) needs to be built up on this basis. Production of written language, however, is confined to German, with the obvious exception of Danish as a subject. Although pupils may sometimes make rough notes in Danish, all notes for use by others — for example in summary of group work — are in German. All written work for scrutiny by the teacher is in German. The question then arises as to how normative in response to such work the teacher will be.

Given the relatively limited amount of German spoken in the school by the Sønderjysk speaker and a further limitation on the situations in which his spoken German is corrected to the teacher model, it is worth considering the relative importance in the learning process of spoken and written language. Correction in the written language is (probably) more thorough and more regular. The amount of written language produced may be comparable to the amount of spoken, although there are obvious difficulties in measuring. It is certainly the case that a more formal variety of Hochdeutsch will be required in writing than speaking and a better approximation to the standard norm, which is moreover limited to semantic and syntactic levels. Since handwriting is taught by teachers of German, a graphemic level is also susceptible to normative correction, although attitudes are less strict. In short, it is possible that the written language is of relatively greater significance for the Sønderjysk speaker's learning of German than it is for the native-speaker. Although pedagogical conclusions might follow from this, the tentative nature of the argument influences me not to pursue them here.

The language component in the subjects German and Danish

We saw above that the syllabus for German avoids using the term "Muttersprache" (*mother tongue*) with a series of descriptive phrases, but leaning heavily on the Schleswig-Holstein documents, the implication is very clearly that the subject is to be treated as the mother tongue. I suggested at that point that German for most pupils could be regarded as a Second Language. We are now at the point where some observations of how German is in fact taught can be considered.

Let me list and comment on some of the traits of the teaching. First, the teachers are not trained as Second or Foreign Language teachers and speak of the teaching as "muttersprachlich". On the other hand, one teacher's comment modifies this by saying that one can rely on pupils' "Sprachgefühl" only up to a certain point, after which it is necessary to give them rules to learn. This the teacher considered to be a non-mother tongue procedure. Although native-speakers may also in fact be given rules, it is the teacher's perception which is important. The text books used are imported from Germany and used at the stage and rate expected of German pupils. However, one teacher said that at the sixth year level the text books made demands on the pupil which are too high, with the result, as I saw for example, that they needed to have a humourous text explained which was clearly intended to be read and immediately understood. The use of mother tongue text books is not in itself significant, since there may not be Second Language text books available; it is rather the combination with teachers' training and approach which is important. The use of mother tongue text books in other subjects is susceptible to the same comment. The use of German as a metalanguage for explaining Danish text books has already been mentioned too.

Despite the teachers' training, experience in the school leads them to adopt certain techniques which belong to Second Language teaching. As we saw above, interference is tolerated if correction would be inhibiting for the learner. Pupils' not feeling inhibited is a psychological priority for the Second Language teacher which need not be so high for the mother tongue teacher. The latter need not fear that his pupil is solely dependent on teacher attitudes for further progress. Interference is, however, anticipated and made conscious for the pupil. For example, a contrast between Danish "risikere" and German "riskieren" (*to risk*) is accompanied by the warning not to be tempted to put an extra "i" in the German word. On another occasion a list of verbs was to be completed with dependent prepositions, many of which, if translated directly from Danish, would be unidiomatic. Another teacher, when marking essays, has made a collection of interference phenomena. All teachers acquire a stock of knowledge of items easily identified in the written language, but phenomena not the result of loan-translations scarcely appear in teachers' deliberate anticipations of problems. The contrastive analysis is post hoc and limited.

The teaching of Danish follows a similar pattern. The teachers are trained as mother-tongue teachers. The syllabus says that Danish must be considered the mother-tongue because of the examinations. Mother-tongue text books are used in both Danish as a subject and in certain other subjects, at the same stage as in Danish schools, although it is the combination with teachers' approach that is significant.

On the other hand, teachers learn to anticipate interference from German and from Sønderjysk. For example, I observed a lesson with final year pupils in which extracts from their essays were isolated for comment on interference phenomena. At the opposite end of their learning of the written standard, pupils are introduced to reading in their third year. This process is quite different from the process in the mother tongue since they have been learning to read for two years in German, and the learning for most is considered to be essentially complete. In learning to transfer the skill, pupils first meet words where all the letters are pronounced "as in German", before moving to words with "silent h and d". In the course of this third year pupils are brought to the point of using mother-tongue text books intended for the third year in Danish schools. A great deal of reading is done in this year, which is thought also to serve the purpose of reducing interference from Sønderjysk.

The status of Rigsdansk is closely connected with the position of German. As long as the German language is seen to be the main and perhaps only difference between a minority school and others, any weakening of the position of German will be perceived as an attack on the very being of the school and rebuffed accordingly, despite the many other features which give the school its special character. The syllabus for Danish claims that the teaching must be seen as mother tongue teaching because it leads to the examinations which all Danish pupils take. This is not, however, the fundamental point. It is not the status of the teaching but of the language which is at issue and it is not for examination reasons but for sociolinguistic reasons that the language needs status. The starting point can be found in the second of the aims of the "Schul- und Sprachverein": "to introduce pupils to the Danish cultural and language world and to prepare them for life as citizens of this state" (cf. pp. 21–26).

The "language world" referred to here contains many language varieties with many registers. A citizen of the state needs to be able to use as many of these varieties and registers as possible in order to acquire access and opportunity to enjoy the range of professional, educational and economic lives which the state and society offer. This is not to say that the "wrong" accent will prevent an individual from taking up opportunities for ever, for Danish society is not as rigid as in the past. Nonetheless, dialect speakers in general do perceive their dialect as a possible barrier, even if, as in Sønderjylland, there is a certain pride in the regional dialect (Nyberg, 1980 and 1981). Therefore, a Danish citizen needs confidence in his use of a number of varieties: dialect, spoken and written standard in informal and formal registers over a wide range of situations, or domains and the confidence that he knows when each is appropriate. Such confidence would also reduce some of the tensions in his relationship to dialect, and increase his opportunities in career and social terms (Pedersen, 1977:114). The speaker of Sønderjysk is thus already in need of considerable help, even without the additional factor of German. In the school at the moment, that help is limited and pupils feel that they are not proficient in standard language:

> "also ich kann nicht so gut Dänisch (...) Sønderjysk, das ist auch was anderes; ich weiss nicht, ich kann auch nicht richtig (Dänisch reden) also wenn wir hier in der Schule Dänisch haben, das kann ich nicht richtig reden; man geniert sich auch ein bisschen dafür ..."
>
> *("well, I can't speak Danish so well (...) Sønderjysk is different; I don't know, I can't speak Danish properly, so when we have Danish here at school, I can't speak it properly; you feel a bit ashamed of that too ...")*

Pupils are probably most conscious of phonetic and phonemic differences between dialect and standard and at this level those with the experience find that they can adapt quite quickly. Whether speakers of the standard would also accept the Sønderjysk speakers' pronunciation is a different question, and the unconscious influence of language attitudes on people's perceptions of other people is well known (Lambert, 1967). It is, however, more than a question of phonemic level; at semantic and syntactic levels, of which speakers are less aware, adaptation of the standard through conscious learning is much more difficult. Pupils need that unconscious control of the standard which comes through use rather than through study. It would not, therefore, be adequate simply to increase the amount of time spent in study, i.e. the number of Danish lessons on the timetable. Pupils need to use the standard in interaction with standard speakers, in a range of situations and using formal and informal spoken and written registers.

Let us consider some of the implications. On the assumption that school is the only place where productive competence can be furthered, it is evident that improvements in pupils' standard Danish would need a change of school language policy. More Rigsdansk would have to be used in operating the school, in teaching and learning. More study of the dialect issue — questions of interference, discussion of status and appropriateness, analysis of linguistic attitudes — would require separate treatment from learning involving the relationship with German. This would mean a further dimension and responsibility in the subject Danish. This could mean an increase in time allocated to the subject which would in present circumstances be perceived as a weakening of the German character of the school. If it were accepted that the minority character of the school is not dependent only on the language issue but on such things as syllabus, teacher origin and teacher training, then this kind of suggestion would not be perceived as weakening the fundamental nature of the school. The suggestion that pupils need to interact with speakers of standard Danish, to be taught by such people, has different implications. The nature of the school is in reality much determined by the fact that a majority of the teachers are German nationals and that all the teachers except one were trained in the German educational tradition. To bring in Danish standard speakers, by implication trained in the Danish tradition, would be to alter the situation fundamentally to a degree which the minority would find unacceptable. A compromise might be sought through those teachers born and educated in Sønderjylland/Nordschleswig — in minority schools — and then trained in Germany. These teachers could be in a position to provide the environment of standard Danish from which pupils can acquire adequate control themselves. These teachers are in many other respects, too, in a better position to understand the school and its pupils than teachers from Germany. Their full value has yet to be realized.

At the end of Chapter 3 (pp. 63–64), after analysis of curricular thinking evident in syllabus documents, I began to analyse the definitions of the teaching of German and Danish. I have demonstrated in this chapter that linguistic behaviour in the school is inconsistent with the curricular philosophy because of the actual linguistic competences of pupils. The linguistic policy is, we have seen, closely connected with perceptions of the nature of the school as preparation for and introduction to two cultures. It is time now to examine more closely the question of culture and cultural transmission.

The literature component in the subjects Danish and German

There is an evident assumption in curricular documents and in the general rhetoric of the minority that language and culture are two sides of the same coin. I shall question this assumption with respect to some aspects of culture, but begin nonetheless with one aspect where the assumption is justified: literature. In keeping with the European tradition the teacher of Danish or German language is also the teacher of Danish or German literature. There are obvious good reasons for this, but it is a tradition, not an inevitability.

In both Danish and German syllabuses the language takes priority. In fact in the aims of Danish teaching quoted from the Ministry of Education's recommendations (pp. 54–62), there is no reference to literature or to culture. The emphasis is on creating linguistic competence in a variety of forms and the ability to evaluate and act in societal contexts. The school's own aims supplement this with reference to both "Sprachwelt" (*language world*) and "Kulturwelt" (*cultural world*) (cf. pp. 21–26). The aims of German teaching are subdivided into three sections, two referring to linguistic competence and one to cultural awareness, acquired through examples of texts (pp. 54–62). This initial difference widens when one analyses the approaches to language evident in the popular introduction to the syllabuses. The emphasis in the Danish is on linguistic skills, on language as a means: "et middel til erkendelse af deres egen og andre menneskers situation . . . et middel til at erhverve viden . . . en støtte for begrebsdannelsen . . . et redskab for kontakt og kommunikation" ("*a means for apprehending their own and other people's situation . . . a means for acquiring knowledge . . . a support in the formation of concepts . . . a tool for contact and communication*"), (quoted in German in the syllabus). In the German syllabus, although there is recognition of recent views of language and the consequent stress on experience rather than analysis, the point of view does not give up entirely the notion of understanding the rules of language which underlie linguistic acts. In both Danish and German, texts are considered to be the basis for inductive learning, but although German refers to a multiplicity of text types, the implication is that text means written language. In the Danish syllabus, however, the notion of text is extended deliberately to include: "skrevne og talte ordtekster, lyd, f.eks. i form af 'lydbilleder', samt tegnede, fotograferede og filmede billedforløb" ("*written and spoken word-texts, sound, for example in the form of 'sound-pictures', together with drawn, photographed or filmed picture sequences*") (in German in the syllabus, quoted from the Ministerial Vejledning Dansk, 1976:23). This widening of the concept serves in the first instance linguistic purposes: to promote a more subtle understanding of language other than narrative, descriptive, emotive in literary texts. The effect, however, is also to widen the concept of "culture", first to include under "literature" both classic and trivial literature, and second to include under "text" linguistic, visual and aural artefacts. In the second case the artefacts are usually in a trivial rather than classic genre, photography in advertising, for example, rather than photography as fine art.

Teachers have, of course, some latitude in their interpretation of the documents, although the state examinations constrain them. From observation, submissions of lists of texts prepared for examination, and interviews, there is a clear impression of a difference of approach in the teaching of German and Danish in the school. That difference results in pupils being exposed to different interpretations of the notion of literature. It would, however, be a simplification to suggest that German teachers do not treat anything but classic literature, or that Danish teachers do not teach classic literary history. Pupils find it difficult to verbalize the difference and the following is one of the best:

"Ja also im deutschen Unterricht da sind ja eigentlich mehr, sozusagen so, oft ältere Texte oder, von ... von Goethe haben wir nun nichts aber, ... mehr längere Texte und so, und vielleicht auch mal Gedichte oder, die schon alt sind und im dänischen Unterricht da sind wir dann, oft neue und, neue Texte, also mehr protestantisch oder von einer Gruppe die gegen irgendwas protestieren, modernere Texte gebraucht, aber hier wird auch viel mehr verlangt in Dänisch, in Dänisch in der Prüfung als Deutsch (...) da soll man auf alles eingehen, auf die Form auf die Schreibweise ob da sich Reime sind, das Bild wie es aufgebaut ist ob man sehen kann welche Bedeutung es hat, welche Bedeutung es hat für die Menschen oder ..."

"(Yes, well, in the German lessons there are really more, well, as it were, older texts, by ... well we don't have anything by Goethe but, ... more longer texts and perhaps also poems which are old, and in the Danish lessons, there we have often used new, new texts, more protestant or by a group who are protesting against something, but the demands are much greater in Danish, in the Danish exam than in German (...) there you have to consider everything, the form, the style, whether there are rhymes, how the picture is structured, whether you can see what meaning it has, what meaing it has for people or ...")

It is important to remember that the German examination is a foreign language examination, but the wider concept of text in Danish is evident here. Another pupil explains the difference by saying there are more novels in German and more Sachtexte (translating Danish sagtekst, meaning non-literary text) in Danish and when asked about his general impression of German and Danish literature, he says: "also ich kenn' die dänische Literatur fast nicht, ganz ehrlich zu werden (oder in Deutsch) ja da wissen wir es gut" (*"well, I hardly know Danish literature at all, to be quite honest (or in German) yes there we know the literature well"*).

The general impression can also be formulated as a greater tendency in Danish towards a sociological theory of literature and in German towards textual analysis and biographical and historical approaches. These differences reflect in part the differences in educational philosophy and teacher training in Denmark and Germany. Of the teachers of Danish responsible for the older pupils one was entirely trained in Denmark and the other was trained in Danish teaching in Denmark. (It is only in the last ten years that training in Danish teaching has been available in Schleswig-Holstein, in the Pädagogische Hochschule, Flensburg.)

It is appropriate that the philosophy of Danish teaching involves the preparation of pupils for life in Danish society whereas German teaching puts more emphasis on "culture" rather than "society"; this is in keeping with the aims of the minority schools and with the lives of the vast majority of pupils. Those pupils who eventually settle in Germany are less well served.

I have so far avoided definitions of "culture" or "Kultur", as they are many and varied. It has, however, become evident that "Kultur" as presented in the subjects Danish and German can be more and less inclusive with respect to the status of the texts: whether they rank as "high" or "trivial" literature. The tendency in Danish to deal also with non-linguistic aspects of culture takes us to the next stage of the discussion. "Kultur", whether "high" or "low", includes artefacts which are non-linguistic; music and the fine arts are examples. But if "Kultur" is interpreted in the anthropologist's sense, then it includes social relationships, customs and tradition, food and eating habits and much more. Schools share with parents the responsibility of initiating pupils into all aspects of culture. The question then arises whether and how the minority school can accomplish this kind of task.

The school as a mediator of Danish and German culture

It is one of the purposes of the school to prepare pupils for Danish citizenship and introduce them to the Danish "cultural world". In this context "culture" is best interpreted in a wide sense, for introduction to the fine arts cannot be considered adequate preparation for citizenship. The general character of the analysis so far suggests that the school is only partially succeeding. On the one hand, it equips pupils with Danish qualifications, it educates them in a school system which is Danish in its organizational character, it introduces them to social issues through "Samtidsorientering", it gives them teaching in the standard language and prepares them to use it in a range of contexts. On the other hand, there is an underlying educational philosophy which is not Danish, the teaching of History and to some extent "Samtidsorientering" does not do Denmark full justice, pupils feel that the standard language is foreign to them and the introduction to literary and non-linguistic cultural traditions is almost non-existent.

Where the school does treat non-linguistic culture, it is largely German. One of its strongest areas of experience is music. There is, however, as we saw in the introduction to the syllabus, an awareness of a duty to keep the German folksong tradition alive (pp. 54–62), and in practice it is only rarely that, with the co-operation of the Danish teacher a Danish folksong is learnt. The same bias exists in the school's choral work. The visual arts are taught for performance, rather than through study of artefacts, and therefore there is no clear purpose of transmission of one culture or the other; the syllabus is essentially the same as in Schleswig-Holstein.

With respect to German culture the school's purpose is to introduce pupils to the German "cultural world" and "to reinforce the German sense of community". We meet again the problem of deciding what "German" refers to: Minority, the Federal Republic, the two Germanies, German-speaking countries and so on. Whatever the extent of the reference, in the context of sustaining a sense of having something in common, the concept of "culture" can also be interpreted along the continuum from "high art" to the anthropological "way of life". However, there is not the same pressing need to prepare pupils for citizenship as there is from the Danish point of view. In general terms the analysis has suggested that the school fulfils this task adequately, especially if "culture" is interpreted not too widely. The presence of German teachers brings a German philosophy in both strictly pedagogical terms and with respect to behavioural expectations; the linguistic training is largely adequate for pupils' second language needs; the German historical, musical and literary historical traditions are given considerable prominence; even German social issues, which are not perhaps strictly necessary for those who are not going to live there, are treated to some extent.

The question as to how successful the school is in the shared task of pupils' socialization, preparation for life in society after school, is difficult to answer. This is, of course, not unique to this situation. My analysis suggests that in terms of Danish society as a whole — where the centre of gravity is a long way to the north and east of Sønderjylland/Nordschleswig — the school's preparation is inadequate. The same applies *mutatis mutandis* with respect to preparation for life in German society. Although the school does not set out to do this, there is a small minority of pupils who will want to settle in Germany eventually. Some teachers believe that the school in fact prepares pupils well for life in Sønderjylland/Nordschleswig, especially if the individual continues to be a member of the minority, but that it does not do an adequate job otherwise.

In purely linguistic terms, the position is clearer. Pupils' mastery of German is less than is needed for living in Germany — they do not have the necessary range of varieties — and their control of standard Danish can only be inadequate, even if they achieve well enough under the special conditions of examinations. In the final section of this chapter I will review pupils' own perceptions of their languages in order to throw light on the issue of linguistic socialization and language attitudes.

Pupils' perception of their language

After nine or ten years in the German school in Tinglev/Tingleff, pupils speak German, Sønderjysk and Rigsdansk — and English learnt as a foreign language from the seventh year. Their perceptions and feelings about their languages vary from individual to individual and I intend to give some insight into the variety in the next chapter. Here, I want to abstract to a level of generality which still accounts for a majority of pupils.

> "Ich meine ich habe nur eine Muttersprache und das ist Sønderjysk ... (Deutsch) das ist auch eine Sprache die nebensächlich auch dazugehört, ein bisschen am Rande."

> *("I think I have only one mother tongue and that's Sønderjysk ... (German) is also a language which in a subsidiary way belongs too, a bit on the edge.")*

This is the position of most pupils who speak Sønderjysk at home: some differentiate more in their account of the position of German, depending on how much German is current alongside Sønderjysk in the home. The Sønderjysk which they speak is, however, different from that of their Danish neighbours; it is an indication of people's ethnic identity that their

Sønderjysk is influenced by German, whereas the Danish Sønderjysk speaker is perceived as having more Rigsdansk in the dialect:

"Man kann das immer auch schon hören von der Sprache her, finde ich also, denn wenn Dänen, auch wenn die Sønderjysk sprechen zu Hause, da ist immer dann wieder ein dänisches Dialekt wieder eingebaut und mein Sønderjysk da ist wieder mehr Deutsch drin, also mit deutschen Wörtern.

("You can always hear it already from the language, I think, because if Danes, even if they speak Sønderjysk at home, there is always a Danish dialect built in, and my Sønderjysk there is always more German in it, I mean with German words.")

The cause of this difference is attributed to schooling, essentially to the influence of the teachers' language. In the German school, the interference from German is accepted among the pupils themselves and is reinforced by the relatively closed social networks within which many of them live — it is possible for a pupil to spend all his school and free time among peers from the school. The fact that pupils watch almost exclusively West German television and read the minority's German-language newspaper doubtless contributes to the situation. They say that German words "slip out" in their Sønderjysk, or that they find they do not know a word in Danish and have to circumscribe the concept or simply let the German word slip out. This can cause annoyance for the speaker:

"Wenn man Sønderjysk spricht, da kommt oft ein deutsches Wort dazwischen, dann verstehen sie also nicht, die die aus der dänischen Schule kommen, verstehen dann einen nicht, und muss man irgendwie umschreiben und dann weiss man nicht das richtige Wort dafür, kennt man nur das Deutsche . . . (. . .) ja da ist man irgendwie, 'ach Scheisse', nicht?"

("When you are speaking Sønderjysk, there often comes a German word in the middle, then they don't understand, those who are from the Danish school, they don't understand you, and you have to circumscribe and then you don't know the right word for it, you only know the German . . . (. . .) yes, well then you feel somehow, 'well, shit!', you see?")

However, it is often the case that the other does in fact understand the German word and accepts it. Or it can cause laughter and mockery; it will depend on the relationship of the two people. When this might happen in speaking standard Danish, usually with someone from outside Sønderjylland/Nordschleswig, the speaker has to eliminate German words from his conversation more deliberately. This is not to say that he eliminates German influence entirely.

Although the speaker may feel annoyed or, more commonly, simply aware that this is one of the factors which makes him different from the majority, one pupil was more outspoken in his evaluation:

"die von der dänischen Schule haben, die haben ein Sønderjysk mit ein bisschen Rigsdansk, also Hochdänisch; das hört man sofort, die haben eine feinere Sprache, wir haben ja so eine Sprache die eine Altmodische ist, und die haben eine feinere Art sich auszudrücken als wir haben."

("the people from the Danish school have, they have a Sønderjysk with a bit of Rigsdansk, that is standard Danish; you hear it immediately, they have a finer language, we have a language which is old fashioned, and they have a finer way of expressing themselves than we do.")

In this account, the higher status of Rigsdansk is the cause of the evaluation, rather than the influence of German; the others speak better because they have Rigsdansk expressions, rather than saying we speak worse because we have German expressions.

Turning to Rigsdansk, we find that pupils are usually insecure about their ability to speak the standard language:

"ich komme mir wirklich blöd vor wenn ich da Hochdänisch sprechen soll, das ist eine ganz Fremdsprache für mich."

("I really feel stupid, when I have to speak standard Danish, it's a quite foreign language for me.")

Yet the few who have occasion to speak Rigsdansk over a concentrated period feel they can adapt to the linguistic environment; it remains unclear whether their interlocutors agree. They feel nonetheless that they ought to be able to speak Rigsdansk: to speak Sønderjysk when the other is speaking Rigsdansk is not appropriate in the experience of one pupil, and this is doubtless due to attitudes to dialect formulated by another pupil as follows:

"(Sønderjysk) das ist eine Sprache für sich selbst, die die Dänen nicht richtig respektieren, oder sie wollen es nicht respektieren weil sie es nicht

((Sønderjysk) is a language in itself, which the Danes don't properly respect, or they don't want to respect it, because they can't understand it; and then

verstehen und da wird dann *there is a contest about who*
Kampf gemacht, wer wohl die *speaks the proper language,*
richtige Sprache spricht, die *the proper Danish language.)*
richtige dänische Sprache."

The opportunities to use Rigsdansk outside school are limited. The receptive knowledge is not increased through television or other means and so the difference between these pupils and their Danish peers is caused mainly by the difference in schooling. For those who want to remain in Sønderjylland/Nordschleswig — for example in agriculture — the issue is of little significance. For others who say they would prefer to pursue the sort of career which is not tied to this region and who nonetheless say they want to stay here, the insecurity in Rigsdansk is, I suspect, a contributing factor, even though it can be overruled by other forces.

There is little intention among the Sønderjysk speakers of living in Germany. In fact their personal experience of Germany is usually limited to shopping excursions, school trips and occasional visits to friends or relatives. Their linguistic experience varies, to some extent but not entirely as a consequence of their proficiency in German. At one extreme is the pupil who claims to speak Danish and German equally well and that native-speakers do not notice that he is from Sønderjylland/Nordschleswig; his intonation pattern is, however, distinctly Nordschleswig German. A more frequent experience is formulated thus:

"man ist nicht so sicher wie *("you don't feel as sure as . . .*
. . . hier da weiss man da, da *here, you know, you don't*
braucht man nicht so sicher zu *need to be as sure, here you*
sein, da kann man . . . da *can . . . over there they can*
drüben da können sie es per- *speak perfect German, and*
fekt Deutsch und hier viel- *here perhaps not quite so per-*
leicht nicht ganz so perfekt, da *fect, so you feel a bit unsure,*
ist man ein bisschen unsicher *but it's O.K. (. . .) I can under-*
aber das geht (. . .) (ich kann) *stand everything and can ex-*
alles verstehen und kann mich *press myself, well, if . . . then*
auch ausdrücken, ja wenn es *re-formulate or somehow, it's*
. . . dann umformulieren oder *always possible.")*
irgendwie, das geht immer."

In my earlier analysis (pp. 63–64), I suggested that the school offers a limited model of German, Hochdeutsch, appropriate for only a limited number of domains. Pupils discover this when they experience the colloquial language, which they can usually understand due no doubt to television, but which they cannot produce. They cannot, therefore, be linguistically integrated, although prolonged residence would improve their position as it would for any second language speaker of German.

The subjective experience of the three languages or varieties is strikingly summarized by one pupil who identifies very clearly with the minority and its schools — "ich fühle mich hier gut" ("*I feel fine here*").

"ich spreche lieber Deutsch als Hochdänisch; ich finde, dass Deutsch mehr meine Muttersprache ist als Hoch- dänisch, aber meine richtige Muttersprache das ist also Sønderjysk."

(*"I prefer speaking German to standard Danish; I think that German is more my mother tongue than standard Danish, but my proper mother tongue, that's Sønderjysk."*)

Finally, the question arises whether pupils consider that bilingualism is advantageous. The general response to the simple question is that it is advantageous, because it offers better job opportunities, and the example of import–export work is given. Yet this reminds one of the school's own presentation of the advantages of bilingualism through the biographies of former pupils in the school handbook, or of the advertisements which attempt to attract non-minority pupils into the schools. Everyone thinks of this argument but it applies in fact to few, and the rest have not usually considered the bilingual factor in their deliberations about a career. The advantage of being able to continue one's education in either Germany or Denmark applies likewise to fewer than the number who mention it. The possibility that there might be psycholinguistic, sociolinguistic or cultural advantages or disadvantages is not mentioned and this is scarcely surprising because the notion of bilingualism is not something they have given serious consideration to, or been encouraged to do so by their teachers. In this respect the school fails to help pupils to come to terms with their own identities and capacities. This is, however, not surprising in the context of my earlier analysis of curricular thinking (pp. 54–62), where the pupils' bilingualism was treated simply as a problem to be solved as quickly as possible, as an unfortunate complication in the teaching situation.

The problems which bilingualism might bring in other ways than in the classroom are not very clear to pupils. German-Danish bilingualism is so relatively common in the region that it is not admired, whereas other forms of linguistic competence are. For example, my own ability to speak two or three languages — and the fact that my children are bilingual — is admired as much here as in traditionally monolingual environments. Yet those who admire are just as competent themselves but do not value their abilities. In such an environment, the inevitable problems of bilingualism are highlighted and the compensating enrichment left in the dark. One pupil added another dimension by saying that Finnish-Danish bilingualism is better than the German–Danish bilingualism of the border region:

"da besteht ja kein Zusammenhang zwischen Finnisch und Deutsch oder Dänisch (. . .) da sind andere Weltansichten und hier ist das alles zu kompakt eigentlich und zu ähnlich also bei mir so weit ich sehe kein Unterschied mehr."	*("there exists no connection between Finnish and German or Danish (. . .) there, there are different views of the world and here everything is too compact, really, too similar; so in me as far as I can see there is no difference.")*

The similarity which he describes is one of the factors which make the individual's experience of living in the minority, attending a minority school and speaking the minority's languages an extremely difficult one for him to conceptualize and describe. It occurred in pupils' response to the question about what is particularly German in their school. It occurs in adults' accounts of what membership of the minority means in terms of daily life. It is an issue which I will address in the final chapter again.

Finally, although it would be a common sense hypothesis to believe that having the school language as one's dominant language — coming from a German-speaking home — would be educationally advantageous, pupils do not usually believe that this is the case. In fact for some it is seen as a problem when learning Danish, i.e. the standard language, at school. It would be extremely difficult to test such hypotheses because of the many variables and the low numbers involved. It is, however, both a warning and a tribute to the school that one of the most perceptive pupils said:

"es ist natürlich schwer zu sagen oder (. . .) manche können ja entweder . . . oder die können nicht richtig Dänisch und nicht richtig Deutsch, also von der Grammatik her und ich glaube dann wäre das einfacher für die gewesen, wenn die nur mit einer Sprache also . . . und würden in den Fächern besser zurecht kommen."	*("it is of course difficult to say (. . .) many can either . . . or they can't speak Danish properly or German properly, that is with regard to grammar, and I think then it would have been easier for them if they had just (learnt) with one language . . . and would cope better in the subjects.")*

This is the warning; the tribute is in the fact that the pupil would still want to send his own children to a minority school despite potential problems:

"denn das ist, also es ist so immer drin in uns."

("because it is, well it is always inside us.")

5 On Leaving School

Introduction

The preceding chapters have described aspects of the minority and in particular the characteristics of one school. I have suggested that the school plays a significant part in the formation of pupils' relationship to the minority, whether that relationship is strong or weak. It is therefore particularly interesting to see how pupils respond to a new environment when they leave the school. The environment may constitute a complete change for them — for example, if they had spent school and free time within the minority networks and now enter a Danish education institution — or the environment may be essentially the same but more homogeneous — this is the case for those who go on to the German Gymnasium (Sixth Form College). One might speculate about the psychological, linguistic and social adjustment required of pupils to succeed in their new environment, about the effect that change may have on their relationship to their school and the minority. So much will depend, however, not only on the fact that they went to the German school but also on family influence and commitment to the minority, that it is fruitless to attempt to categorize and to find correlations — particularly when the numbers involved are low. My approach in the following pages is therefore to describe and analyse the results of interviews with pupils and former pupils, to point out areas of experience which they appear to have in common and others which are unique to individuals. There are two main sections: interviews with young people who left school one or two years ago, and interviews with a group after a few weeks in their new environment, a group who had also been interviewed before leaving school.

The former pupils

The following account is based on interviews with eight former pupils, one interviewed alone, two others together and the rest as a group. They were all successful in their new environment in so far as they felt settled-in and making satisfactory progress. They all, but to differing degrees, felt themselves to be committed members of the minority, at least to the extent that they would want to send their own children to a German school. The majority were attending a Danish Further Education institution (Handelsskole, Commercial College), one was at the Gymnasium, one was an apprentice mechanic and one was in agriculture. The proportions reflect roughly the general tendencies among pupils leaving the school in most years. One of the interviewees was clearly identified by himself and by others as being German-speaking and it is not surprising that he was the one at Gymnasium. The others were identified as Sønderjysk speakers, although two of them said they spoke both Sønderjysk and German at home.

The most striking difference in the new environment is, of course, linguistic, and the contrast is sharpest for those at the Handelsskole. They move from a school where German is the official language to a school where all those functions are in Rigsdansk, and German (unlike Rigsdansk in the German school) becomes a foreign language. At the Gymnasium, more German is spoken by pupils than at the school in Tinglev/Tingleff — probably because of a higher proportion of German-speakers — but the German-speaker said that there was still a lot of Sønderjysk spoken in the breaks. For those in work, the use of German is non-existent or at best used when there is contact with customers from Germany; Sønderjysk is the dominant language. In the context of the earlier discussion of pupils' attitudes towards Rigsdansk, it will be clear that it is at the Handelsskole that the linguistic change and challenge are greatest.

These students have a clear advantage as far as German as a foreign language is concerned. Indeed they are disparaging about the standard of the German of their teachers as well as fellow students. On the other hand, their attitude with respect to Sønderjysk, which they clearly prefer to Rigsdansk, is defensive, for they are sometimes attacked:

"Man hört oft an der Handelsschule mit Kameraden die nur Hochdänisch sprechen, wenn man die dann Sønderjysk anspricht, dann kommt es so: 'Snak da dansk'."	(*"You often hear at the Commercial College with friends who only speak standard Danish, if you talk to them in Sønderjysk, then you hear: 'Speak Danish'."*)

As far as Rigsdansk is concerned, they "try" to speak it, especially with teachers, some of whom are more tolerant than others towards Sønderjysk. As a final line of defence, however, they assert that no-one can forbid them to speak Sønderjysk, even in the examinations; the issue of their competence in Rigsdansk is obviously problematic. Furthermore, when writing in Rigsdansk, they find that their Germanisms are noted by teachers, a weakness which clearly identifies their origins.

The change to a Danish school also brings out contrasts of a non-linguistic kind. Although pupils in the German school know of the custom in Danish schools of pupils' using Du and first names to teachers, the moment when they have to do it themselves is a difficult one. It creates a short period of re-adjustment, which includes also a new attitude to "discipline":

"Ich glaube man lernt mehr wenn die Diziplin strenger ist, auf der Handelsschule da kann man sagen was man will, da passiert nichts." *("I think you learn more if the discipline is stricter, at the Commercial College, you can say what you want, nothing happens.")*

However, the Gymnasium student had a similar experience when some of the teachers introduced this custom too. As far as relationships with their fellow students are concerned, the Handelsskole students found that they were easily identified as coming from the German school, partly because of the phenomenon of lexical interference from German in their spoken language. This led in the early period to unpleasant attitudes among the Danes, reminding them of rivalries with pupils from the Danish school when they used to catch the same bus to Tinglev/Tingleff. The response to this situation is described as follows:

"da muss man sich erstmal einleben und die heute, die müssen auch einsehen, dass man nicht anders ist als die." *("then you just have to get used to things, and people today, they have to realize that we aren't different to them.")*

However, not all had this experience to the same extent — it is partly a question of how the individual interprets the attitudes of others — and all agreed that relationships with fellow students were soon very good, whether the number of "Germans" in the class was large or small. The fact that the Handelsskole also contained a greater proportion of Danes from outside Nordschleswig, who have less prejudice *vis à vis* the minority, may also contribute to the harmony.

For those in employment, working in isolation and less identifiable as German, the pressures and problems are not so immediate. There is still the phenomenon of lexical interference, experienced as a lack of vocabulary, but it need not be conspicuous. Nonetheless, other people soon know who is German and who is Danish; in a relatively small community nothing remains hidden long. When one's identity is known, it can lead to new friendships. For example, one person working in a village some kilometres from home found that, when his German identity became known — through people asking where he went to school — then he found himself being invited to the homes of other Germans in the village. The sense of belonging together comes through talking about common school experience and a feeling that "sie verstehen einen besser" (*"they understand you better"*).

All those who leave the German environment in their daily life experience a period of re-assessment. It is more important to those who continue to be closely involved in the minority during their free time, but it happens to all through the contrasting new experience. There is first a new perspective on the school they have left, expressed above in terms of attitudes to discipline, or below with respect to size and school relationships:

"damals als ich in der Schule war, da habe ich darüber gelacht, jetzt muss ich doch sagen, irgendwie da ist, da ist mehr Ordnung drin in der deutschen Schule (. . .) in der dänischen Schule, so da einige die werden so beiseite, hier wird keiner beiseite geschoben."

("When I used to be at school, I used to laugh about it, but now I have to say, somehow there's, there's more order in things in the German school (. . .) in the Danish school, some are pushed aside, nobody is pushed aside here.")

The move to a geographically new environment as well as a new kind of social institution takes students away from Tinglev/Tingleff where there is a large German community and where it is possible to live mainly within that community. Pupils experience their German identity more clearly when they are in other parts of Denmark, and their Nordschleswig identity when they are in Germany, but it is possible to have a similar experience, even while remaining in a German school, the Gymnasium:

"in Tingleff habe ich mich nicht so besonders Deutsch gefühlt aber als ich nach Apenrade kam, wo ich denn also . . . da war so, in Apenrade sind weniger Deutsche als in Tingleff, da fühlt man sich irgendwie doch mehr als Deutscher."

("in Tingleff I didn't feel so specially German but when I went to Apenrade, where I . . . there it was so, that there are fewer Germans in Apenrade than in Tingleff, then you feel yourself somehow more German.")

The strongest experience comes from the starkest contrast — in the Handelsskole:

"Man muss sich behaupten, deshalb wird das Gefühl fur die deutsche Minderheit stärker.
Ich glaube, das ist auch weil man, hier ist man gewohnt Deutsch zun sprechen, dann kommt man wie wir auf eine andere Schule auf eine dänische Schule, und da ist irgendwie 'ich bin aus einer deutschen Schule, jetzt muss ich mich behaupten', und ich glaube, das ist ziemlich ausschlaggebend, dass man, *wenn* man sich behaupten kann, dass man sich danach fühlt, 'ich habe mich, ich habe mich bewährt'."

("you have to assert yourself, that's why the feeling for the German minority gets stronger.
I think it is also because you, here you are accustomed to speaking German, then you go like us to another school, to a Danish school, and there it's somehow 'I'm from a German school, I must assert myself', and I think that's fairly decisive, that you, if you can assert yourself, that you feel afterwards 'I've, I've proved myself.")

However, not everyone is successful in this process, the pressures of which are clear in the emphatic "if you can assert yourself", and this speaker, whose description met with approval from the others, could also describe how others had not succeeded. They had cut themselves loose from the minority, perhaps because they were from a different area, where there are not so many Germans.

To summarize, the process of leaving the school and settling into a new environment has certain features which are peculiar to the minority pupil, as he examines the period in retrospect. The features are linguistic, psychological and social, adapting to an environment where Rigsdansk or Sønderjysk is dominant, where peers are Danish and usually in the majority exerting certain pressures to conform. The response varies according to the amount of pressure and the Handelsskole is clearly the most problematic situation. Yet in retrospect it is quite possible that certain aspects of experience are "forgotten", re-interpreted or suppressed. In order to get closer to the experience, I consider now another group of pupils, whom I interviewed two or three weeks before they left school and four or five weeks after they had begun work in their new environment.

Pupils in the 10 Klasse — before leaving school

I interviewed 21 pupils from the year-group of 29 over a period of several days at the end of May and beginning of June. During this period they were free of lessons and came to school only to take their oral examinations. I had observed their classes many times during previous weeks and on one occasion taught some of them in an English lesson. I interviewed them all singly, except two pairs. All but five agreed without hesitation to having the interview recorded — four of the five were the two couples, who were particularly nervous. I had assured them when I first arrived, and explained in outline what I was interested in, that their anonymity would be protected. About five weeks before the interviews I had asked them to keep a record of their language use for one week. This had given them a clearer idea of my interests and also caused them to give some thought to their language use. During the interviews, I used a series of prepared questions but took them in any order, depending on the drift of the conversation; I did not necessarily use all the questions in an interview nor did I deliberately use always the same formulation. The interviews lasted between 20 minutes and 45 minutes, depending on the willingness of the pupils to speak and on the atmosphere established. No-one was unwilling to talk, but some were more nervous than others. Those who I saw were not willing to be interviewed were not put under any pressure by me: of the nine I did not interview, two or three were clearly unwilling, two I had spoken to in depth on previous occasions, and the others were not available. I suspect some of the latter group were unwilling and some were simply not present when I hoped to see them.

I do not claim, therefore, that the interviewed group were representative or a defined sample. Their experience and their opinions are nonetheless important for that. They are representative in the sense that they cover the whole spectrum of family background, career intentions, commitment to the minority, language use and so on. My intention is therefore to give an account of their interviews which does them all justice, maintains their anonymity and is also a comprehensible and relatively complete picture. I shall do this by using certain themes, which reflect something of the format of the interviews.

I start with the question of "Haussprache" (language of the home). This is a concept which is familiar to pupils, not least through its use by teachers, and a concept through which they habitually identify each other. It is used together with other terms to refer to those pupils who do not speak Sønderjysk at home, but because it is used alongside the terms

"Lehrerkind" (child of teachers), "deutscher Staatsbürger" (German national), it is not used accurately. There are pupils in the group who speak German at home and yet are not thought of as being "deutschsprechend". These pupils have spoken Sønderjysk since early childhood through contact with neighbours and are perceived as Sønderjysk speakers as far as informal conversation is concerned. Of those who are perceived as "deutschsprechend", some are purely so and are unwilling to speak Danish at all and some are prepared to speak Danish, both the Rigsdansk which was their first introduction to Danish at school and the Sønderjysk which they have adopted since in their conversation with friends. Those who are unwilling to speak Danish are also clearly committed to a career in West Germany; those who speak some Sønderjysk would prefer to stay in Sønderjylland/Nordschleswig.

When the concept of "Haussprache" is used of the self, it becomes less ambiguous; the majority claim to speak only one language. Only one or two are clearly aware that there are particular members of the family with whom they speak another language. One pupil said that the topic caused shift in language even with the same interlocutors. It was the request to keep a language diary which had helped him to realize this. Most other pupils said the keeping of the diary had not caused surprises; one said he now realized that he spoke less German than he had thought. The level of language awareness, therefore, is worth consideration (Byram, 1985).

With respect to interlocutor, pupils identify certain individuals as being German-speakers, with whom they say they speak German. Observation shows, however, that they also address them in Sønderjysk, especially in a group conversation, and then switch to German: the switch does not necessarily take place at the moment of turning the conversation to them. When reporting on their language use, pupils said they used German during the lessons and Sønderjysk during the breaks, but in fact they often use Sønderjysk among themselves during the lessons; they recognize this when asked for detail. Similarly one pupil said, when discussing the balance and proficiency of himself and his peers in German and Sønderjysk, that they speak German six hours a day. Most pupils said that they were not surprised by their own language use when filling in their language diaries and for those who are Sønderjysk speakers this meant that they estimated the amount of German *used* (Sprachgebrauch), (a term deliberately chosen to be all-embracing and explained as such), at between 15% and 30%. I strongly suspect, from classroom observation, that the amount of German *produced* by pupils is much below this: in many lessons only a few pupils would contribute orally and some pupils scarcely contributed at all in most lessons. The production of written German increases the amount, and could be just as significant (cf. pp. 72–73). The difference between receptive and productive uses of the language is surely unusually large, since the "compensatory" periods of oral production during breaks at school and at home are almost exclusively in Sønderjysk for the majority.

When asked which language they spoke at home, pupils gave the following answers:
Sønderjysk: 11, German: 5, both Sønderjysk and German: 3, Rigsdansk: 2. Of the "Germans", two only were identified by others as German-speaking. The diary of one of the other "Germans" shows that he speaks German with those identified as "German"; usually German with others like himself with German "Haussprache" and with one Rigsdansk speaker who does not speak Sønderjysk; and usually Sønderjysk with all the others in the class. As he said in the interview, "es kommt darauf an" ("*it depends*").

The last remark is interesting because it indicates an awareness of the complexity of the issue and has methodological implications. As described above, pupils identify individuals as "German-speaking" and claim to speak German with them. Similarly, pupils can answer direct questions about what language they speak at home, which is the sort of question which questionnaires to bilingual speakers often contain. They also completed language diaries, apparently without much difficulty. However, when pressed to think more carefully and monitor their language more consciously, or when observed in actual conversation, it was quite evident that their initial responses to questions or diary-keeping did not reflect accurately their actual behaviour. This is not, of course, to suggest any ill-intention on their part, for I believe they co-operated willingly. Those who did not complete the diary were not put under any pressure to do so. The problem lies in the fact that their own awareness is a simplified one. They know that one of their languages is dominant in one of their relationships but do not monitor their language closely enough to be aware of interference and code-switching. Their possession of two languages obliges them to categorize their relationships broadly according to language but they do not, and need not, analyse their language use in detail. The degree to which this issue affects individuals will vary: for some the dominance of one language in a relationship will be almost complete, only affected by uncontrollable interference. One pupil, however, found it impossible to keep a diary because he realized in the attempt that there were many switches in his conversations with the same interlocutors, particularly at home, switches which seemed to be topic-dependent. I strongly suspect that other pupils may have the same experience but, in the retrospective completion of the diary — even if done very soon after the event — they perceived themselves as speaking, say, Sønderjysk when in fact the occurrence was not so simple. Language diaries and questionnaires can reflect the individual's perception of his language use, but not the reality in all its complexity.

I also asked pupils how they felt when speaking German in Germany. One of the purposes of this question was to establish whether the language marks a boundary (Barth, 1969) between themselves and West Germans. The answers ranged from an assertion that there was no difference felt, that Germans do not realize that the speaker comes from Denmark, through a recognition that people hear a difference but that one should not be embarrassed and should indeed assert one's ability to speak German, and on to the other end of the spectrum, a feeling of considerable insecurity when speaking German "over there". The answers reveal that it is a question of proficiency and confidence, rather than "Haussprache", although this factor is clearly involved. Of the four or five pupils who said there is no difference for them in speaking German in Germany, one speaks mainly Sønderjysk at home; the latter also claimed that people do not realize he is from Sønderjylland/Nordschleswig — yet he has a recognizable accent. The fifth pupil is also a Sønderjysk speaker, who said he speaks both languages well and when in Germany speaks "immer Deutsch und dann fühle ich mich irgendwie mehr Deutsch als ich hier Deutsch fühle" (*"always German and then I feel somehow more German than I do here"*). This pupil insists on speaking German, even when Germans speak Danish to him. This suggests confidence and commitment to German, despite having a recognizable accent. The sentiment is echoed by another Sønderjysk speaker:

"ich geniere mich jedenfalls nicht mein Deutsch anzuwenden gegenüber Deutschen (...) dann macht es ja auch nichts, wenn man wohl merken kann, dass ich Däne bin."	(*"I'm not ashamed anyway to use my German vis à vis Germans (...) then it doesn't matter if they can probably notice that I'm a Dane."*)

Is it, however, simply coincidence that both these pupils intend to specialize in languages in further education? For one of those with German "Haussprache", the pressures of the situation are more worrying:

"das ist etwas anderes in Deutschland, Deutsch zu reden, finde ich, ich habe da ein bisschen merkwürdiges Gefühl, also ich bemühe mich, so gut Deutsch zu reden wie ich	(*"it's something different to speak German in Germany, I think, I have there a rather strange feeling, so I make an effort to speak German as well as I can (...) so I often feel like*)

kann (...) dann fühle ich mich
oft wieder als Ausländer da,
ein bisschen ein anderes
Gefühl wieder, in Deutschland
Deutsch zu reden."

*a foreigner there, it's a bit, a
different feeling, to speak German in Germany.")*

When, in order to get nearer to that feeling, I suggest it might be
something to do with the "Umgangssprache" (colloquial language) and
"Slang", this pupil agrees, saying "man hat nicht denselben Dialekt wie die
Deutschen" (*"we don't have the same dialect as the Germans"*). Others also
attempt to describe the difference with terms such as dialect, "Sonder-
sprache" (special language) and even speed of speech. For a few, this is a
matter of adopting to the style of the Germans and then feeling comfortable; for most it is a barrier.

I asked some pupils the same question with respect to Danish, that is
how they feel when speaking Rigsdansk outside Sønderjylland/Nordschles-
wig; not many have much experience of this. The responses were not
unlike those for German, but with the difference that only two speakers
have Rigsdansk as their "Haussprache" and feel that there is no difference;
neither of these considers himself a member of the minority. However, one
Sønderjysk speaker who had said that it is conspicuous if one speaks
Hochdeutsch (standard German) when others are speaking colloquially,
also said that the colloquialisms in Rigsdansk are also to be found in
Sønderjysk and this gives some common ground. Although only one pupil
said that Rigsdansk felt like a foreign language, all but the two already
mentioned said that speaking Rigsdansk is difficult, and that they very
rarely do so. Two with German "Haussprache" foresaw problems when
they would start in a Danish further education institution, one of them
suggested that the main problem would be breadth of vocabulary. Since
they tend to read only German books and newspapers, and watch only
German television, their receptive knowledge is not strengthened outside
school either. Although not directly asked, several pupils said they would
have liked more Danish at school, especially "wenn man nicht so gut ist"
(*"if you are not so good"*), in German and Danish as subjects; two said
they thought there should be more subjects taught in Danish, even up to
half the timetable.

With respect to Sønderjysk, a majority of pupils made the distinction
between their own Sønderjysk, with a strong German influence, and that
of their Danish peers, with Rigsdansk. Some, however, neither volunteered this distinction nor recognized it as valid when I suggested it to
them. For the majority, especially those who identified closely with the

school, the distinction is valid, and is one of the ways by which they recognize another member of the minority.

Pupils' linguistic experience outside Sønderjylland/Nordschleswig is one of the most significant factors in their identity. There are many other factors which help them to keep themselves separate from the Danes. The distance created by Rigsdansk keeps them separate from Danes from outside Sønderjylland/Nordschleswig. Most, if not all, have been the object of verbal abuse in the past, although this appears to be soon forgotten. For those who live out in the country, or in the hamlets and smaller villages, contact with minority members may well be greater, but friendship with peer-group Danes is very frequent: "ich habe wirkliche Freunde da, und dann macht es ja nichts aus." (*"I have real friends there, and then it doesn't matter."*) For some the question of whether someone is German or Dane is of no importance and, apart from going to the German school, they do not identify with the minority. One of these claims to speak all three languages equally well, an indication, I suspect, of identity rather than proficiency. For most, however, their position becomes clear when they are away from Sønderjylland/Nordschleswig and, although there are many kinds of experience involved — for example the uncomfortable formality of social relations in Germany — it is in the feelings aroused through speaking that the issue of identity is encapsulated. There is no simple formula. Here are a few descriptions:

"ich fühle mich mehr Deutsch als Dänisch, oder so, als Nordschleswiger fühle ich mich."

(*"I feel more German than Danish, or well, I feel I'm a Nordschleswiger."*)

"(in Denmark) dann fühlt man sich mehr Deutsch, (in Nordschleswig) eigentlich ́ auch mehr Deutsch, also ... (in West Germany) als dänischer Deutscher ... ich werde wohl gern hier in Dänemark (meinen Beruf haben) lieber in Nordschleswig."

(*"in Denmark you feel more German, in Nordschleswig also really more German, or ... in West Germany, as a Danish German, ... I would like to make my career here in Denmark, preferably in Nord-schleswig."*)

"für mich ist das Gebundensein eigentlich so, weil ich eigentlich kein Vaterland

(*"for me the feeling of being tied is really so because I really have no fatherland or whatever*

habe oder so ... weil in Deutschland da fühle ich mich da noch so ein bisschen Dänisch und in Dänemark da fühle ich mich wieder ganz klar Deutsch und das ist einfach die einzige Stelle wo man wirklich hingehört."	*... because in Germany I feel always still a little Danish, and in Denmark I feel quite clearly German, and here is simply the only place where we really belong.")*

For those with German citizenship there is a tendency to feel much more clearly German, but it is no more than a tendency. It is, however, quite clear that the majority feel linguistically out of place in Germany, that the problems of Rigsdansk keep them at a distance from many Danes, and that this distance is reinforced by the option of feeling "German" in the sense of belonging to the majority or, for those with German "Haussprache", through a more purely linguistic identity.

It is in fact difficult to discern any pattern in the interrelationship between language, commitment to the minority, place of abode, social status and so on. Schulte-Umberg's attempt (1975) to analyse the influence of family and school on ethnic identity remains unsatisfactory. He suggests that the family has a key position in the formation of a child's ethnic identity, confirming a common-sense hypothesis, but cannot be more precise than that. With respect to schooling, he considers only the reasons for parents' decision to send their children to a German school, and not the influence on the children's ethnic identity which the school might have. Toft (1982:47) asked parents in his sample whether their children were members of the minority and compared this with school attendance. 88.5% of those attending the German school were thought by their parents to be members of the minority. This tells us, however, nothing about the kind of membership, nor the influence of school; the other 11.5% may, for example, have been turned away from the minority by their very experience of school.

The interview material which I collected can give a different kind of picture. It can give an overview of the multiplicity of attitudes to minority membership existing in one group of school pupils as they are about to leave school. How those attitudes have developed and whether they will change afterwards remain unanswered questions.

If we take a starting point in home language, there are two pupils living in the town who both have German as the home language. One of them prefers very much to speak German, although he has spoken

Sønderjysk since early childhood. He reads almost exclusively German and watches only German television. Outside school, however, he has little formal contact with the organizations and networks of the minority. He sometimes visits the youth club, but never goes to any of the functions of the BdN. His parents are probably members of the BdN, but he hardly seems to know or care. He estimates that he speaks 90% German in the course of a day. The second pupil uses the minority networks in the town to the exclusion of almost all others. He is a regular visitor to the youth group, he plays sports in the minority's clubs, and scarcely speaks to anyone from the majority in the course of a normal day. He estimates, however, that he speaks less than 50% German on most days, and that Sønderjysk and a small amount of Rigsdansk dominate his speech. This pupil's commitment to the minority is very real, but he feels no "duty" towards the minority: he would, and does, take a role in organizational matters in the clubs he uses but rather out of interest in the sport, not in order to help maintain the minority as such.

A third pupil seems to have a greater sense of duty. His father is an active member of the BdN, and he himself is familiar with its activities. Judging by the articulate and thoughtful nature of his responses, he has given much consideration to the minority and his relationship to it. He is aware, for example, of the formation of a "political youth forum" in the last two years and is thinking of taking part. Yet he lives in a small village where although there are several German families, the friendship networks are more open and the amount of German spoken is minimal. At home he speaks Sønderjysk. German is used only on formal occasions, an important birthday, for example, and then only as a token, during the words of welcome and the toasts. He is already a member of the BdN in his own right and so are his older brothers and sisters, and through the school and sporting clubs he has often visited Germany, but rarely individually and has little personal experience of daily life in Germany. He thinks the minority will continue to exist for a long time, but that it will become smaller and smaller. He says, without bitterness or accusation, that many young people no longer feel drawn to the minority, that they marry into Danish society and thus "da kann man noch fragen, ob es noch eine richtige Volksgruppe ist, (. . .) oder ob die Volksgruppe erhalten werden bleibt" (*"you can then ask if it still is a proper minority (...) or whether the minority will be maintained"*). Another pupil from a similar farming community and with a similar interest in the minority speaks German at home and in the course of a normal day estimates that he speaks at least 70% German. In contrast to the previous one, he feels that he speaks as good a German as is spoken in Germany though he speaks a lot of Sønderjysk with friends, both Danes and Germans. Though country life involves him and his family in contact with Danes, he is very aware that most of their leisure time is spent in the company of other Germans. The difference between the open networks of economic life and the closed networks of social life is apparent in his description of the talks organized for the minority:

"die sind nur für die (Volks-gruppe), also Dänen können natürlich auch mitkommen aber das tun sie nicht, meis-tens sind nur Mitglieder vom Bund (deutscher Nord-schleswiger) da."

("they are only for the minor-ity, well Danes can of course come too, but they don't, usually there are only members of the BdN there.")

There is no prohibition of entry, but the expectations are quite clear; it also happens in reverse:

"aber andererseits kann ich mich auch nicht an ... be-teiligen an, oder ich tue es auf jeden Fall nicht, an dänischen Vorträgen."

("On the other hand, I can't take part in ... or at least I don't do it — in Danish lec-tures.")

The resulting closed networks are evident to this pupil, and the consequent separation:

"Die heute hier aus der Volks-gruppe, die treffen sich ja oft so, zum Beispiel haben wir ein Kartenklub da bei uns in der Nähe (...) und da treffen sich auch ausschliesslich Leute aus der Volksgruppe, ja die sind sehr viel unter sich, das finde ich auch, die mischen sich nicht so mit den Dänen (ist das ein Vorteil?) nicht unbe-dingt denn das kann ja auch so schlimm werden, dass sie sich total davon absondern ..."

("People today here from the minority, they often meet each other, for example there is a card club near us (...) and there, there are only people from the minority who meet, they are often together, I think so too, they don't mix with the Danes, (is that an advantage?) not necessarily, because it can become so bad that they cut themselves off completely. . .")

In marked contrast to this pupil, whose family and social life brings him often in contact with the minority's events, there is another who distances himself from his parents as far as the minority is concerned: "eigentlich gehöre ich zur Volksgruppe durch meine Eltern, aber ich stehe nicht wie meine Eltern, ich stehe nicht so doll dazu" (*"in fact, I belong to the minority through my parents, but I'm not like my parents, I'm not so committed as they are"*). For him being in the German school means that he has learnt German, and nothing else. His friends are Danish, he thinks of his social environment as Danish and the minority plays no further role in his life.

For those from an agricultural background, there is a branch of the minority, the agricultural society, which plays a significant role. This is particularly the case if the pupil intends to work in agriculture and for one such pupil it is the only link with the minority outside school. For adult members of the minority in agriculture this is often the only regular contact with a minority organization.

Next, there is the pupil who has occasional contact with the youth club, but is otherwise little involved and even negative in his attitudes. He feels that the school should teach more Danish and that to begin in the third year is too late. He is perhaps one of the least successful in academic terms and would send his own children to a Danish school, provided it were small. If he were living in Tinglev/Tingleff however, he would send his children to the German school, because the Danish school is too big. For him the question of membership of the minority is not important and so he does not care whether his friends belong to the minority or not.

Finally, there is a group of pupils who could be too easily identified to be described in detail. They include those for whom the school has served the purpose of preparing them for higher education either in a Danish or a German institution, and for whom the question of being a member of the minority is of a much lower priority. For them, academic success, or failure, is what the school has to offer. Force of circumstances may have brought them to the school and the same kind of force may take them into Danish or German schools after leaving this one. The issue of belonging to the minority or not is one they would rather forget.

Post-school experience

One of my main reasons for choosing to work with this group of pupils was my hypothesis that the transition from school to a new environment would be a period when certain phenomena otherwise latent would be especially apparent. In particular I had hypothesized that any link between language and identity would come to the surface when a major change in linguistic environment took place. In fact, I found scarcely anything to support this hypothesis in its simple form although the change of environment — both to a Danish environment and to a more homogeneously German one — was interesting in other ways.

A second round of interviews took place some four weeks after the beginning of the new school year. The interviews were again based on a number of prepared questions but did not rigidly follow a pre-determined format. The questions were formulated in part to test my hypothesis on language and identity, in part to confirm and deepen some of the information in the first interviews and in part as a result of observation of two of the new institutions to which pupils had gone. There are, in fact, two main groupings: those who go on to the German Gymnasium in Aabenraa/Apenrade, and those who go to the one-year basic vocational training (Erhvervsfagliggrunduddannelse, EFG); the majority of these specialize in commercial studies. I therefore visited the Gymnasium and the particular Handelsskole (Commercial School) which most of the interviewees attend because they live in its catchment area. The visits included observation of classes, one lesson of teaching, and discussions with the Principal and some staff. Each visit lasted two days. These visits afforded some insight into the institutions attended by 12 of the 19 pupils who were interviewed for a second time: eight were at the Gymnasium, four on the commercial course. Of the other seven, three were in work, one was at another commercial course, one at a technical EFG course and the fourth in a Danish Gymnasium. The pupils were interviewed for the most part in pairs or in groups. One was interviewed at home, two in the Handelsskole, and the rest volunteered to come back to the Tingleff school in the afternoon. The group interviews had the advantage of creating a more relaxed atmosphere — evident from some use of Sønderjysk among themselves — and the disadvantage of not necessarily obtaining as full an account of individuals' experience and thoughts as might have occurred in private. On the whole, however, the pupils knew each other well enough not to have to hide much, although I felt that two of them might have said more in private. This is a methodological problem of finding the most favourable balance.

The German Gymnasium serves the whole of Sønderjylland/Nordschleswig. It is the pinnacle of the minority's education system and for many people is a symbol of the full status of the system. Without the prestigious Gymnasium, the system would be incomplete. The fact that the system does not include some of the other post-compulsory institutions — in particular the Handelsskole which many pupils attend — is not so detrimental to the system. Yet this means that pupils may attend the Gymnasium more because it is German than because it offers precisely the education they wish for. One pupil felt that too much emphasis was given to the Gymnasium as a post-school option and any reference to other alternatives was minimal and even negative.

In comparison with Tingleff school, the Gymnasium pupils felt that it was a natural continuation in many ways. Yet they could also identify ways in which it was "more German", if asked to think in such terms. The answers suggest that the presence of a greater proportion of "German-speakers" gives the Gymnasium an atmosphere of being "more German". The German speakers were, in fact, both from Sønderjylland/Nordschleswig and from Germany. The difference was perceived by those who have German as "Haussprache" and also by those with Sønderjysk "Haussprache". It is the fact that those from Germany speak more fluently and also that some of them speak no Danish at all which makes them influential. The significance of the latter was particularly clear in the teaching of geography, taught in Danish by a temporary teacher. Some pupils in the class could not understand and a running translation and a written summary had to be provided. This is a very clear indication that the linguistic norm is now German and an illustration of the influence of the German-speakers on the linguistic life of the school. The peer group reinforces the influence of the teachers. For those who speak Sønderjysk at home, the norm creates a new atmosphere, noticed by one of the Tingleff German-speakers:

"Ich merk's, bei den andern also, wenn die Dänisch reden, hier da hatten sie nicht sofort umgeschalten auf Deutsch wenn ich kam oder so, da haben sie weitergeredet auf Dänisch (...) aber jetzt, jetzt im Gymnasium da sind ja viel mehr deutsche Staatsbürger, und auch die Sprache, ... und die ganzen Deutschen von den Volksschulen, die Deutsch zu Hause sprechen, sind ja fast im Gymnasium (und die, die zu Hause Dänisch sprechen) bleiben bei Dänisch zu reden,

("I notice it in the others, when they speak Danish, here they didn't use to change immediately to German, if I appeared, they would continue to speak in Danish (...) but now, now at the Gymnasium there are a lot more German citizens, and so the language ... and all the Germans from the lower school, who speak German at home, are almost all at the Gymnasium and (those who speak Danish at home) continue to speak Danish, that is Sønderjysk ... well

also Sønderjysk . . . also bestimmt ein bisschen mehr Deutsch reden jetzt, weil ihre Klassenkameraden auch Deutsch reden, nicht? und da können sie nicht jetzt Sønderjysk zu den (reden)."

certainly they speak a little more German now, because their friends speak German, you see? and so they can't speak Sønderjysk to them.")

So there are now quite clearly three categories: those with German nationality and coming from Germany, those living in Sønderjylland/Nordschleswig — some of whom have German nationality — and speaking German at home, and those who speak Sønderjysk. The latter group were the large majority in the Tingleff school but suddenly are no longer so, and are clearly aware of this:

"Das ist jetzt mehr Deutsch, finde ich, also die meisten, ich glaub', das sind nur drei von meiner Klasse, und wir sind dreizehn, die sprechen nur Danisch, (...) und darum, also in den Pausen sprech'ich eigentlich auch nur Deutsch."

("It's more German, I think, so most of them, I think there are only three from my class — and there are thirteen of us — who speak only Danish (...) and so in the breaks I speak really only German.")

But it is not only a question of quantity but also of the quality of the norms set up by the native-speakers in the peer-group.

"Ich finde, auf dem Gymnasium wird man eigentlich viel mehr dazu gezwungen, sich mehr gezielt auszudrücken, seine Formulierungen besser zu bedenken (...) auch weil die andern Schüler also oft auf einem sehr· hohen Deutschniveau sind (...) man traut sich nicht etwas zu sagen, weil man also sich der Formulierungen nicht sicher ist, und das also, das könnte einen auch hemmen."

("I find that at the Gymnasium you are really forced much more to express yourself precisely, to think over your formulations better (...) also because the other pupils are often at a very high standard in German (...) you don't dare say anything because you're not sure about the formulation and that could inhibit you.")

The teachers, too, are felt to be more demanding in their expectations, especially if they are recently from Germany. This impression was confirmed by one teacher who found he needed to be more explicit in his instructions than in a German school.

In the linguistic environment, then, the Gymnasium presents a change and a challenge for some pupils — a challenge which can be inhibiting. Yet paradoxically they had not experienced the school as being "more German" because of this, even though most would suggest that the language is the main German characteristic of their Tingleff school and would argue that to have less German language in the school would make it less German. Nor did they feel that speaking more German made them feel more German in themselves. For some the Gymnasium is a natural continuation of their school career and provides an atmosphere with which they can readily identify, providing greater linguistic harmony between school and home. For those who speak Sønderjysk and whose "German" identity is not so firm, the environment is less comfortable, both linguistically and ideologically. There will come a point, said one pupil, where a decision has to be made, a point which may be created by the need to make a political decision "also, da muss ich mich entscheiden, ob ich jetzt Deutsch oder Dänisch bin, und diese Entscheidung würde mir unheimlich schwer fallen" (*"well, then, I have to decide, whether I'm now German or Danish, and that decision would be extremely difficult for me"*). For such a pupil the political expectations which some, perhaps many, members of the minority place upon the Gymnasium are particularly problematic. At a public debate on the Gymnasium, where the unexpectedly large attendance was evidence of the importance of the Gymnasium in the minority, it was stated that the Gymnasium should produce the future leaders of the minority, a political élite to maintain the minority. As the pupils themselves become older and more conscious of the political reality around them, and as they move into a linguistically more German environment, the issues of identity and allegiance become clearer.

For those who go into a Danish environment, the situation is at first glance the reverse of the Gymnasium environment, but is in fact more complex. The language of their school is expected to be Rigsdansk in all classroom and teaching-linked domains. In informal domains, there is also Sønderjysk, but not exclusively as it had been at the Tingleff school; Rigsdansk and approximations to Rigsdansk are also part of the informal domains. For the small minority who speak mainly or exclusively German at home, the linguistic expectations of peers have a similar effect to those of the Gymnasium, but this time with Sønderjysk as the norm:

"na ja, ich versuch' mich   (*"well, I try to express myself*
genauer auszudrücken, aber   *more precisely, but that is well*

das ist eben doch mal, manchmal also wo man die Wörter so aus dem Deutschen ableitet, nicht direkt auf Deutsch sagt (...) wenn ich jetzt nicht das genaue Wort auf Dänisch weiss, und aber auf Deutsch (dann drehst du das ein bisschen als ob es Dänisch ins Dänische, mit dänischer Aussprache?) ja ... (...) die andern verstehen ja wohl was ich meine ..."

(so, sometimes where you transfer the words from German, don't say them exactly in German (...) if I don't know the exact word in Danish, but do in German (then you twist it a bit as if it's Danish, into Danish with Danish pronunciation?) yes ... the others probably understand what I mean.")

For another pupil, who speaks Sønderjysk at home and does not identify with the minority, the more homogeneous linguistic environment has brought greater clarity and awareness of his own language and of the interference from German in his Sønderjysk:

"und wenn das passiert, dann denke ich auch darüber nach (...) wir haben so ein Mischmasch zwischen Deutsch und Dänisch gesprochen, früher in der Schule."

("and when that happens, then I think about it (...) we spoke such a mixture of German and Danish before, at school.")

Another pupil said he felt more and more secure in Rigsdansk because of the new environment and teacher expectations, and a third, who was in work, and who had said he felt insecure in his German in the first interview, was clearly happier with just one language:

"man wird auch viel mehr sicher wenn man nur Dänisch spricht, mit der Zeit, dann weiss man zuletzt alles."

("you also become much surer if you only speak Danish, in time, then eventually you know everything.")

This pupil was, however, referring to Sønderjysk. Those in the Handelsskole who were hearing and using much more Rigsdansk than before, found it a "strange" experience (ein merkwürdiges Gefühl). In particular they had problems with terminology which they had learnt in German and which was not immediately recognizable in Danish. One area of particular interest is the fact that the Latin-based terms for grammatical concepts are learnt in the German school, whereas the Danish teachers use purely

Danish terminology. This was particularly problematic in German grammar lessons.

The German lessons are in fact problematic in other more fundamental ways. From learning it on the assumption that it is their mother tongue, they now move into a situation where it is treated as a foreign language. I suggested earlier that the mother-tongue approach is inappropriate, even though the pupils do not recognize this. The foreign language approach is even more so, and the pupils recognize and resent it. They feel that they have little to learn, although they recognize that grammatical analysis may be useful in the written language. For those with German as the home language grammatical analysis is, in fact, annoying because they feel they know the language but still have difficulty with analysis. They tend to find the pronunciation of other pupils amusing and the mistakes made by non-native-speaker teachers irritating. They find the task of translation particularly difficult, yet it is an examination requirement and thus, on the whole, they feel that they have no advantages to compensate for their disadvantages in Danish. The strength of feeling was evident when a pupil at another Danish school said he had a native-speaker as German teacher; he was congratulated on his good luck. In short, the German lessons provide no bridge between the German and Danish schools and the pupils move quite abruptly from a situation of hearing and using a lot of German to one of none at all.

They do not, they claim, speak German among themselves, although evidence from teachers at the Handelsskole, who hear German pupils speaking German in the breaks, suggests that this may be an initial reaction, an unwillingness to be different, which will change as they gain more self-confidence in their new surroundings. In fact, most said they did not miss speaking German. For those in work, this was particularly true, but also for some of those in the Handelsskole. Three pupils said that they think in German and therefore miss the use of the language, but they were not exclusively pupils with German as home language or even pupils with a strong German identity.

The question of identity becomes an important one in the Danish environment. For those who have little or no allegiance to the minority, it provides the first step towards moving into the majority's social institutions. There is a tendency for all the pupils in Danish schools not to advertise their German identity. Some cling to the anonymity more than others. They believe that their teachers, except perhaps the German teachers, do not know, although they recognize each other from their language:

"das ist bei mir eigentlich auch, die sagen, dass ich mit einem kleinen deutschen Akzent eigentlich spreche ... einige Wörter, also wie Kemi, da sag' ich Chemie noch immer, Psychologie statt psykologi."

("in my case it's the same, they say, I speak with a little bit of German accent ... some words like 'Kemi', I say 'Chemie' still and 'Psychologie' instead of 'psykologi'.")

The degree to which an individual feels different and ill at ease will doubtless depend both on linguistic factors and on his self-confidence in the identity, whether it is German or Danish. Perhaps those find it most difficult who are in the process of shaking off their connections with the minority, and, on the other hand, those who have a firm German identity and also have German as the home language:

"also ich fühle mich doch ein bisschen anders auf einer dänischen Schule also, aber das ist schwer, das finde ich nicht (...) vielleicht auch eben weil man denkt, dass die andern finden, dass ich irgendwie anders bin."

("well, I do feel a bit different in a Danish school, but I don't find it's difficult (...) perhaps also just because you think that the others think that I'm somehow different.")

For one of the pupils in work, speaking no German at all and with no particularly strong connections with the minority, the lack of German language and the Danish identity of those he works with make him feel less and less German. Thus in general, the move into a Danish linguistic and social environment can be difficult, can create a sense of being different and can lead to a need for anonymity.

Some indication of how a Danish institution receives the German pupils was evident from the Handelsskole. The Principal and teachers are aware of the pupils, and operate with the concept of "the German pupils" as one of their means of dealing with them. On the other hand, they try to avoid using the concept publicly. Thus they do, in fact, quickly realize, within a few days, who is German, despite what the pupils themselves think, but they do not use the knowledge in public. One teacher said the German pupils are over-sensitive and need careful handling. They do, however, correct Germanisms in the pupils' work and draw attention to them; they give advice about academic options on the basis that pupils already know German; they can help pupils to find work with employers who particularly welcome German pupils. They recognize German pupils not only because of their lack of proficiency in Rigsdansk and of a "frame of reference" for cultural or literary allusions, but also because of their particular pride in Sønderjysk. Some teachers also find difference in behaviour, in a "gammeldags" ("*old-fashioned*") courtesy, in their not being so "snakselige" ("*talkative*") as Danish pupils but therefore "ikke sprudlende" ("*not sparkling*") either. Conversely, the pupils feel that the school is not so well-disciplined and orderly. It is in such remarks that the unquantifiable and almost invisible differences between the two cultures experienced by the pupils becomes most apparent. It is the experience which lies behind and below the obvious differences and difficulties, and is responsible for some of the transitional unease which surfaces from time to time.

Throughout my conversations, there was a constant problem in the use of the adjectives "German" and "Danish". The adjectives — whether used in German or Danish — are almost inseparable from the homonymous nouns "German (language)" and "Danish (language)". All discussion of German or Danish experience — and especially of German or Danish schools — was constantly slipping between the adjectival and nominal usage. Furthermore, the adjective "German" can mean Nordschleswig German or Federal Republic German; similarly "Danish" can mean Sønderjysk Danish or Rigsdansk Danish. Clearly the language and culture are interwoven, but just as evidently there are non-linguistic aspects of culture and behaviour which are around the language. It must be remembered that these aspects play their part just as significantly as the language even though less obviously to both participants and observer.

When, therefore, pupils indicate their sensitivity to linguistic norms, there is a strong probability that they are equally sensitive to other cultural norms, even though not as aware of them. The Sønderjysk speakers in the Gymnasium who feel a need to formulate their ideas carefully are perhaps "accommodating" (Giles & Powesland, 1975) not only linguistically. The German speaker who formulates his Sønderjysk more carefully is acting in a similar way. On the other hand, those former pupils who explained their need to assert themselves and their self-confidence in the Handelsskole are refusing to go beyond a certain point in accommodation to their new environment. The language is in both situations a symbol and essentially unquantifiable. Thus although it would be possible to measure changes towards the norm which any individual might make, the degree of change, the quantity of variation is meaningless without the context of the individual's identity and allegiance to the minority, which in turn is made up of a number of factors, including family relationships, employment or academic ambitions, educational success or failure and so on.

6 "Language and Culture" in the Minority

The "basis" of the minority

Die Grundlage einer Volks-
gruppe wird immer die
Sprache und die durch sie ver-
mittelte Kultur sein.
(Nissen, *Der Nordschleswiger*,
Nov. 1982)

*(The basis of a minority will
always be the language and the
culture transmitted through the
language.)*

This statement, taken from a speech made to representatives of the
minority from all the local groupings in Sønderjylland/Nordschleswig, is
the simplest formulation of a belief which clearly underlies and could be
documented from any number of speeches, written statements, editorials
and so on. That belief also influences the actions of many members of the
minority, officials and ordinary members alike, although it is possible to
argue, as some members do, that cultural activity is in practice subordinated to political activity, whereas it should be the reverse (Brons,
Nordschleswig 82, 1982). In earlier chapters I considered the nature of the
school and its contribution to the realization of this "basis of a minority"
and it became apparent that a much more differentiated view is needed of
"language and culture"; this is also the case in the wider context of the
minority.

One might even cast more fundamental doubt on the underlying
belief. The view that cultural activity is in reality often subordinated to
political activity is in practice well-founded. It is the point of view which
maintains that cultural activity would be impossible without political power
and representation. One of the principal purposes of political power is to
maintain the financial standing of the minority, for it has in itself no
economic force through which to create the finance it needs. The raising of
monies from regular contributions and occasional sponsorships is insuf-

112

ficient for the needs of the minority as it at present functions. Thus, the fundamental doubt would be that the true basis of the minority is in the political and economic position it has acquired rather than in the language and culture. This kind of analysis of the minority — of the significance of its economic and financial basis for the character of its organizations and the nature of the relationship of individuals to the organizations — has not yet been carried out. Neither the sociologists nor the political analysts have considered, for example, the significance of the fact that there are major subsidies obtained from the Federal Republic of Germany. In how far does that fact determine the linguistic and cultural orientation towards the F.R.G.? Does financial dependence inhibit cultural independence and the creation of a Nordschleswig identity for the minority? Informal observation suggests that these questions are at least worthy of consideration. They cannot be answered here in any clear-cut way, for the path from financial subsidy to the detail of cultural events — choice of music for concerts, policy on book-buying for a library — or to the realization of linguistic norms, is a long and complicated one. The flow of influence along that path is doubtless neither in one direction only nor unaffected by currents from other sources. Cultural and linguistic phenomena are not determined in some simplistic way by financial arrangements, but they are not independent either and that factor should be borne in mind. Without financial subsidy, the minority could not exist as it does. Indeed without financial subsidy, the minority might not exist at all. Yet the members of the minority would not cease to exist; they would have to reinterpret their identity in different economic circumstances. The shared contemporary perception — the word "ideology" is shunned by the minority because of its negative connotations — remains nonetheless that "language and culture" are the foundation of the minority. It is therefore necessary to analyse what is meant by this phrase.

Concepts of culture

The use of the definite articles in Nissen's phrase "the language and the culture transmitted through the language" begs many questions. Some of them were already evident in the discussion of language and culture in the school. Whose language? Which varieties of that language? In which domains of social interaction? Whose culture? What kind of culture? Only culture mediated by language? And more fundamentally, is a particular and different language really *a sine qua non* for the maintenance of a minority (Anderson, 1979)? Again, I do not suggest that I shall answer those questions in the following pages. It will be my purpose to describe some aspects of the actual practice of the minority from which it will be evident that those questions are valid ones and that the slogan "German language and culture" requires some analysis.

I do not want to suggest, however, that such analysis is absent within the minority itself; indeed the notion of "culture" is frequently debated, even if the notion of "language" is usually assumed to be a fundamental, simple concept. The most frequent contributors to the debate are teachers, even when culture beyond the bounds of school-work is concerned. This reflects the fact that cultural events usually take place in school buildings, organized by committees where teachers are active. It also points to the absence of other groups of people in the minority who professionally or otherwise might be deeply involved in social and cultural analysis, critique and debate. The minority is largely dependent on the teaching profession for its cultural and intellectual activity, as is openly recognized. The dangers are also recognized. One headteacher complained that such activity should not be a part of the teacher's contract:

"Das darf nicht sein. Ich wünsche mir doch auch, dass alle Lehrkräfte irgendwie gut verteilt einen kleinen Job übernehmen, den sie auch wirklich mit Freude ausüben. Wenn wir sie zu viel drängen und wir haben dann eine Lehrkraft, die uns alles verdirbt, weil sie es nur macht, um ihren Platz zu behalten, kann das auch nicht gut sein." (Uth, *Der Nordschleswiger*, March 1980)

("That should not be so. But I also hope that in some way well distributed teachers will all take on a little job which they really do with pleasure. If we force them too much, and we then have teachers who spoil everything because they are only doing it to keep their job, that can't be any good either.)

The strength of the implied expectations and pressures on teachers is here quite clear.

Before pursuing the analysis as such, let us consider what cultural activities take place. Rather than attempting a definition of culture through which to select activities, I propose to give an impression of the range of activities which members of the minority might be involved in. All of them might be perceived as "furthering German culture"; an oft-used phrase is "die deutsche Kultur pflegen". The most widespread bearer of German culture is the daily newspaper, *Der Nordschleswiger*, which informs about events in Germany as well as in the minority. It has a print of just under 4,000 copies, with almost 3,500 being sent out by post to regular subscribers. It gives notice of and then later reports on most if not all events in the minority. For someone living in Tinglev/Tingleff, for example, activities are available at village, municipality and regional level. In a regular diary for the area for March–June 1983, there are over 50 meetings listed. They range from handicraft activities in preparation for Easter, through social evenings for BdN members, confirmation services, committee meetings, shooting club championships, school carnivals, youth club meetings, meetings for retired people, to the annual major event for the whole minority, a youth and sport festival one Saturday in July. Some of these 50 events are similar to each other, for example the numerous school carnivals, and are thus intended for a part of the population only. Not included in the list are such things as the weekly sports club meetings, training and playing sessions, or the occasional village theatre group presentations, usually light farce. Another major missing item is the programme of the agricultural society for the area, which appears to lead a separate existence in many ways, even though some of its activities, for the women members especially, are not specific to agriculture. Another kind of regular meeting is found rather more in the winter season, when evening classes in, for example, first-aid, English for tourists, macrame, are offered in the schools. All the activities mentioned so far are largely "internal" to the minority, organized as part of the life of its institutions and organizations.

The question arises to what extent these activities are "German". One area where, again, school-teachers and school-children are much involved is sport. In essence there is nothing specifically German about the sports which are played, and members do not experience them otherwise; indeed even the use of the German language is confined to training sessions, if the trainer is a teacher, and to the formal occasions of committees or festivities. What is German is the fact that the people involved belong to the minority and feel content and secure in each other's company. This applies in varying degrees to all the internal activities. It is the environment of the activity rather than its content that is German. Not even the amateur theatre groups confine themselves to German plays, and though the plays are given in German, rehearsal takes place as much in Sønderjysk as German. All these cultural activities tend, therefore, to sustain the sense of a German community within Sønderjylland/Nordschleswig. They do not, however, promote specifically German culture nor do they produce specifically Nordschleswig German cultural artefacts.

That which is specifically German tends in fact to come from outside, from the Federal Republic and Schleswig–Holstein in particular. It is German in two ways: it is produced by Germans — actors, musicians, lecturers from the University of Kiel, writers reading from their own books — and its content is usually from the German cultural tradition. In the latter case, "German" includes contributions from German-speaking countries other than the Federal Republic, although the German Democratic Republic hardly appears. The status of the culture offered is "high" or "classic". Whether the material is modern or not, it is clearly within the classical canon. Although there are lectures on popular topics, they are surrounded by a certain formality. In short, whether it is a Strauss operetta, a lecture on the heathlands of Europe, a Shakespearian drama, Dürrenmatt's "Die Physiker" or Haydn's "Creation", the tone is clear: "culture" is high culture.

There is, however, another significant source of German culture: the three channels of West German television. The quality of reception is high throughout most of Nordschleswig and members of the minority watch almost exclusively German television. Through television much of the cultural spectrum is completed. Some of the creative arts, such as film and rock music, which are not offered in the Nordschleswig programme, are represented on television; others, such as jazz or modern poetry, are not. The classical canon is filled out by lower status art and entertainment. But all this is limited to the one medium, television, which gives its own format and distortions to every kind of art. Although television gives people in Sønderjylland/Nordschleswig the opportunity to share with West Germans a great deal of their cultural opportunities, it does not simply transpose West German culture into the area; there are still large gaps in the spectrum. Furthermore, this medium allows in the culture as in the language, only receptive knowledge, and there is always the sense of looking across the border, of not being fully involved. This is crystallized, for example, in the nightly weather-forecast, which covers the whole of Germany, including the G.D.R., but which does not go beyond the German–Danish frontier. Although it is still possible in practice to anticipate the weather north of the border from the forecast, the sense of being excluded is quite clear. Television offers, therefore, a somewhat vicarious cultural experience and its role should not be over-estimated.

The essence of the account so far can be summarized as follows. There are two kinds of cultural event: those with a source lying outside the minority and those internal to the minority. The external events are either imported specifically for Nordschleswig, in which case they are classical culture, or they are received in Nordschleswig though intended for West

Germany. These two categories cover much of the spectrum of culture, from entertainment to "high" art, but some genres and media are not represented and there is a vicarious element and a dependency relationship to this imported culture. The internal events are specifically German and have a recognizable minority character, but in the format rather than in the content. They further the sense of a German community (die deutsche Gemeinschaft) but do not produce any counter-balance to the dependency relationship to imported culture. When one considers the size and the social structure of the minority, the lack of independent "high" culture is not very surprising. It has neither the intellectual traditions nor the cultural institutions — galleries, museums, theatres — which are the backdrop to artistic endeavour. In this respect it differs from some other minorities whose cause has been championed by gifted individuals making significant contributions to the fight for survival (Gras & Gras, 1982). Its intellectuals are mainly teachers whose contribution has been limited to historical research and writing, an important task in any society but which is so laden with the emotions of the last 60 years that its status is somewhat unclear.

At another level, the high proportion of people living in rural surroundings might lead one to expect activity within the traditional crafts. There is little evidence of this however, and the proximity and mixing of German and Danish rural populations over many centuries means that such craft artefacts would not be specifically German. They could at best be independent of the imported culture.

Given the relatively small size of the minority, the absence of its own artists and craftsmen of whatever kind is not very surprising. Yet Emil Nolde was born in one of the border villages, and in the final analysis the existence of artistic genius is independent of surroundings. The absence of a local culture is due more to other factors. After all, it is possible to stimulate local culture by sponsorship, through artists-in-residence, travelling exhibitions and so on. The more fundamental reason is bound up with the philosophical, political and economic orientation of the minority.

Culture and language policy

In an information publication of the BdN, the first aim of the minority is said to be:

"Aufrechterhaltung und Ver-   (*"maintenance and deepening*
tiefung der geistigen und kul-   *of the spiritual and cultural*
turellen Verbindung zum   *link to the German people*

deutschen Volk ohne Iso-
lierung dem Norden
gegenüber."
(Informationsunterlagen,
1982:6)

without isolation vis à vis
Scandinavia.")

The same publication includes the statement of the basic principles of the
minority's political party. In the second section, on "cultural policy" —
which, significantly, appears before economic and social issues — the
following statement appears:

"Die Schleswigsche Partei tritt
ein für die deutsche Kultur-
arbeit in Nordschleswig, deren
Hauptaufgabe die Erhaltung
und Pflege der deutschen
Sprache ist."
(Informationsunterlagen,
1982:14)

("The Schleswig Party sup-
ports German cultural work in
Nordschleswig, the principal
task of which is the mainten-
ance and cultivation of the
German language.")

The tendency to make the concept of culture subordinate to concept of
language is here very plain. It is similar to that which was found in the
declaration of the aims of the schools, and has the same weakness: the
exclusion or at least the down-grading of non-linguistic aspects of culture.
Furthermore, although the notion of "link" in the first quotation need not
involve dependency, the sheer size of the minority compared with the
rather nebulous entity "the German people" tends to rule out any notion of
"link" on equal terms.

I have already suggested that, in contrast to the debate on the meaning
of "culture", there is little clarity or even realization of the complexity of
the notion of "the German language". The same can be said of the concept
"the German people". In practice the schools provide a model of what "the
German language" is for its pupils. If we now consider how the concept of
"the German people" is realized in practice, the reasons for the emphasis
on the language as the repository of culture will become clearer.

The most obvious reference group for "the German people" is the
political entity of the Federal Republic of Germany and the federal state of
Schleswig–Holstein. There have been many indications of this in preceding
pages, from the financial support and sponsorships, through the use of
West German school books by Schleswig–Holstein teachers, to television
and cultural imports. There are, however, other definitions of "German"
which go beyond the Federal Republic. One definition takes its starting

point in the history of Sønderjylland/Nordschleswig. Rather than arguing that the area is historically part of some German political or racial entity — a tactic which used to be used but has now lost its appeal — the approach is through the notion of "Gesinnung" (*"convictions and attitudes"*) — which is in accord with the declarations of 1955 in Bonn and Copenhagen. Thus in January 1983, the front page of the local section of *Der Nordschleswiger* was devoted to a lecture by a Kiel University historian, with the title: "Deutsche Nordschleswiger können sich mit gutem Gewissen als Deutsche bekennen" (*"German Nordschleswigers can call themselves Germans with a clear conscience"*). The emphasis is here that, where biological, religious and cultural distinctions cannot be clearly drawn, what is important is "Gesinnung". This is the criterion for identity and as such evades the difficulty that the home-language or mother-tongue cannot be used as a criterion.

Yet we have seen again and again that the language *is* used as a criterion, perhaps because "Gesinnung" is too private and also because that privacy is protected by the minority's own legal foundation, the Bonn–Copenhagen declarations. Therefore it is not surprising to find that a second definition of "German" is based on the notion of language. Again it is in the words of an outsider to which *Der Nordschleswiger* gives prominence that the clearest statement is to be found:

"Im Gegensatz zu fast allen Völkern dieser Erde hat sich unser Name, das Wort "deutsch" nicht aus einem Stammesnamen oder der geographischen Bezeichnung eines Siedlungsgebietes entwickelt. Wir nennen uns so nach unserer Sprache." (Klein, *Der Nordschleswiger*, Nov. 1982)	(*"In contrast to almost all other peoples of the world, our name, the word 'German', has not developed from a tribal name or from the geographical designation of a settlement area. We get our name from our language."*)

This definition was echoed in another lecture in April 1983 as part of a series discussing aspects of the minority. The first speaker, a representative of an organization (der Verein für das Deutschtum im Ausland, VDA), which aims to support German-speaking minorities, went on to suggest that the Prussian, the German-Swiss, the South-Tiroler, the Alsacer and others have a common heritage. Clearly, if the Nordschleswig minority wishes to be included, it needs the language as a link. It is evident that this is indeed the wish. There are frequent visits to these other minorities. *Der*

Nordschleswiger reports on the political and cultural fortunes of, for example, South Tirol and the German minority in Belgium. The VDA sponsors visits to West Germany. Yet there remains the problem that German is not the daily language of most members of the minority. This astounded one leading politician visiting from South Tirol, which led to an editorial in *Der Nordschleswiger* calling for more stress on the significance of German, for example through the schools (Oct. 1982). The same attitude is apparent in attempts to introduce more German into the sports club, in the stress that youth work should take place within "a framework of German language" (cf. pp. 51–54). Yet it has to be admitted that this is not a realistic aim.

A sociolinguistic view

The visitor from South Tirol could not understand why people did not use their German. The sociolinguistic explanation is to be found in the notion of diglossia: "Deutsch ist unsere Sonntagssprache" (*"German is our Sunday language"*), as one lady put it (Fishman, 1980; Søndergaard, 1981). For those members of the minority who have Sønderjysk as the home language, German is the H language, to be reserved for formal, institutional occasions. To attempt to introduce German into L language contexts is to attempt to break down the diglossic distinction, which is sustained by a whole range of complex emotions, attitudes and habits. Thus the diglossic position of German within the minority's activities can be justifiably used to link the minority into the concept of "German" which is defined through language, "der deutsche Sprachraum" (*"the German language area"*), but it also leads to comparisons with other areas. Those comparisons, with South Tirol (Egger, 1977), with German-speaking Belgium (Nelde, 1979) — where German has both H and L language functions — are not always satisfactory for the minority. They lead to a feeling that more German ought to be used, could be used. This seems particularly evident for those with German as the home language, that is taking both H and L functions. They are the ones who in editorials and committees call for the use of German in daily life.

It is claimed that more German is in fact being used by pupils to each other in some schools. Yet this should not be equated with a change in habits of Sønderjysk speakers. The only ones of the group interviewed in Tinglev/Tingleff who had ever changed the language in which they habitually addressed any one individual, were those who had begun to use Sønderjysk with some friends who had German as the home language. The force at work here is that of accommodation to the norm set by the majority of the speakers (Giles, Bourhis & Taylor, 1977). The use of more

German in óther schools is more likely to be due to an influx of German-speakers and the accommodation of the Sønderjysk-speakers to the larger numbers than to any fundamental diglossic shift for the Sønderjysk speakers themselves.

Within the minority as a whole, and outside the H language contexts, all the indications are that the Sønderjysk speakers are in the majority. The statistics available in Sievers (1975) and Toft (1982) support this, despite the limited sample-base. Toft (1982:44) claims there is a fall over three generations in the use of Sønderjysk and a rise in German as the home-language. Given the limits of his sample (1982:26) and the fact that there is a change of only 1.7% fall in the use of Sønderjysk and 4.1% rise in German, the significance must be doubtful. On a conservative estimate, about two-thirds of the minority speak Sønderjysk as their L language and German as their H language in minority affairs. Furthermore, productive proficiency in German even as H language is not equivalent to that of the native-speaker. The teachers recognise the difference between native-speaker pupils and others very easily. At the lexical level, school pupils are often deficient in comparison to native-speakers (Søndergaard, 1980). In terms of register and variety, I have shown above that pupils do not have the opportunity to develop in the same way as a native-speaker, although the areas where they have most opportunity coincide with the formal use of German. I have also shown from interview material that some pupils feel insecure in their use of German, although much less so when on home ground.

It is evident then that there are considerable expectations and pressures on minority members to use German. The demand is made in a linguistically undifferentiated way, but the expectations are that at least in formal contexts — for example committee meetings and speeches — German must be used. Indeed the wish is that German should become the language of informality within the minority's institutions, as the following editorial indicates:

"Die deutsche Sprache darf aber nicht nur die Festtags-sprache der deutschen Volks-gruppe in Nordschleswig sein, sie muss auch in der täg-lichen Arbeit der deutschen Institutionen und Verbände benutzt und gepflegt werden."
(*Der Nordschleswiger*, April 1983)

(*"The German language should however not be simply the language of festive days, it must also be used and culti-vated in the daily work of the German institutions and asso-ciations."*)

This view is clearly different from that which describes German as the "Sunday language", and the use of the near-synonym "festive day" suggests that the concept is familiar and the view it represents is widespread. The assertion that this view is unsatisfactory, made in the official organ of the minority and repeated often elsewhere, is likely to make the Sønderjysk speaker feel inadequate. His productive proficiency in German as a formal language, and all the more so as an informal language, is not up to native-speaker standard, even when he is in school and using German every day. After leaving school, those who do not continue in a German institution will begin to feel even more insecure, particularly if they do not spend some of their leisure time in minority activities. Furthermore, some of the "middle" generation who were educated in the post-war years did not have satisfactory German school education and in some cases had to go to a Danish school. For these people, proficiency in the H language in formal contexts is also quite problematic.

The logical consequence of this situation would be that proficiency in German is a pre-condition for occupation of a position of importance and influence in the institutions of the minority, be they political or cultural. This is not to say that there is an explicit ban on those who are not proficient. That would be unacceptable and indeed it is unlikely that any member of the minority has consciously formulated this kind of thought. Much less do I wish to suggest a theory of conspiracy against the Sønderjysk speakers. Furthermore, it is evident to and accepted by all that Sønderjysk has an inevitable place in Sønderjylland/Nordschleswig, even though its dialectal status can lead to deprecatory remarks. There is and has to be, therefore, tolerance even within the official attitude towards Sønderjysk:

"Hier soll kein Bann gegen die plattdänische Umgangssprache vieler Angehörigen der Volksgruppe ausgesprochen werden. Sie hat ebenfalls ihren festen Platz im bunten Bild unserer nordschleswigschen Heimat."

(Der Nordschleswiger, April 1983)

("There shall be no ban uttered here against the 'dialectal' Danish colloquial language of many members of the minority. It too has its safe place in the varied picture of our Nordschleswig home.")

Nonetheless the hypothesis that proficiency in German is a key to power within the minority is a logical one given the conglomeration of factors outlined so far. Let it be clear, however, that the language factor, though powerful, is not the only decisive one. The personality of the individual, his position as a member of a well-known family, for example, may be factors strong enough to outweigh the language factor. It should also be made clear that proficiency in German cannot in practice be easily distinguished from other rhetorical skills. And finally there is no difference in essence from the role of linguistic and rhetorical skills as a pre-condition to a position of power in many other, monolingual societal groupings.

However, in this particular situation, the role of language is especially evident because of the contrast between Sønderjysk and German. The testing of such a hypothesis is difficult. First, it is difficult to isolate linguistic proficiency. Second, since the hypothesis includes the notion that no member of the minority is consciously aware of the role of language, a short and simple question is not possible; the possibility of being misunderstood is strong. Third, this kind of analysis, which implies that certain members of the minority might be excluded from full participation on linguistic grounds, is not likely to be acceptable to everyone and therefore evoke an evasive reply. The adduction of evidence is hence not easy or likely to be conclusive.

If the hypothesis is correct, then those best placed linguistically to take up positions of importance are those who have the widest command of the varieties and registers of German: the native-speaker German nationals and the indigenous speakers with German as home-language.

The opinions of informants were divided. On the one hand one told me his son had said he would never allow himself to be elected to a committee because he did not speak German well enough. On the other hand, another from the same generation said that in the meetings of his school governing board, a mixture of German and Sønderjysk is spoken, and that one member, a Dane, speaks no German at all. Another informant said:

"Wenn zwei Kandidaten sind, der eine ist dänisch, oder von dänischer Schule, davon geht man immer aus, und dann der in der deutschen Schule, und der in der deutschen Schule überhaupt nicht dazu taugt, dann wird er gewählt, das tut er . . . weil der andere, der weiss nichts über die Kultur,

("If there are two candidates, one is Danish or from a Danish school, you always start from that assumption, and then the one from the German school, and the one in the German school is no good at all, he is still elected, he is . . . because the other knows nothing about the culture, how is

wo soll er das auch her wissen, und deshalb ist es immer so, ... vielleicht geht's in den ersten Stufen, aber dann weiter hoch, überhaupt nicht."

he to know, and that's why it's always like that ... perhaps it's possible on the first levels, but higher up, not at all.")

This suggests that the crucial factor is schooling, that language cannot be separated from school, and second that more tolerance would be shown in the lower levels of the hierarchy. We must differentiate between local and central committees and groupings. Several informants suggested that the language is not a problem, citing examples where individuals making a speech have openly said they have prepared their notes in Danish and would prefer to speak Sønderjysk, for which there is general understanding. Most of the school-pupil informants said they did not think that lack of proficiency in German would matter, but many of them have little experience of the political life of the minority and, feeling they had to give an answer of some kind, usually said it was not important. Those who were more closely in contact through their own and their family's political activity lent support to the hypothesis:

"Das glaube ich wohl, dass das eine Rolle spielen kann, ob man sehr gut Deutsch oder nicht sehr gut Deutsch ... ich glaube auch ... viele die nicht so gut Deutsch können, die haben Hemmungen also aufzustehen und etwas zu sagen, also ihre Meinung zu sagen, weil sie haben Angst, wenn sie nicht richtig deutsch ... dass sie sich blamieren oder so, und auch finde ich, die anderen in der Volksgruppe sollten das mehr tolerieren, weil sie sind ja vielleicht durch den Krieg, in der dänischen Schule gewesen oder so, also nicht durch eigenes Verschuld."

("I do believe that it can play a role, whether you can speak German well or not very well ... I also think ... many who can't speak German well, they have inhibitions about standing up and saying something, to give their opinion, because they are afraid if they can't speak German properly ... that they might show themselves up or something, and I also think others in the minority should show more tolerance, because they've been, because of the war, in a Danish school or something, so it's not their own fault.")

Although this quotation is in places quite definite in tone, the hesitation and qualification in the first sentence is an indication that the notion is a new one, which the informant has not much considered before. Yet the fluency and tone of the rest suggest that the notion, once raised, corresponds to actual experience. The same happened with another informant:

"Das kann gut sein, denn die haben wahrscheinlich Komplexe dann, weil sie sich nicht so gut verständigen können mit den anderen und gerade das Beispiel da, im Vorstand, da wird ja nur Deutsch gesprochen und da sind ja oft Lehrer und so, und die sprechen dann sowieso Deutsch (...) auch in kleineren Dörfern, wenn da ein deutscher Lehrer hinkommt oder neu zukommt, das passiert natürlich nicht oft, dann dauert es eigentlich nicht lange, bis er mit im Vorstand gewählt ist, und ich glaube auch oft das ist so, die Leute, die denken dann, 'Na der ist Lehrer, der versteht was davon, der wird sicher gut sein im Vorstand' ..."

("That could well be, because then they probably have complexes because they can't communicate so well with the others, and precisely that example, in a committee, there, there is only German spoken and there are often teachers and they speak German anyway (...) in small villages too when a German teacher comes, or comes new, it doesn't happen often of course, then it's not long before he is elected on to the committee and I think it is often the case, people think 'Well, he is the teacher, he understands things, he will certainly be good on the committee'")

Yet, at this village level, the teacher may also be at a disadvantage, says the informant, because he cannot speak Sønderjysk with the villagers. Again, we must note the hesitant beginning, but also the spontaneous introduction of the issue of the role of the teacher, associated with the use of the German language. There are pressures on the teacher from the official organs of the minority, as we saw earlier, which seem to be echoed among ordinary members. Linguistically as well as in other respects, the teacher is best equipped to fulfil the demands made by the officials, often teachers themselves, that more German should be used.

It seems reasonable to differentiate, in accordance with these indications from informants, two organizational and sociolinguistic levels: at a local level, Sønderjysk is acceptable even in formal contexts, although German is the norm; at central, regional level the requirement is much stronger that German should be the only acceptable language of formal discourse, and indeed where possible should be used in informal contexts. This situation, combined with professional pressures and expectations, puts the teaching profession in a strong political position. In an article based on his sociometric study of the farming community, Toft also differentiates between two levels of influence:

"Von einer politischen Dominanz von bäuerlicher Seite kann also nicht ohne weiteres gesprochen werden, insbesondere dann nicht, wenn man die Zusammensetzung des Vorstandes und der Ausschüsse des BdN betrachtet. Anders ist dies auf örtlicher Ebene (...) Hier sind die Landwirte im Vergleich zu ihrer Bevölkerungsstärke in der Volksgruppe deutlich überrepräsentiert. Auf überörtlicher Ebene sind vor allem die Lehrer der deutschen Schule sehr stark vertreten; geringerer politischer Einfluss geht von den sonstigen Berufsgruppen und nicht erwerbstätigen Personen aus. Insgesamt kann nicht von aussagekräftigen Unterschieden gesprochen werden (...)"

("One cannot speak simply of a political dominance by the farming sector, especially if one considers the composition of the committee and sub-committees of the BdN. It is different at a local level (...) Here the farmers are over-represented in comparison to their numerical strength in the minority. At a level higher than the local level, the teachers from the German schools are especially strongly represented; there is rather little political influence from the remaining occupational groups and people not gainfully employed. On the whole one cannot speak of significant differences (...)")

(Toft, 1981:82–87)

Although Toft finds no significant differences from group to group, despite his reference to the teacher-group, it is my hypothesis that such differences would be found if some measure of proficiency in German were used to categorize, rather than professional status; that is, a sociolinguistic categorization rather than a socio-economic one.

The somewhat complex analysis presented above may be summarized as follows. There is a demonstrable desire on the part of officials of the minority to change the status of German within its organizations. As well as being the formal language, it ought to be the informal language for all members, irrespective of their home language, i.e. of their dominant language in daily life outside the minority's institutions. This desire stems from the minority's wish to link itself with other German-speaking groups — political nations and linguistic minorities — through the definition of a reference group which says that "German" means "speaking the German language".

One result of this requirement is that people with Sønderjysk as their dominant language — particularly if their German is, relative to the minority's norms, weak — may feel insecure in the situations where German is required. This sense of insecurity would doubtless spread to others if the desire to introduce German more widely were made into a requirement. In short, other things being equal, low proficiency in German is an inhibiting factor in obtaining a position of power within the minority. I have suggested, however, that the argument applies in different degrees at local and central levels. I have also taken into consideration the fact that language proficiency — in terms of lexis, syntax, sociolinguistic competence — cannot be distinguished in practice from rhetorical skills and personality traits. It seems to me nonetheless clear that the logic of the argument is supported by some evidence from informants, even though conclusive evidence cannot be expected, for reasons given earlier. Speakers with German as their dominant language — of whom the teaching profession are one clearly identifiable group — are most easily able to fulfil the minority's official linguistic expectations. For them it is a matter of shifting register but for Sønderjysk-dominant speakers it is a question of switching code, from L language to H language. Teachers are also under professional pressure to take on positions of responsibility and power. It is therefore not surprising to find the teaching profession well represented at the central level of control, together with other people who are essentially "German-speaking".

That linguistic proficiency, coupled with rhetoric and personality, is a *sine qua non* of political power is commonplace enough. However, the situation is here significantly different in that circumstances of upbringing — the "choice" of home language — tend to exclude some people from the acquisition of the necessary linguistic ability. In fact, for the majority of the members of the minority, there is no "choice"; they cannot choose to bring up their children in German, because it is not emotionally their mother-tongue and they are not sufficiently proficient in the linguistic aspects of child-rearing. Thus, the more the official organs of the minority require the use of German, the more the majority of its members will feel linguistically excluded from positions of responsibility and power, and the more the vacuum will be filled by German-speakers.

Policies in Minority school and society

Finally in this chapter, I want to consider the relationship between the conceptions of "language and culture" in the school and in the minority as a whole. In many respects the parallels are evident and to be expected. Although there may be debate about the organizational relationship between the school system, the "Schul-und Sprachverein" on the one hand, and the political system, the "Bund deutscher Nordschleswiger" on the other, the practical relationship is clearly a close one (cf. pp. 14–20). Indeed the whole question of the school's role within the minority society throws light on the issue of how any school system relates to the society of which it is a part. In this case the degree to which the school is intended to reflect the ideology of the dominant group in the minority is more explicit than in many other societies. It has become evident in previous chapters from observation and interviews that the school is an independent interpreter of the ideology and thus in its turn modifies the ideology as it is passed on to younger generations.

The obvious parallels need no detailed enumeration. The evidence on which the comparison is based was presented in Chapters 3 and 4. There are H and L languages in the school as in the minority. For the Sønderjysk speaking majority, H and L are two different languages; for the German-speaking minority they are paralleled by different registers of the same language. The attempt to impose German in L functions within the minority contrasts with the evidence from Tingleff school where German-speakers tend in fact to acquire Sønderjysk as their informal variety due no doubt to their willingness to adapt to the majority surroundings. There is also evidence that teachers accommodate to the use of Sønderjysk as the informal language with pupils and among themselves.

With respect to German culture, it is generally the case that the imported culture in school is "classic", as in the minority. Although there is some importation of non-classic culture for the schools as a whole, the internally created culture of the Tingleff school, through the activities of the youth club in extra-curricular time for example, is not specifically German. This too is the case in the minority. Exceptions exist, but the general tendencies are clear.

There is one major difference between the school and the minority community which is easily overlooked because so obvious. "Language and culture" can refer in the school to both German and Danish language and culture; this is stated in the aims and realized in the teaching. In the minority, however, the phrase refers exclusively to "German" although the precise meaning of "German" is, as we have seen, not always clear. The school aims to prepare pupils for life in two cultures with two languages. The minority focuses on German culture within a Danish polity; it keeps a distance between itself and Danish culture. The school in fact prepares its pupils for life in the Danish polity through the Danish school subject "Samtidsorientering", but it also includes the Danish culture mainly through the subject Danish which the minority excludes from its way of life. To invite a Danish author to give a reading of his work in the German library in Aabenraa/Apenrade, for example, would be unthinkable. However, although the school includes Danish culture and language in its teaching, we saw that the scope and depth are limited. This is hardly surprising in the light of the minority's attitude, which the school clearly reflects and on which it appears to have no influence.

In Chapter 4 (pp. 73–77 and 80–88) I considered the linguistic needs of the individual pupil as they may arise from life in Danish, German or Nordschleswig society. It is evident from the present chapter that the needs of the minority — that the school should reflect a German language and culture in a Danish polity — are at odds with individual pupils' needs. At the moment, the needs of the pupil give way to the needs of the minority and as long as the minority keeps Danish culture and language at arm's length — perhaps because they are seen as a threat — the minority will have a blind spot in its view of the language curriculum of the school. This is evident in the frequent assertion that any change in language education policy will change the nature of the school beyond recognition and lead to the downfall of the minority. Consider the following statement from this point of view:

"Wir sind uns bewusst, dass gerade auch unsere Arbeit in der Landessprache von grösster Bedeutung für den weiteren Lebensweg unserer Schüler ist. Dieser Unterricht kann nicht gut genug sein. Wir müssen aber auch sehen, dass eine Veränderung unserer Unterrichtssprache (z.B. vermehrt Dänisch auch in anderen Unterrichtsfächern: Erdkunde, Geschichte, Mathematik ...) die zeit-

("We are aware that precisely our work in the language of the country is of the greatest significance for the future lives of our pupils. This teaching cannot be too good. We must however also see that a change in our language of instruction (e.g. increased Danish in other subjects: Geography, History, Mathematics ...) would limit the time allowed our German language. All the declarations of our decision-making bodies

lichen Möglichkeiten im Bereich unserer deutschen
Sprache beschränken würde.
Alle Aussagen unserer be-
schlussfassenden Gremien sind
dahin gegangen, dass wir als
deutsche Schulen in Nord-
schleswig mit deutscher Unterrichtssprache unsere besondere Aufgabe haben – eben
keine 'Sprachenschule' zu
sein."
(Sönnichsen, *Der Nord-*
schleswiger,
March 1983)

have pointed in the direction
that we as German schools in
Nordschleswig with German
as the language of instruction
have our particular task — pre-
cisely not to be 'language
schools'.")

The blind spot is caused by the fact that the German language is singled out
as the characteristic par excellence of the German school; therefore any
reduction in German language would be a loss to the "Germanness" of the
school. However, I demonstrated in Chapter 3 that there are many factors
which make the school German, especially the teachers' training in the
German educational tradition. Although this may not be so easily recognized as the fact that German is used as the formal language of the school,
it is at least as important, and indeed more fundamental in influencing the
character of the school. Were this analysis to be accepted, the blind spot
would disappear and a more flexible approach to language policy would be
possible.

This is in fact unlikely to happen as long as the needs of the minority
are put before the needs of the individual, most evident in such statements
as the following:

"Schule ist kein von der Volksgruppe losgelöster Teil, sondern muss sich auch nahtlos
und harmonisch in die
Gesamtpolitik der Volksgruppe einfügen. Damit fällt aber
gerade dem Schul- und
Sprachverein eine besondere
Aufgabe zu, die bisher nicht
immer so gesehen wurde. Auf
Dauer lässt sich Schule näm-

("The school is not a separate
part unloosened from the
minority, but rather it must fit
in with the total policy of the
minority seamlessly and har-
moniously. But this means that
a particular task falls to the
Schul- und Sprachverein,
which has not always been
seen. In the long run, that is,
the school cannot be adminis-

lich nicht nur schulisch und *tered only educationally and*
pädagogisch verwalten." *pedagogically."*)
(Kracht, *Der Nordschleswiger*,
March 1983)

This is an explicit statement of how the Headteacher of Tingleff school
views the relationship between school and community, especially the
community's political organizations. It is evidently at odds with the policy
of the "Schul- und Sprachverein", but is a realistic statement of the
implications of the situation when seen from the viewpoint of the minority
as a whole.

7 Ethnicity, Language and Schooling

Membership of the Minority

Preceding chapters have treated the minority largely in an institutional perspective. It is the purpose of the present chapter to analyse the nature of individual minority membership in order then to consider the nature of the minority as a social group.

A large part of the preceding discussion of the minority's institutions has been concerned with the problems inherent in a "different" and a minority status. The school in particular has to attempt to resolve potential linguistic and cultural deficits arising from difference. Yet for the individual member of the minority, disadvantages might well take a second place to advantages, if a calculation were to be made, although as Midgley (1980: 120) says, people do not choose a way of life after rational calculation or by some kind of cost-benefit analysis. Membership of the minority is experience which is simply there, is immediate and defining for an individual's whole life, of which it is a part. It is not inevitable: it is possible to avoid it by passing over to the majority. But for those who choose and accept it, there is no sense in treating it as a source of advantage or disadvantage. Thus, the question I put to pupils in the tenth year, as to the advantages and disadvantages of being in the minority, is one which they had not considered in a calculating manner before. The question has to be asked in the full consciousness that it is an observer's question and one which allows description of membership in just one way; there are other ways which are open to a participant, and which might be best expressed through the complex means of art and literature. This must be borne in mind in the following.

The pupils could most often think only of advantages in being in a German school. They were aware of problems — and in the course of an interview were usually quite open about them — but wanted to be positive about their experience when asked to weigh pros and cons. They found it relatively easy to think of their bilingualism, the good teacher-pupil ratio, the visits to Germany and so on. They and their parent generation find it less easy to pin down the sense of well-being which membership brings. Yet it is that which is the incalculable, the experience which is fully accessible only to the participant.

In the past, the pressure and threats from the majority created a need to "hold together". For the older generations this seems to be diminishing and is perhaps regretted:

"Das war dies, . . . als man nach dem Krieg, als das alles kaputt war, alle naher zusammenfanden, und wer dann wirklich noch nach war von all den, und das war irgendwie interessant, ein Gehörigkeitsgefühl, nicht? Das war's wirklich. Was man jetzt eigentlich entbehrt, auch meist"	*("It was that, . . . when we after the war . . . when everything was destroyed, all the schools and everything, . . . when we came nearer together, and found who was really left from everybody . . . and that was somehow interesting, a feeling of belonging. It really was. What we miss, really, now").*

For younger generations it is replaced by friendship, by a feeling of belonging together. It is strongest in those who feel fully committed, like the pupil for whom there is no real alternative to the German school despite language problems (cf. pp. 82–88). It is also evident in those who feel no commitment to the minority as such yet continue to visit the youth club. In this latter case the feeling is perhaps indistinguishable from that of any former pupil of any school, who feels an emotional attachment. Where on the scale of commitment that feeling becomes the special sense of belonging to a minority is hard to say. It is however a feeling which is conscious and acknowledged, and the ease with which the term to describe it — Gehörigkeitsgefühl (sense of belonging) — comes into conversation, demonstrates that people know and value it.

On the other hand, the sense of belonging can also be experienced as a restrictive influence. The restriction comes from within and without the minority. The full value of membership comes only with full commitment, the notion of "sich dafür einsetzen" (*"commit oneself. . ."*), or "aktiv sein" (*"be active"*). This leads to a sense of duty to fill the necessary offices, to a tendency to be inward-looking and exclusive (cf. pp. 94–103 for a discussion of closed networks). It is difficult if not impossible to belong to minority and majority, to straddle the boundaries between the two groups (cf. pp. 149–54). From within the minority, there are these pressures to fulfil duties and roles. From outside the minority there is a tendency to hold at a distance, to categorize people as minority members rather than to use other social categories through which to perceive them.

There is a sense of rivalry between majority and minority group. At a local level the possibility that the Danes want to found a "fritidshjem" ("*a place where children can go after school*") has to be countered by a similar German initiative. At a regional level, the establishment of a Danish research institute north of the border is reflected in the founding of a German institute south of the border.

The sense of belonging is made more complex by the inheritance of attitudes connected with post-war events. The fear of black-listing made most members reticent about their membership in the past (cf. pp. 10–13 and 14–20), and the influence of those events is still evident today in all generations. Some people hide their minority identity, and there are many degrees of "Bekenntnis" ("*declaration of belonging*") between that and complete openness. The possible demise of the minority because of the falling numbers leads the opinion-makers to argue that membership must become "eine Selbstverständlichkeit" ("*a matter of course*"), that members must have "Mut zur Bekenntnis" ("*courage to make an open declaration of belonging*"). There is, however, something strange in the constant debating and defining which go on (cf. pp. 14–20): the constant appeals that membership must be "selbstverständlich" put that quality itself constantly in doubt. Significantly, those young people who are secure in their minority identity, who are most likely to sustain the survival of the minority, find the constant debating superfluous. When asked what they thought of the debate about identity evident in *Der Nordschleswiger* and elsewhere the pupils gave immediate and heartfelt replies: "ich find' das Quatsch" ("*I find it stupid*"), "überflüssig" ("*superfluous*"), "warum, was hat man davon" ("*Why, what is the point?*"). They made disparaging remarks about the meetings of the BdN with its parochialism, and equally critical comments about Danish festivities with the strongly nationalistic singing of Danish folk songs. To my suggestion that the debate is necessary to the survival of the minority, some responded by grudging agreement, but there was also agreement that there is talk and talk and little happening, that the conception of the minority held by older generations is not their conception. For them the principal issue is speaking German but accepting that they live in Denmark, that they are Danish. Is this the rejection of older generations which any groups of young people manifest? Or is it a sign that the minority is changing and must change? Whatever the answers, it is clear that these young people have a burden to carry, but that they carry it lightly.

Their own analysis of the burden is just as revealing. They attribute more influence to home than school. They can identify pupils whose parents are "Danish" and are therefore themselves "Danish". The degree of their own "German" identity depends on how much their parents "sich dafür einsetzen" ("*commit themselves*") how "aktiv" they are. For the pupil who is going on to the German Gymnasium but whose parents are not "aktiv", there will be, he knows, a moment of decision. He feels perhaps more Danish than German, but the decisive moment will come when he votes in local elections, whether he votes for the German party or not. Whatever the degree of their commitment, however, they welcome the breaking down of barriers between themselves and their Danish peers. It is possible to accept others and remain what one is:

> "ich akzeptiere den einen und den anderen, auch, also man soll ja wohl seine Richtung haben, das find' ich da wohl, aber man soll auch einander akzeptieren."
>
> *("I accept everyone, too. You ought to have your own direction, I really think that, but you have to accept each other")*

Clarifying and defining "your own direction" is not, however, always easy. Categories and labels do not readily make a good fit with experience. There have been several surveys which have included questions about self-categorization. Each appears to have a predilection for a particular range of options. Willkommen (1975:143) has: German, *German* North Schleswiger, German *North* Schleswiger, North Schleswiger, Schleswiger, Dane. Toft (1982:38) attempted a two-dimensional account by asking about "Nationalgefühl" ("*national feeling*") and "nationale Gesinnung" ("*national commitment*") but admits that these two cannot be clearly contrasted. Under the first heading, he has four possibilities: German, Danish, other, none. Under the second, he has also four options: Danish, Neither/Nor, less German, German. He hopes to bring out subjective values by this method of cross-tabulating, demonstrating his awareness of the difficulties, but it is noteworthy that 9.2% of his informants did not answer the question about national feeling. Zeh (1982) has three categories: German, Dane with German language, Dane. I suggested my own four categories to the pupils; German, German North Schleswiger, Danish North Schleswiger, Dane. But more important than the categories were the pupils' reactions.

Although they were willing to accept them as useful, they were not always at ease with them. One preferred the category "North Schleswiger" and found the sub-division into German and Danish awkward, a distinction he did not want to make. If required to make a decision — as a questionnaire inflexibly would — then he would feel bound to say "German North Schleswiger". A questionnaire would therefore be unsatisfactory. A different reaction came from other interviewees. They found the notion of "Danish North Schleswiger" odd, and their immediate response was to say "ich bin Nordschleswiger" (*"I am a North Schleswiger"*). When pressed to consider the sub-division, they agreed that:

"doch da'st doch ein Unterschied, doch der Unterschied zwischen Deutschen und Dänen in Nordschleswig, also unser Nachbar zum Beispiel, der ist eingeborener Sønderjyde aber er ist auch sehr dänisch und wir sind auch Sønderjyder aber deutsch ... ja wir sind deutsche Nordschleswiger, nein wir sind Nordschleswiger, also deutsch, die anderen sind Sønderjyder."

("Yes, there is a difference, yes the difference between Germans and Danes in North Schleswig for example our neighbour, he is a native Sønderjyde (South Jutlander) but he is also very Danish and we are also Sønderjyder but German ... yes we are German North Schleswigers, no we are Nordschleswiger, that is German, the others are Sønderjyder ...")

The final analysis is significant, i.e. that "we" are Nordschleswiger, using the German word, "the others" are "Sønderjyder", using the Danish word. This indicates that the expression "dänischer Nordschleswiger" — being a translation of "Sønderjyde" — misses the point. The full force of the distinction between minority and majority in the geographical area of Nordschleswig/Sønderjylland is carried in the symbolic switch from a German word to a Danish word.

In the final analysis, however, there is a certain impatience in young people's attitudes to the whole issue of identity and nationality. The following statement from one pupil was applauded by others in the group:

"dänisch oder deutsch, ich bin beides, sage ich immer und wenn einer jetzt total national dänisch ist, dann bin ich total national deutsch und wenn einer jetzt total national dänisch ist, dann bin ich total national dänisch, ich mach'

("Danish or German, I am both, I always say, and if somebody is totally nationally Danish, then I am totally nationally German and if somebody is totally nationally German then I am totally nationally Danish; I always

immer Protest, ich finde es
egal, also, ich finde alle Menschen sind gleich, ich mach'
kein' Unterschied . . ."

*protest, I think it doesn't mat-
ter; I think all people are
equal; I don't treat them differently . . .")*

Yet even the latter pupil is expressing a feeling that there is a difference, that they have to find a place between two cultures, as well as between two languages. There are several identifiable attitudes to the fact of living between two cultures. At one extreme, there is a belief that German culture in Nordschleswig should be no different from the culture of Germany or other German-speaking areas. The concept of culture involved here is rather the "classic" or "high" culture discussed above (cf, pp. 113–17). A mid-way position is taken by those who wish to see the two cultures run in parallel, both accessible to all members of the minority, but both essentially separate and clearly identifiable. This is in essence the official view of the minority, proclaimed in the aims of the schools. A third position is in the attempt to fuse the two cultures, to perceive them both as contributing to the individual's culture, offering greater richness and complexity. In this case the problem is in the incompatibility of beliefs from two cultures. In practice it is possible to hold some beliefs and drop others, while maintaining the "bridging" identity of "Nordschleswiger". This position involves the perception that there is in fact little difference between the two cultures except in superficial, material ways. Several informants suggested this spontaneously, which contrasted strongly with the views of Danish teachers at the Handelsskole, several of whom asserted that there are wide differences between German and Danish culture. The latter were referring to social attitudes, degrees of formality and values; behind their views there probably lies, too, a wish to keep a certain distance between the two cultures, an apprehension towards the dominant neighbour. The former were referring to cultural artefacts, to artistic traditions and to standards of living. Their views of Germany and "German" culture are probably coloured by the ambiguity of "German": the "Nordschleswig German" culture is in this respect much influenced by Danish culture. When they speak of "German" culture it is not always clear to either listener or speaker which "German" is meant.

In all this, the geographical proximity to the border is a decisive factor. Several informants described how members of their families who had moved to other parts of Denmark or Scandinavia had become "less German", a trait they recognized from the use of Danish in letter-writing but also from diminished interest in the affairs of the minority. Those who moved to the Federal Republic, however, became "more German", both in their language use and also in their heightened interest in the minority, signalled by their continuing to subscribe to *Der Nordschleswiger*. In both cases, "German" means above all "Nordschleswig German", although the ambiguity remains inherent.

This account of minority membership would be incomplete without some mention of the burden of animosity involved, even though it is a difficult issue to document. The usual position, and the widely-held view promoted for outsiders (apparent in Krejci & Velimsky 1981, for example) is that the difficulties and problems of the past have now been laid to rest. There may be a degree of rivalry, but the enmities created by historical events are past. Now it is doubtless the case that the open clashes, the avoidance of contact in public or private, the prohibition of mixed marriage are much reduced and have almost entirely disappeared. Nonetheless the problems of the past are not forgotten. Among the oldest generation it is still possible to revive the indignation verging on fanaticism at the re-drawing of the frontier in 1920. Among the youngest, I often heard of unpleasant experiences of name-calling and insults on the streets. I even noted a difference in attitude to myself when I was briefly mistaken for a German academic by Danes. The young people shrug off these experiences with understanding and tolerance: they cannot accept blame for events years before they were born. Nonetheless, it is experience they have to live with all the time. As one person from the middle generation said, it is not possible to be taken for what one is as an individual; one is always categorized as a member of the minority. The overriding significance of membership is, in all its facets, a dominant dimension of people's lives.

The Minority as an ethnic group

At first glance there is little if anything to distinguish a member of the minority. The complex history and the relatedness in racial and cultural terms of West Germanic and North Germanic peoples are the reasons for the lack of physical distinction and for the lack of noticeable difference in many aspects of culture: housing, dress, food. Fink (1964) has, however, shown that the establishment of a language border for the church after the reformation is reflected in the position of today's frontier. North of the border Danish came to be used in schools, south of the border Low German was the official language. The religion was, however, Lutheran to the north and south. The division was as much administrative as cultural, although it doubtless partly reflected and partly determined the dominant language of the population.

The minority is an ethnically distinct group in the sense that the members of the minority consider themselves to be so. For them the cognitive category of "deutscher Nordschleswiger" contains a set of attitudes, opinions and beliefs which are attributed to them by themselves and outsiders. Mitchell (1974: 2) contrasts this cultural phenomenon of "cognitive ethnicity" with a structural category or principle which is helpful in understanding people's behaviour — i.e. by attributing people's behaviour to their adherence to an ethnic group — and which he terms "behavioural ethnicity". Cohen (1969 and 1974) has suggested that cognitive ethnicity is essentially descriptive and circular:

> "What it says is that people act as members of ethnic categories because they identify themselves, and are sometimes also identified by others, with these ethnic categories. How do we know this? The actors say so, or so they act." (1974: xii)

In this critique of a view represented by Barth (1969), he suggests that this can only be the first stage of establishing ethnic categories, and that further analysis must follow. Cohen himself defines ethnicity as a political phenomenon, as strife between ethnic groups which in turn he defines as:

> "an informal interest group whose members are distinct from the members of other groups within the same society in that they share a measure of (. . .) compulsory institutions like kinship and religion and can communicate among themselves easily." (Cohen, 1969:4)

It will will be clear that my emphasis is on "cognitive ethnicity" and although the political dimension of the German minority's activity has not gone unnoticed, Cohen's definition would be too restrictive. In previous pages the raw data for a "cognitive map" of minority membership has been presented. My intention now is to draw the map more precisely.

Barth's main criterion in distinguishing an ethnic group is that of self-ascription:

> "(it) has a membership which identifies itself, and is identified by others, as contributing a category distinguishable from other categories of the same order." (Barth, 1969: 11)

There are other features, such as sharing biological origins, being biologically self-perpetuating, sharing cultural values and institutions, having a shared field of communication and interaction. But by placing the emphasis on how groups are socially effective, how they maintain themselves, rather than on the goods, values and beliefs which they share, Barth comes to view those phenomena as crucial which help the group to maintain their boundaries. The phenomena which mark a boundary may also change, but the sense of belonging within the boundaries remains. Self-ascription is very plainly the basis of membership of the German minority: "Bekenntnis" (*"declaration of commitment"*) is the key concept which is protected by the Bonn-Copenhagen declarations.

Consequently an "objective" analysis of markers of difference is inadequate; there may be many or few cultural differences, but some are selected as significant by the members themselves and some are not. In the case of the minority the number of differences is small, and the differences are slight. In this, the German minority is like many others where the number of "distinctive" features is usually much lower than the "non-distinction". (Alcock *et al.*, 1979: 182). In much of their daily life adults may activate none of the differences. What is significant, however, is the emphasis given to differences by the members themselves. The objectively minimal use of the German language is perceived as highly important, as is the fact of having been to a German school. In fact, the indications from previous chapters are that attendance at school is the defining primary characteristic but that the consequent ability in German language is perceived more readily as the boundary phenomenon. These, for the individual, are the means of marking difference, of realizing self-ascription *vis à vis* others. Within the boundaries thus marked there are activities and cultural stuff which "fill out" the membership, but they are not crucial, and not everybody is equally and fully involved. The small number of boundary features is a result of the group's minority status; the number of areas open to it in which to articulate its identity is limited. The special historical situation of the minority, where the effect of the war as we have seen was to make many people hide their identity, has meant that people emphasize boundaries only in favourable situations. The tendency of members to have a strong German flavour in their Sønderjysk — whether uncontrollable or unconsciously perpetuated remains unclear — serves as an indication of identity, *vis à vis* other members. It serves, however, as an internal indication, something which is a semi-public marker. It is perhaps also a consequence of history that the institutions of the minority are often only semi-publicly marked.

In short, the fact that in many respects the members of the minority are indistinguishable is not important. What is important is that they declare themselves to be members, that they have features of their lives which they take to be indicators of identity. Because of their minority position and because of their historical situation those features remain largely covert. It is only in secure surroundings — among friends at work, with neighbours — that the main features are made public: attendance at German school and use of the German language. As I have shown above it is the historical circumstances peculiar to the area which have made ethnicity prominent: the search for mutual reassurance after the events of 1920 and 1945. There is some evidence that ethnicity is becoming a much less prominent category of social interaction. Social contact between Germans and Danes is certainly less fraught with animosity than a generation ago, but it has not disappeared. Another indication is the voting patterns for regional and national elections. The votes which used to be cast along ethnic lines are now split among parties which represent the usual range of left to right-wing groupings. Within the minority, there has appeared a "political youth forum" which attempts to create a context for left-wing politics, and yet maintain allegiance to the minority. These are the indications that social class allegiance is gradually becoming more prominent as ethnic allegiance diminishes in importance.

De Vos & Romanucci-Ross (1975) argue that ethnicity can be as powerful a force as social class because it is one of the orientations open to an individual in identifying with a group. Where the configuration of circumstances is such that ethnicity is a more powerful source of group allegiance, the social positions and opportunities open to the individual are dependent on his ethnic identity. Where the ethnic group is a minority, with only limited spheres of social action within their control, then the individual is restricted to the social roles within those spheres. In the case of the German minority, the spheres in question are cultural and educational and the roles open are cultural and educational; administrator or teacher — as occupations — and political or cultural leader, as a leisure-time activity. Not all occupations are ethnically coloured; for example, opportunities in shop-floor factory work are not dependent on ethnic identity. On the other hand there is a grey area where employers from the minority are thought to favour applicants who are from German schools. There are some occupations, though, notably in the state sector — railway, police, for example — where it is believed by members of the minority rightly or wrongly that minority membership is a hindrance, at least if the job is sought in the border area. Thus the individual may find membership of the minority an intolerable constraint, not allowing sufficient range of occupational choice. Komjathy & Stockwell (1980: 165) suggest that the intellectuals of the East European German minorities between the two World Wars were similarly frustrated by the incompleteness of their education begun in minority schools and by the lack of opportunities for them in their host states. They indicate parallels among ethnic groups in the United States.

Where there is constraint, the individual may well reject minority identity, and pass over into the majority. Elklit & Tønsgaard (1979: 85) identify in fact three groups: the Germans, the Danes and those who are neither/nor; the latter group is relatively small, 22 from 609 interviewees. It is significant that from within the minority the third group is not perceived in the dichotomy of minority/non-minority; they are classified as part of the majority, of "the Danes". The option of being "neither/nor" at least in some domains is, however, open and perhaps reinforced by what Fishman (1980: 10) calls "ethnically neutralised" behaviours which are typical of contemporary social development. The geographical proximity of the border and the prominence of ethnicity are nonetheless pressures which probably account for the low numbers in Elklit & Tønsgaard's third category, and its not being perceived from the minority viewpoint. On the other hand, Elklit & Tønsgaard's suggestion (1979: 100) that this group represents a transfer phase does not do justice to the tradition in the area according to which some people choose to remain distant from the whole issue of ethnicity.

Svalastoga & Wolf (1963: 145–47) consider that there are three causes of change: school attendance in the other school system, marriage with a partner from the other group, living in a milieu where the other group is dominant. Elklit & Tønsgaard also underline the significance of home and school (1979: 104). In practice it is in mixed marriages that there are crucial decision to be made.

The choice of school for children of a mixed marriage is important not only for the children themselves but also for the parents. It can bring out into the open the demands that the marriage makes with respect to ethnic loyalty. Some couples discuss the question before marriage, others face it only at the moment of choice of Kindergarten or school (cf Søndergaard, 1983). It means a shift towards the other identity for one of the partners, but not necessarily a total change since in other issues, where neither minority nor majority perceive the features to be ethnically significant, the individual can maintain allegiance to the original way of life. Another kind of situation arises when a couple who both went to a German school may decide to send their children to the only school in the village, which is Danish, rather than make them conspicuous and cause them unacceptable inconvenience by sending them to another village with a German school. Nonetheless they would like their children to learn German and will "never raise the Dannebrog in their garden". Because ethnic identity is composed of both origin and self-ascription, there is in a sense a limit to the change of identity: biological origins cannot be denied. Furthermore school attendance reinforces the biological criterion, is an extension of it, because school attendance is determined by parents. Elklit & Tønsgaard (1979: 104) suggest that home is a primary factor and school secondary, but this comes from their reliance on statistical analysis of a rather limited number of informants, in which they do not consider directly the relationship between school and home. It is clear from my work that parents consider that school shall complete the influence of the home, and that school depends on parental co-operation. The relationship is of mutual dependence in which school gives the "finish" which is visible to members of the minority: linguistic competence in German and experience of German culture. A person who changes identity cannot make up the loss, cannot catch up on the education process missed in childhood.

For those who stay in the German minority, their ethnicity determines some social roles. Where, as in the minority, an ethnic group has only a limited number of domains in which to realize its identity, the influence of ethnic identity is restricted. Nonetheless, it can be completely dominant within the domains in question. Pupils may spend school and leisure time entirely within minority social domains if they live in a place like Tinglev/Tingleff where there are sufficient members to people the minority's own institutions. Adults can scarcely do this — with the possible exception of teachers and cultural administrators. There are degrees of commitment to the "content" of ethnic identity, once the boundary markers have been established. And because the minority realizes itself only in certain domains, there are degrees of boundary crossing; a mother may agree to send her children to a German school but not perceive the German language as a part of her identity, even though she speaks German as well as or even better than her husband who does identify with the language.

In his discussion of non-minority groups, Barth (1969: 28) establishes:

> "a somewhat anomalous general feature of ethnic identity as a status: ascription is not conditional on the control of any specific assets, but rests on criteria of origin and commitment; whereas performance in the status, the adequate acting out of the roles required to realise the identity, in many systems does require such assets."

The assets he exemplifies are material: land-ownership and rights. In the case of the German minority material assets are held in the name of the group — schools, newspaper, sports grounds, etc. — but the individual does not need to have material assets. He does need a capacity: to speak German acceptably. I argued in Chapter 6 (pp. 120–27) that there is a requirement on members to be able to use German adequately. The degree of adequate mastery remains unspecified and exceptions are allowed, but these points reinforce rather than reduce the significance of the requirement. There are other phenomena described in earlier chapters which fill out the framework but which are not boundary markers. The list includes: watching West German television, the Patenschaften (sponsorships), the newspaper, *Der Nordschleswiger*, journeys to Germany and links with other minorities — the German ones through the V.D.A., others through die Föderalistische Union Europäischer Volksgruppen (F.U.E.V.) — and attending minority cultural events.

Features such as partial passing and partial determination of societal life indicate that minority ethnic identity is a special case of ethnicity. It is worth quoting Barth at length:

"Many minority situations have a trace of (. . .) active rejection by the host population. But the general feature of all minority situations lies in the organization of activities and interaction. In the total social system, all sectors of activity are organized by statuses open to members of the majority group, while the status system of the minority has only relevance to relations within the minority and only to some sectors of activity, and does not provide a basis for action in other sectors, equally valued in the minority culture. There is thus a disparity between values and organizational facilities: prized goals are outside the field organized by the minority's culture and categories. Though such systems contain several ethnic groups, interaction between members of the different groups of this kind does not spring from the complementarity of ethnic identities; it takes place entirely within the framework of the dominant, majority group's statuses and institutions, where identity as a minority member gives no basis for action, though it may in varying degrees represent a disability in assuming the operative statuses. . . .
But in a different way, one may say that in such a poly-ethnic system, the contrastive cultural characteristics of the component groups are located in the non-articulating sectors of life. For the minority, these sectors constitute a 'backstage' where the characteristics that are stigmatic in terms of the dominant majority culture can covertly be made the objects of transaction." (1969: 31–2)

Now this throws considerable light on the situation in Sønderjylland/ Nordschleswig and the role of the school in particular. Some of the account is applicable: rejection by the host population; activity in the total system organized by the majority; prized goals are outside the field organized by the minority's culture and categories. But some of it has to be modified. Essentially the cultural characteristics are in non-articulating sectors of life:

culture in terms of the arts, sport and so on is a duplicate of the majority's culture and there is scarcely any meeting of ethnic groups in these activities. The sports clubs compete against each other or against clubs from Germany rather than within the leagues and competitions of the majority. The schools, however, function at an organizational level within the Danish system — within the Lov om friskoler (Act on private schools) — and this serves as a basis for articulation of the minority's ethnic identity both vis à vis the majority's political institutions and with respect to members of the majority who wish to send their children to a German school. The school has something of the character of a majority institution; it is comparable with other private schools. The same applies to other minority institutions, such as the youth organizations or the agricultural society; they have an organizational foothold in the majority system, but they duplicate the majority group's institutions. In a village where there is, for example, a German shooting club but no Danish one, individuals use the minority institution much as they use German schools, with emphasis on their majority-linked status. This linking into the majority system provides a political basis, on which the political party functions, and which justifies the claim to representation at governmental level (through a special office in Copenhagen) even though the political mandate has been lost. Therefore Barth's characterization of the minority's sectors of activity as "backstage" is not appropriate; nor is Cohen's (1969) emphasis on the informality of intra-group ethnic relationships. Organizationally the minority has moved "upstage" — a few of its members can use their minority identity as a status in the majority organizations — but the content of the organizations remains of little significance to the majority group. It is, as Barth says, stigmatized and covert but it is not hidden entirely from view, for it occurs within visible institutions. Access to the institutions for non-minority people is de facto closed, although individuals are tolerated. Where the number of individuals threatens to change the character of the institution, there is consternation. There has been considerable debate in recent years as to whether the schools should open up to the majority (Søndergaard, 1983). It is a policy forced on them by the circumstances of falling pupil population. This pragmatic response has brought out into the open the essential nature of the schools as closed minority institutions. When numbers of non-minority pupils become large, there are demands from the minority to reverse the policy.

Shifting the emphasis from anthropological literature, we find that a taxonomic approach throws a different kind of light on the minority. Krejci & Velimsky (1981) paint on a wide canvas, using statistical material to demonstrate that the issue of ethnicity arises in many different forms throughout Europe. The size in terms of people affected is reflected in the following:

"As a result of the redrawing of boundaries the percentage of population belonging to ethnic nations without state or self-government in Europe decreased from about 26 per cent in 1910 to only about 7 per cent in 1930." (1981: 63)

The minority in Sønderjylland/Nordschleswig were part of that 7%; the total of people affected was some 78 million. As a result of both wars, some 80 million people achieved improved political status with respect to their ethnic identity, whereas 6 million people belonging to former ruling nations, including Germany, were ceded to other states, in this case Denmark. Plainly, the number of people involved in Sønderjylland/ Nordschleswig, even when the group was at its largest, was relatively tiny. This may be one of the most prominent reasons for the "almost idyllic" position of the minority in the eyes of Krejci & Velimsky (1981: 193). In one of their general tables, the minority does not even figure as a "sizeable" minority, which they define as being at least 100,000 strong. On the other hand it is part of the ethno-linguistic community which is among the most divided — the German community. It is spread over 12 states, as a full nation — e.g. in West Germany — in a multinational state in Switzerland, and in minorities in, for example, France, Belgium, Italy. They distinguish two attitudes to self-identification in all ethnic groups: those groups which see themselves as several different nations or, where a minority, as separate ethnics — for example France and Belgium with a common language; those groups which consider themselves as one nation with fragments existing as minorities — for example, Sweden with a minority in Finland. It is interesting that the German community splits into both these categories, unlike almost all others. There are then two kinds of relationship with other members of the community open to the minority in Sønderjylland/Nordschleswig. It can first define itself as a fragment of one of the several independent nations — and for geographical and historical reasons choose the Federal Republic of Germany; but this tends to exclude a relationship with other states: Austria, the German Democratic Republic, and German Switzerland. In practice individuals tend to belong to family and friendship networks in Schleswig Holstein and Nordschleswig/ Sønderjylland, which Søndergaard (1981: 82) calls the Schleswig basis of the minority. The second relationship at group level is with other "fragments" with minority status. In this case it does not matter whether the other groups identify with the same state or not. Thus there can be close relationships with and interest in South Tyrol Germans, who identify with Austria, and also with Belgian Germans, who identify with the Federal

Republic. Alcock *et al.* (1979: 179) use the term "kin-culture" where a number of minorities have "a distinctive historical cultural family".

In their taxonomy, Krejci & Velimsky distinguish between "objective" and "subjective" factors. They accord greatest significance to the latter, "the subjective factor of (national) consciousness" (1981: 45) which in the total or almost total absence of objective criteria and recognition by other people is nonetheless the decisive element in the long run. They thus give, in their wide geographical and historical perspective, support to Barth's emphasis on self-ascription. Their approach, however, leads them to concentrate on their objective criteria: territory, state, language, culture and history, and then assume that where these are present, there is also national consciousness "the presence of which is not easy to ascertain" (1981: 45). Where the group is not well established by the five criteria, they suggest that another factor is vital for national (ethnic) consciousness. They assume its presence:

> "in the case of those ethnic groups which in addition to some objective characteristics do possess a cultured élite capable of defending in an articulate way their claim for a separate ethnic identity." (1981: 45)

In Nordschleswig terms, this suggests that the lack of political factors — having territory and state status — is made up by the continuous efforts of the Bund deutscher Nordschleswiger and of *Der Nordschleswiger* to articulate the identity of the minority. It is noticeable how much and often the issue of identity is debated in the minority; as we saw above (pp. 132–38) the slogan is that German identity should be "eine Selbstverständlichkeit" (*"a matter of course"*) and yet that naturalness is constantly defined as if it were not so plain. Krejci & Velimsky's remark indicates that this may be a necessarily continuous process, in the absence of other features.

Despite the advantage of the broad canvas, they lack the detailed knowledge which would prevent some of the inaccuracies: they suggest that there are 30,000 in the minority; they talk of "reciprocal arrangements" between the two states. It is also evident from the large number of qualifications they have to make to their tables that generalizations and taxonomic categories are to be treated with extreme care. In the final analysis the individuality of the ethnic group and of its members cannot be ignored.

Turning our attention back to the individual, we find a different aspect of the cultural content of the ethnic frame-work. Through his ethnic identity, the individual shares certain "value orientations" (Barth, 1969:14) or "common meanings" (Taylor, 1971): the beliefs and expectations about conduct and standards within the social domains of the ethnic group. These are the parameters which the individual who ascribes himself to membership of the group expects to judge and be judged by. In the Nordschleswig situation, the dominance of the school means that notions about appropriate education are at the centre of the orientation. Thus the fact of having been to a German school is not only a boundary marker, it is also a shared experience which gives the feeling of harmony described above (pp. 132–38). That feeling of harmony comes from the general agreement that the German school is more ordered, formal, teaches more, gives a firmer sense of values; this becomes particularly evident to individuals when they meet different value orientations in Danish education (cf. pp. 89–93). It is reinforced by the sense of rejection by the majority and serves as a haven of mutual support under majority pressure. Those who cannot find that mutual support in their environment — living or working in a Danish milieu — can resolve their problem by passing over into the majority, although they cannot deny their origin and schooling.

I have already suggested that there are some indications that the pressures which have in the past served to make ethnicity prominent over class adherence are weakening. In general where ethnicity is not at issue, because the society is homogeneous or because one belongs to an overwhelming majority, other categories such as religion, profession, social class will claim attention. The individual needs to identify with at least one of these groups. De Vos & Romanucci-Ross (1975: 17) suggest, however, that there are differences in historical orientation. Religious and political groups may well be future-orientated, towards a universalist Christianity or a Marxist classless society, for example. Ethnicity is past-oriented, "primarily a sense of belonging to a particular ancestry and origin and of sharing a specific religion or language". It is certainly the case that older generations in the German minority sustain their ethnicity through reference to the past, not only with respect to ancestry but also with respect to perceived ill-treatment at the hands of the majority. The sense of heritage — although not the resentment from ill-treatment — is particularly strong among the children of land-owners, especially if the individual is returning to agriculture himself. The teaching of history, and the history of Nordschleswig in particular, is likely to support this orientation. On the other hand, there is a lack of interest among pupils in a guilt-laden past which cannot be interpreted to the advantage of the group; all the more so when in practice there is more general German history than Nordschleswig history or Danish history (cf. pp. 80–82). Thus the past-orientation with reminders of the Second World War in particular is not an advantage for the

Nordschleswig minority. The gradual decrease in numbers staying in the minority — not only due to population change — may well be due in part to this past-orientation. Yet the past-orientation is an integral part of ethnicity because of the general biological criterion and, in the German minority, because of the "creation" of the group through historical events.

The response, as indicated in Chapter 6 (pp. 113–17), is to attempt to change the orientation from "German" to "Nordschleswig", although I argued there that the basis for this re-orientation is thin. It is the intention that, again, the school should be an instrument. Changes in curriculum content, particularly in history and "Samtidsorientering", have been effected as a conscious attempt to create a local identity. There is official recognition that Nordschleswig German is different from West German standard and a tendency to nurture the regional dialect. The tendency is not, however, clearly and explicitly thought through. There is a potential clash of standards and models with pedagogical consequences which are not yet fully realized: is a regional standard to be encouraged by teachers who speak West German standard? The way in which the theoretical reorientation is realized in practice will clearly vary. The central position of the school in this and many issues means that teachers have considerable influence in their practice. But it also means that children, as school-pupils, are in the front line of any attempt to steer or modify the life of the minority as a whole. Schools in any society are a tempting locus for politicians and other social theorists. They are relatively easy to influence, especially where there is a good deal of central control, and there is a temptation to model the society through its children. This is evident throughout Europe, particularly in the reforms of the last two or three decades, and the minority is no exception.

Language as a symbol of ethnicity

It has been evident throughout this account that the German language plays a special role in the minority. It was mentioned by some pupils as the only thing which makes their school German. It is the topic of newspaper articles and editorials. It is on the educational agenda for debate. It is, in short, a feature of the cognitive ethnicity of the group, for it is one of the subjects of the shared meanings of the group and therefore a factor in any individual's understanding of himself and his allegiance to the minority. It is in fact commonplace to treat the terms "ethnic minority" and "linguistic minority" as synonymous (cf. Stephens, 1976). It is necessary, therefore, to review the precise role of German in the minority as an ethnic group.

Language is frequently the most prominent feature of a minority and even where the language is all but lost the memory of it can be a linguistic marker (Gullick, 1979). On the other hand ethnic consciousness can survive after the language has disappeared (Anderson, 1979). Language has the advantage of being evident and observable for all concerned whereas minority members may not be as conscious of other ways in which they distinguish themselves from the majority. It has been evident from preceding chapters that language is perceived by many members of the minority as a symbol of belonging and is as such a boundary phenomenon. The school is thought to socialize pupils into the minority, provided that the family sustains the impetus and commitment. The ability to speak German is seen as the principal outcome of having been to a German school. A member of the minority who cannot speak German adequately is an oddity, although historical events have created the exceptions among those who had no opportunity to go to a German school. The notion of what is adequate is therefore adjustable. Linguistic competence is, on closer examination, accompanied by cultural competence. In this respect, those who have married into or otherwise joined the minority remain slightly different, however well they speak German, because they do not have the same cultural competence. That competence comes from learning German in a German school, which is an experience for most of learning German as a second language, though taught ostensibly as if the mother tongue. It is, however, difficult for those involved to observe their cultural competence, difficult to define it despite its being experienced as part of any inter-personal relationship. The similarity between German and Danish popular culture in the area exacerbates the problem. Consequently the language is held up as the principal criterion of membership. The result is that many individuals experience a sense of unease about their German. They say that it is the main thing, yet feel there is something else. They perceive a high level of ability in the language as an indicator or the vitality of the minority and hence perceive any change of the balance between German and Danish as an attack on the life-force of the minority. Thus even the young interviewees were often unhappy with the thought that more Danish should be introduced as a teaching medium in their school, despite their acknowledgement of their personal language problems and despite their desire to be more open towards the majority society. They considered that less German in the school would mean the school were less German, even though some of them thought they would be better equipped for further vocational study if they had more Danish. Thus essentially their reaction is typical of official policy (cf. pp. 128–31).

In this tangle of impressions and opinions, is there a simple answer to the question of what is fundamental to the ethnicity of the minority, which phenomena are essential boundary markers? It is the dominant outcome of my account that members of the minority are recognizable by their cultural and linguistic competence, and that those competences are acquired only through attendance at a minority school. The obfuscating factor in the situation is that members of the minority can easily perceive their own and others' linguistic competence but not their cultural competence, even though the two are inseparable and interdependent. Therefore linguistic competence takes on a greater significance. The significance is disproportionate in functional terms because their linguistic competence is not realized except in the context of a limited number of cultural events, as far as the Sønderjysk-speaking majority of members are concerned. For a minority of German-speaking members, however, it is realized and put into practice much more widely and this fact reinforces the perception of all members of the potential role of language. In short, the language becomes a symbol. Edwards (1977: 262) refers to the communicative-symbolic distinction which is not uncommon in ethnic minorities undergoing language shift. Some symbolic usage of the language in specific domains, such as religion, may exist long after the daily usage in other domains has disappeared. In the German minority case, however, it is not language shift which has created the distinction, and the situation is more complex. For those with Sønderjysk dominant, Edwards' distinction holds, except that the domains are educational, religious and "cultural", and that the dynamic of language shift as a cause of this distinction is not present. For those with German dominant, however, there is no question of the language being restricted to symbolic domains and, in the sense of Edwards' distinction, it is firmly communicative. It is the existence of two kinds of speaker in a relatively static configuration which makes the situation unusual. It makes the symbolic function appear potentially communicative although the apparent potential cannot be realized and is in fact confusing and misleading. It is misleading because it raises false hopes and diverts attention from other features of the group which give it its particular ethnic identity.

The second important outcome of my analysis is concerned with the educational implications of the symbolic function attributed to the German language. It is not that I have done something which the minority itself does not do. It is an active part of the minority's life which I have attempted to describe. The debate about the role of language in the minority and its schools is part of the life of the minority as a group and of parents, pupils and teachers as individuals.

I have shown that in purely linguistic terms Sønderjysk speakers who form the majority of members do not need their German except for a few

H language purposes (cf. pp. 120–27); elsewhere (Byram, 1981: 180) I have suggested that the lack of social and economic support for the language necessitates an artificial nurturing. The notion that the language is a symbol, that there is an artificiality about its support should not be interpreted negatively, however. From the viewpoint of the minority, as long as language is the dominant perceptible marker, there are no value judgements to be made about the situation: it simply is so. Nonetheless there are problems which they dimly recognize and have to live with. It is evident that a complex of ideas, a false linguistic ideology, obscures certain features of the educational situation with the result that being a member of the minority can have some unfortunate consequences. Perhaps some of those consequences might be reduced, but they cannot be entirely re- moved. For they are inherent in the situation. Ideally, they would be reduced to the point where they are balanced by the advantages of membership (cf. pp. 132–38), so that a degree of harmony is created for the individual.

The details of these educational issues have been dealt with in preceding chapters. It has been shown that the present language policy does not fit the needs of a majority of pupils. It is a policy which supports and is interdependent with the misguided notion that the group is primarily a communicatively linguistic minority. It maintains the dominance of the German language. It has also been shown that there is some debate about the educational problems arising from this policy. The debate is hampered by the unchallenged assumption that the German language is the primary phenomenon which distinguishes the minority and hence cannot be tampered with. It is therefore concentrated on proficiency in Danish, leaving the question of German untouched.

The official response is to argue that there is no problem: pupils do objectively have an adequate command of Danish. Examination results in Danish are held to be comparable with those of Danish schools and therefore there are no grounds for worry. The problem with this approach is that it confuses the subject Danish with the mother tongue and claims that the examination is a valid assessment of the whole subject, and by implication of mother tongue proficiency. There are here two reductions of the concept of "Danish", properly defined as a native-speaker's command of the language. Defined in this way, the language comprises a wide range of varieties, registers and tenors (Gregory & Carroll, 1978) and entails a knowledge of the culture. This is not to expect any given native-speaker, particularly at school age, to be familiar with all aspects of the language and culture. It does nonetheless involve a range of language use which cannot be fully introduced into the classroom, even though the nature of the subject Danish has been re-defined in recent times (cf. pp. 73–80). This is the first stage at which reduction takes place. The second stage is in the process of assessment and examination. It is a commonplace that assessment is selective and tends to deal only with cognitive attainment. Where the assessment is by both written and oral examination, the global assessment which ensues is ill-fitted to reflect accurately the proportions of linguistic inter-personal ability, cognitive and affective aspects of language use and the degree to which the speaker can use the language in non-school situations. The pupils interviewed who had particularly good Danish results, thought they were over-assessed because more attention was paid to what they said than how they said it. For them, the crucial question is how near they can get to the standard spoken language. Yet the assessor may have been impressed by their linguistic flexibility, their bilingualism, their understanding of appropriateness, or by their knowledge of the subject matter irrespective of their use of the appropriate language variety; or most likely a mixture of all of these. Whatever the criteria, the claim that comparable examination results demonstrate comparable mother tongue ability is weak on two counts. First, the pupils themselves feel insecure and this subjective reality is just as valid as objective examination results. Second, the experience of Handelsskole (commercial college) teachers demonstrates that the pupils are not as well-versed in Danish language and culture as their Danish peers. Confusion arises because in one sense there is no claim that examination results prove that pupils command the language and culture in complex ways. The claim is indeed more limited, namely that in the one demonstrable and objective way by which schools can be judged, the German school can compete with its Danish neighbours. In this sense the school is under the same kind of scrutiny as any other in Western Europe and beyond. The ambiguity comes from the terminology. The term "Danish" refers both to the subject and to the mother tongue and culture. A claim that the subject is well learned in the school is open to the interpretation that the mother tongue and culture are well acquired. This is an ambiguity which helps the case of those who wish to argue that there is no "Danish" problem.

The problem does not, however, disappear. It is present in the minds of the teachers even if the official policy represents a harmonious solution to the outside world. It is discussed at meetings and in the staffroom and advice is proffered by one academic adviser (Søndergaard, 1984) whose suggestions for introducing the Danish "play-lesson" in the first two years have been accepted in the past. My own position gradually became one where I was asked for advice. In staffroom conversations everyone has an opinion and as a participant I also formed an opinion, partly as a result of discussion, anecdote, experience, talk with pupils and partly as a result of a more objective analysis of the kind which has appeared in earlier chapters.

The school and ethnic identity

In this section, I shall summarize my earlier observations of the school from the perspective opened in this chapter. I shall consider how the school contributes to the maintenance of those phenomena which either function as boundary markers or are activities which fill out the cultural space designated by the boundaries.

The most evident and most important contribution is in fact to reinforce the boundary phenomena. The German language and culture policy of the school is intended to have two separate but complementary effects. First, for the German-speakers, it provides them with the written language and formal registers of German which are associated with the kind of "high" culture which links the minority with the Federal Republic and other members of the kin-culture. For the Sønderjysk-speakers, it provides them with a language with potentially the same functions as for the German speakers. Thus the acquisition of a linguistic capacity and a cultural awareness which are necessary for minority membership is directly though not uniquely dependent on school attendance. The possibility that this function of schooling is over-emphasized to the detriment of pupils' economic and social opportunities in the majority culture is one of the problems arising from the need to rely on the school so much as a locus of socialization into crucial minority attributes. The school's role is supported by other institutions, such as libraries, lecture-programmes, music recitals, but the school's part cannot be over-estimated.

The teachers are the ones who put the policy into practice and the fact that they have a German higher education and training providing them with the appropriate linguistic and cultural basis is crucial. In addition, many of them have German as their mother tongue and are therefore in a better position to induct German-speaking pupils into written and formal language. A problem arises from the fact that the same procedure is used — or is at least intended to be used – for the Sønderjysk-speaking pupils, for whom mother-tongue procedures are inappropriate. As the school is the only place where native-speaking Germans have a right openly to direct and control the socialization process towards the crucial linguistic and cultural norms, its significance is all the greater.

The teachers also contribute to the activities which "fill out" the ethnic space, activities which do not serve as boundary markers, but which are parallel to majority activities and provide further opportunities to realize ethnic adherence in non-distinctive ways. The teachers provide the lead in sports, youth clubs, crafts, music-making, etc., and use the official networks of the school system to support the informal networks for these other activities.

Finally, some teachers contribute to the continuing debate of the minority's ideas, attitudes, policies and self-definition which maintains a high level of awareness among the membership. They thus form part of the leadership which represents and negotiates for the minority *vis à vis* Danish and Federal Republic authorities and politicians. It is not as teachers that they carry out these tasks, but the school system is the only institution which offers employment opportunities in sufficient numbers to create a broad enough intellectual group for this work.

The school buildings and the school as a self-owning institution within the private education system also play their part. The buildings often provide the forum for the activities mentioned above, although there are some independent and purpose-built facilities. The fact that the schools are self-owning produces a need for committees and officers drawn from minority membership. This creates a formal social institution, with a basis in law, although it is not a crucial, boundary-marking feature, since they function under the law governing all private schools.

Finally, the school has another relationship to members of the minority: it represents a continuity with parental influence. We must be careful to distinguish between adult and child membership of the minority. It is, as we have seen, frequently the case that writers emphasize the significance of self-ascription and biological origins, and a consequent past-orientation. This is to see the issue from the point of view of the adult. For the child, however, self-ascription is rather a misnomer since he is in fact ascribed by his parents to membership. Ascription for the child is a function of biological origins, and parental ascription becomes explicit when the child is sent to school. For at that moment, the element of choice becomes clear to the child. Up to that point, parental ascription was largely if not exclusively a part of the natural unquestioned and unchosen family order. Suddenly the notion of ascription is linked with choosing and attending the German school when the neighbour's child goes to the Danish school. The realization of the significance of that element of choice will, however, be a slow process and often comes to fruition at puberty and adolescence. For the minority child the years of growing up may lead to acceptance or rejection of parental ascription, depending no doubt on its inter-relationship with other factors in the parent-child relationship. In short, it is important to remember that schooling is not a unified and momentary socializing process which confirms parental choice. It is, on the one hand, an extension of parental, or biological, influence and, on the other hand, a process which includes maturation, influence from peers and teachers and hence a potential loosening of parental influence. The process gradually develops the choice made by parents into acceptance or rejection by children; from being "other-ascription" there is change to "self-ascription". The actual strength of the role of school in the whole developmental process of childhood is of course difficult to estimate, whether in this particular context or in general. On the one hand, the number of hours spent in school is relatively small in the life of the child, but on the other it is the strength of influence he allows school to exercise which is more important. This last point is perhaps all the more significant in the minority where the sense of being "different" will tend to encourage stronger acceptance or rejection of the principal perceived locus of the difference, i.e. the school.

The question now arises as to how the school can fulfil the task of mediating ethnic characteristics, of socializing pupils into crucial ways of ethnic behaviour, and also prepare pupils for life in the majority culture. This is to take up again the paradox first noted in pp. 21–26, and underlying much of my account, namely that the school is given two aims which are mutually impeding, if not mutually exclusive. It has now become evident that the school's aim of introducing pupils to German language and culture and of reinforcing the German sense of community is fundamental to the minority's existence. On the other hand, pupils' future economic lives and some aspects of their leisure lives and their social interactions will take place within the majority culture.

Bullivant (1984: 51) divides "educational knowledge" into "instrumental" and "expressive". The former involves "knowledge-for-use" which enables people to take part in social behaviour, to acquire skills for use in work and hence is related to realizing one's life-chances. "Expressive knowledge" is related to socio-cultural values and artefacts, to aesthetic and creative pursuits. There is clearly a relationship between these two which is more complex than "overlap" as Bullivant calls it, since expressive knowledge exchange plays a part in social behaviour and interaction. Nonetheless the division is helpful in pointing up the relationship of curriculum content to the two aims of the minority's schools: instrumental knowledge needs a strong Danish flavour whereas expressive knowledge must be German.

The kind of preparation necessary for interaction with the majority is determined by majority expectations and attitudes which are beyond the control of the minority. Because Denmark is a relatively homogeneous culture and society, all those who wish to take a full part in social life are expected to reach linguistic and cultural standards equivalent to those of indigenous, monolingual and monocultural Danes. The fact that Denmark is not monolingual and monocultural does not change expectations. This general attitude is crystallised in reaction to new immigrants from Mediterranean and Eastern countries, described in a Council of Europe dossier on the intercultural training of teachers:

> "The general attitude towards foreigners is cautious. As a whole the Danish population is very homogeneous and does not easily accept the ways of others. Foreign attitudes and behaviour differing from those of the Danes are not openly criticized, yet the unspoken consensus of opinion in Denmark is: 'If foreigners want to live here, the least they can do is learn the language and adapt themselves to our ways'." (Struwe, 1981: 9)

In view of this kind of majority expectation, the school is right to strive for mother-tongue ability in Danish language and culture. It remains questionable whether this is attainable in entirety, since the standard set by the majority is that reached through continuous Danish mother-tongue and mother-culture schooling. However, I shall argue below that the full range of knowledge and experience may not be necessary.

The school also assumes that its task of induction into minority language and culture requires German mother-tongue ability. It is equally questionable whether this is attainable when it is to happen almost exclusively through schooling. It is also questionable whether mother-tongue methods are appropriate for Sønderjysk speakers, if they are to strive for mother-tongue equivalence. The position is made more complex by the fact that there are German-speakers, too, for whom mother-tongue methods clearly are appropriate. In sheer numbers, the Sønderjysk speakers usually outnumber the German-speakers but this ought not to lead to the conclusion that all pupils should therefore be taught exclusively through second-language methods (cf. Egger, 1977: 126 for discussion of this problem in South Tirol). Finally, the assumption itself needs to be questioned: is mother-tongue equivalence necessary for attainment of the familiarity with those aspects of German language and culture which are the markers of ethnic identity?

In short, present demands on pupils from the minority and from the majority amount to a requirement that pupils become balanced bilinguals. (Baetens Beardsmore, 1982: 9). This is implicit in the aims of the school and is the basis on which they attempt to improve their teaching and on which they are given pedagogical advice (Søndergaard, 1980 and 1984). In practice, teachers recognize that the demands are difficult and perhaps impossible to fulfil. But the dissonance between theoretical aims and practical aims is of the sort which creates unease both for teachers and for pupils. The feeling might be dispelled if the theoretical requirements are examined and refined and so the question presents itself whether the notion of balanced bilingualism and balanced biculturalism is realistic. The question must be asked, however, in the context of ethnic adherence.

Bilingualism and biculturalism

The concept of biculturalism is frequently juxtaposed with bilingualism with reference to immigrant groups (Fishman, 1980). It has also been extended to describe groups of longer standing (Gullick, 1979). Fishman (1980: 5) describes both bilingualism and biculturalism as "*individual* behavioural manifestation" (emphasis in original), and then goes on to discuss societal counterparts: diglossia and di-ethnia. In discussing societal compartmentalization of cultural and linguistic behaviour he points out that in modern societies "many (...) behaviours (and many values and beliefs as well) have become ethnically neutralized because of their widespread ('international') currency" (1980: 10). For the individual, then, it is possible to behave in ethnically marked and ethnically neutral ways and, in the former case if the society has two or more ethnic groups, to behave in two or more ethnically marked ways. Thus in Sønderjylland/ Nordschleswig, a German minority member may go to a German lecture; this is ethnically German. He may go across the border shopping for German goods, as do most of his Danish neighbours: this is ethnically neutral. He may work in any number of jobs which are ethnically neutral. He may send his children to a Danish school; this is ethnically Danish. Thus with respect to cultural behaviour there are two broad categories and the neutral — or "non-distinctive" (Alcock *et al.*, 1979: 178) — category may account for most behaviour. With respect to linguistic behaviour, the existence of three varieties, German, Sønderjysk and standard Danish means that Sønderjysk can be neutral, when used in neutral cultural contexts, but there are some neutral contexts where standard Danish is expected and thus they are given an ethnically marked German dimension if Sønderjysk is used. The correspondences between cultural and linguistic markedness and neutrality are not exact.

In order to be able to take full advantage of socio-economic opportunities, therefore, an individual in a multicultural society must be able to function in the ethnically neutral cultural contexts and his own ethnically marked contexts. This is to assume that all or most crucial socio-economic contexts are ethnically neutral.

Because of the dominance of majority expectations of minority behaviour, Goodenough's (1964: 36) definition of culture is apposite here:

> "a society's culture consists of whatever it is one has to know or believe in order to operate in a manner acceptable to its members..."

Acceptance by members of the majority, whatever the minority individual's subjective experience, is the crucial factor, and acceptance is conditional on acting in appropriate ways. Thus it is quite conceivable that an individual can behave appropriately in ethnically neutral contexts as well as in his own ethnic culture, provided he has sufficient knowledge and experience of the norms of expectations in neutral contexts. In this sense, then, a "balanced" biculturalism means an adequate knowledge of all contexts in which the individual usually finds himself but not a complete duplication of all ethnically marked contexts. In Sønderjylland/Nordschleswig, it is not necessary to duplicate experience of schooling or, more realistically, of visits to the theatre, in German and Danish terms. It is, however, necessary for a German Nordschleswiger to know as much about Danish politics and economics as his Danish neighbour.

A similar argument applies to linguistic behaviour, but the fact that standard Danish is expected in a large number of ethnically neutral contexts makes its range wider and its marking potential greater. Sønderjysk, which is usually ethnically neutral, will not be acceptable at many work places or in political contexts. The range of application of ethnically marked standard Danish is wider than other kinds of ethnically marked behaviour. It is thus necessary for the German Nordschleswiger to know German, Sønderjysk and standard Danish, even though the latter disturbs his ethnic identity. In order to become adequately bilingual then — i.e. a "balanced" bilingual in the domains he normally experiences or aspires to experience — the German Nordschleswiger has to "sacrifice" some of the exclusivity of his ethnic linguistic identity. He has in fact to become trilingual in the three codes of German, Sønderjysk and Danish, even though he does not need competence in every aspect of all of them.

It would be logical to conclude from this that a degree of "bi-ethnicity" is forced upon the German Nordschleswiger through having to know standard Danish. In practice, we saw in earlier chapters that pupils do indeed feel uneasy about learning Danish, yet nonetheless do so because of their acknowledged socio-economic needs. The unease expressed by some informants betrays a feeling that ethnic identity ought to be indivisible, that one ought not to be "bi-ethnic", even though the phenomenon of partial passing is a common feature of minority status.

The answer to the question whether the school's aims of balanced bilingualism and biculturalism are feasible has to be a qualified yes. The notion of "balanced biculturalism" has to be understood as a familiarity with ethnically marked and neutral cultural knowledge and behaviour. With respect to "balanced bilingualism" the learning and teaching of standard Danish is at odds with the notion of indivisible ethnic identity. It is therefore at odds with another aim of the school: to reinforce the sense of German community, i.e. ethnic identity. We have seen from the beginning that the school has to live with a paradox. It is a paradox which is beneath the surface but dimly recognized by those involved. Living with a paradox is difficult, but unavoidable. It involves compromise and unease, which are all the more disturbing because they are unclear and not recognized for what they are. It is no doubt a feature of many minority schools and there are no quick resolutions.

The fact that linguistic code does not coincide with distinctive and non-distinctive domains also raises a theoretical point. If there were simple coincidence, German would be used for minority marked domains, Sønderjysk for neutral domains and standard Danish for majority marked domains. There are two points of divergence: Sønderjysk can be used in minority domains, but only as a spoken language and Danish must be used in some neutral domains, especially those where there is a lot of written language. The "slippage" which causes Danish to invade the neutral domains is caused by the relationship of (spoken) dialect to (spoken and written) standard, between Sønderjysk and Danish: in some neutral domains there are the usual pressures within any linguistic community for the standard language to be used. This "slippage" is a phenomenon symptomatic of the dual role that language plays in ethnic relations.

On the one hand language is perceived by many minorities as an "object", as an organizational feature of the social system which they wish to control, much as they wish to control their own school or theatre or newspaper. On the other hand, language is not a domain of activity in the sense that schooling or newspaper production is. Language is not separable or distinct from other behaviour. Alcock et al. (1979: 182–83) appear to confuse matters in this way when discussing distinctive and non-distinctive parts of a minority culture. They list language as an organizational feature together with, for example, economic, religious, legal, artistic, and compare language as a distinctive part of a culture with "a pattern of factory management" as a non-distinctive part. The point is that language choice is a feature of all organizations and is additional to the question of whether any particular organizational aspect is distinctive or not. Frequently, the majority or standard language will be an automatic and therefore unnoticed choice for non-distinctive organizational activities, and thus the standard language becomes ethnically neutral in those situations. It is the peculiarity of the Sønderjysk–Danish relationship, that in many situations Sønderjysk takes a neutral role but in some situations Danish is expected to take that role. For the German minority member, the neutral role of Sønderjysk is acceptable, but the idea that Danish can be neutral is much more difficult to swallow. It is the addition of the third code in the Sønderjylland situation which makes apparent that in other minority situations the standard code is sometimes ethnically marked and sometimes not.

For language cannot always be a distinctive feature. It is distinctive in some domains and neutral in others. It differs, therefore, from other kinds of behaviour, for example religion, where in a given minority situation a particular domain can be wholly distinctive or non-distinctive. For a given minority, language will be sometimes distinctive, sometimes not. The potential confusion lies in the fact that language is perceived and noticed by speakers only when it is distinctive, and they will insist on preserving language rights for such situations. The range of such situations varies from minority to minority; where most will want their language in school situations, fewer will want their language in legal or scientific situations. The danger is that that confusion also invades academic analysis, so that language is seen as an independent, separable sphere of activity, whereas linguistic behaviour always takes place as part of some other behaviour, and the markedness of the two behaviours may not be identical.

Conclusion

One of the interesting features of the Sønderjylland/Nordschleswig situation is that in some ways it is unusual and in many ways typical. Particular historical developments have produced a minority which does not fit the norms of linguistic minorities, yet its cultural and particularly educational characteristics are not unusual. Thus in some ways it can lead to generalizations and wide-ranging insights and in other ways it remains unique.

One of the unusual features is the relative stability of a linguistic configuration more characteristic of language shift. The stability, as pointed out in pp. 149–54, is largely due to the renewal of German speakers through the mainly educational connection with Schleswig Holstein. The stability is also due, however, to the legal and historical foundation of the minority which guarantees essential cultural, political and educational rights, with the result that the minority can attend to improving rather than defending its situation. Similarly the attitudes of the majority, and their demands and expectations of minority members working alongside them, are stable.

In this situation it is interesting to note attitudes towards bilingualism and bilingual education. For a minority undergoing language shift, bilingualism is threatening because it is a step towards assimilation. In the German minority it need not be looked on in quite the same way, and the fact that individuals' bilingualism may be a handicap could be given more positive attention. For it is as much the social attitudes to bilingualism as the individual's bilingual proficiency which determine success or failure. The positive attitude of parents to immersion programmes in Canada contrasts with the social rejection of the bilingualism of new immigrants in many West European countries; Lambert (1979) has distinguished the phenomena of additive and subtractive bilingualism. Yet the attitudes of the German minority are largely negative, where possible ignoring pupils' bilingualism and otherwise treating it as a problem. Similarly the majority requires native-speaker proficiency in Danish, without giving any credit for individuals' bilingualism as a social, intellectual and cultural enrichment (Lambert, 1978) at best it is seen as a tool for local commercial transactions. Such attitudes and demands are basically unfair to the individual, and are characteristic of many minority situations. Yet the attitudes of the majority can hardly change so long as they are supported within the minority itself. Where a minority has a strong and confident position vis à vis the majority group — which is of course not always the case — then it ought perhaps to make demands on behalf of its individual members as well as on behalf of the group as a whole. Those demands should be based on a positive rather than an apologetic attitude to individual bilingualism. This is then one of the features of the German minority which is part of its particular situation, but it also raises issues of a very general nature for many minorities. Individual minority members should be valued for their bilingualism in much more than utilitarian terms, rather than penalized by demands that they should be able to compete with majority individuals as well as being bilingual. Demands made on their behalf, however, need not be made in the spirit of asking for special dispensation for a handicap, but quite the opposite, in terms which demonstrate the enrichment of the individual through bilingualism.

The role of minority schooling in changing attitudes to bilingualism and the demands made on behalf of individuals is evident and crucial. It has become clear in this account that the tendency to label minorities as linguistic minorities is misleading. The reliance of the German minority in Nordschleswig on its schools and its teachers is perhaps unusually pronounced, but it is nonetheless indicative of the importance of education in the life of any minority. It ought therefore to be evident that close attention needs to be paid to the whole life and functioning of schools in minorities: to their language curriculum, of course, but also to the details of the overt and hidden curriculum, and to the political, cultural and socio-economic environment in which schools function.

The purpose of a case study such as this should be to raise such theoretical issues on which more rigorous theorizing and testing might be founded. It should, however, also remind those who construct theory of the extreme complexity of reality, so that due attention and respect be paid to the significance of individuals' differential experience of reality and the inevitability of mutually contrasting pressures on the life of the individual. For it should not be forgotten that the actors in the situation described also have an interest in the study. They may learn something about their position with the help of an outsider, but he should — and does — in no sense pretend to have captured the definitive account of "the case". For the case is not closed when the outsider goes away, and the best conclusion I could wish for is that this monograph becomes part of the continuing situation it has attempted to describe.

Appendix 1

Fieldwork and Methodology

Ever since Whyte wrote an appendix to *Street Corner Society* in its second edition (1955), it has become the custom to describe sooner or later the ethnographic process in urban and educational studies. (e.g. Hargreaves, 1967; Lacey, 1979; Burgess, 1984). Anthropologists have done so too, but often separately in autobiographies or field-manuals. This account has two purposes: to contribute to the store of knowledge of practical aspects of ethnographic methods, and to support the study by explaining the source of evidence from which the ethnography is written.

Preliminaries

My first visit to the Danish German borderland was some 20 years ago, as a student, to work on a farm south of the border and learn some German. Like many families "my" family has relatives in the German minority and through personal contacts and, during an undergraduate course, from an awakening interest in bilingualism I began to read and talk about the borderland and its people. My undergraduate dissertation, written in 1969, was published some ten years later by a Danish teacher who thought its introductory account of bilingualism and of the bilingual history of Schleswig would be of interest to local people. I visited the region frequently in the intervening years.

From 1973, a chair of Danish was established at the Pädagogische Hochschule in Flensburg and its holder, Professor Bent Søndergaard carried out a series of research projects in the next decade. It was through Professor Søndergaard that, after returning to a University post in 1980, I began to renew contacts with the officials of the German minority. In particular I met and discussed my proposed research with the Schulrat (Education Officer) who has always encouraged research on the minority. For the two years before my fieldwork began I reviewed and extended my reading of the history of the area, looking particularly at anything which dealt with language and schooling.

Access to the school in Tinglev/Tingleff was provided by the Schulrat. I chose it from information about the five town schools and asked the Schulrat to put me in contact. My choice was governed by the following criteria: homogeneity of pupil population — the school has few non-minority pupils; size — being the largest it would give most informants; representativeness of school leavers' career choices — a spread of choices across the options open to them, even though the numbers are too low to meet any statistical criteria. The significance of pupils' career choices was that my hypothesis that the relationship between language and ethnic identity would show at the moment of leaving school, was already formulated as a research focus. Access to the school was then initiated by the Schulrat and continued by an explanatory letter to the Headmaster from me some weeks later. This took place about 18 months before the fieldwork was due to start. Some months before the start the Headmaster was consulted by the Danish Ministry of Education, who were providing part of the funding, about the feasibility of the fieldwork. This gave an official Danish tone to the work which was not likely to help. When the Headmaster told me about the consultation, on my arrival, I explained that the funding was quite unconditional with respect to publication or other-wise of the report and that the original proposal had come from me. I was in no way an agent of the Ministry of Education. I experienced no disadvantages from being supported by the Ministry after that initial explanation and in fact the connection was not mentioned again.

Introduction

More problematic was my introduction to the school. The date of arrival was arranged by letter. I arrived and was introduced to the staff as "der englische Dozent" (the English don) which led me to believe that my explanations of my work and the fact of my arrival had been made known to the staff. This, I later discovered, was not the case. After a further explanation of my work, which obviously but not deliberately left him with an unclear idea of my methods and precise aims, the Headmaster gave me permission to sit in any class provided teachers had 24 hours notice. It was explained to the teachers that I was interested in the language of the children and not in the teaching *per se*. During the first week I observed a number of classes and also offered to stand in for an English teacher who was absent; I taught 2–3 lessons and was also invited to talk to other English classes. Teachers had the impression I was there only for a short period and wanted me to do a guest-appearance. After 3 days I was expected to help myself to coffee during breaks and one of the teachers began to use the "du" form to me — but she was unusual in this. After the first week there were school holidays. After the holidays I continued observation and only after 3 more days did I realize in conversation with one teacher that nobody had known about my arrival or how long I intended to stay. When a number of teachers realized this, especially the English teachers for whom I had taught, there was sympathy for my situation and a change in the relationship.

Stage 2

The next stage came when I met the assembled pupils of the final year and explained what I hoped to do with them. The Headmaster and one teacher were present and the explanation provided greater understanding among staff as well as pupils. In my first explanation I had attempted to explain the rationale for my methods whereas for the pupils I simply told them what I wanted to do. This taught me to stress the processes rather than the reasons on all other occasions. In the following days two of the teachers showed particular interest in my work, asking me in more detail about it, and they also told me about a meeting they were to address on the issue of teaching bilingual children. On another occasion, a teacher made sure I was involved in the staffroom discussion of one of the pupils' assembly productions. A significant point came in a later discussion with the first two teachers when they spoke about the research work carried out by other academics. They talked about the problems and deficiencies — especially academics' lack of understanding of the minority viewpoint — and in this conversation talked of "them" as if I were not one of that kind of academic. Another significant change in my staffroom relationships took place when I was invited to a party. This led to the use of "du" with more and more colleagues, some of whom simply changed, others made a point of formally changing from "Sie" to "du". From that point on I was given more and more information and help in arranging interviews with pupils.

The first round of interviews was with several groups of 3–5 volunteers. These interviews were not taped since some individuals were reluctant. About the same time, pupils kept a diary for a week, attempting to note their language use and topic and interlocutors. At this stage, I began to revise my original plan to choose a small number of pupils for long, depth-interviews to a plan to interview all of the 29 school leavers. The main reason was that it became clear that there was a wider range of backgrounds and experience than expected and secondly that depth-interviews would not be practically feasible or easy to conduct with pupils whose awareness of their own linguistic behaviour was limited. I also began to look for interviews with older generations. Access was provided to families by teachers and by acquaintances of long standing, but there was some reluctance and response was limited although those who did give interviews were open and usually willing to be taped.

The second round of pupil interviews took place before the summer holidays (cf. Chapter 5) and I was given help in the form of a room, lists of examination times and times of pupils' availability. Most pupils were interviewed, but some were more willing than others, some talked more freely than others. Interviews lasted between 15 minutes and 45–50 minutes.

During the whole of this period and into the next stage, I read many of the minority's publications. In particular I read *Der Nordschleswiger* for the preceding 18 months, but I also consulted the minority's year-books and other annual reports. *En passant,* it is interesting to note that this kind of analysis was entirely familiar to me from my work in literary criticism. Common to both pursuits was the notion that (literary or interview/ observational) text has to be interpreted in context, and that a linguistic relationship exists between text and context.

Stage 3

After the holidays, one teacher was absent for a number of weeks. This had been known in advance and it was arranged that I should take some classes during that period. This was the means of more complete integration into the staff. It was helped by the fact that my returning after the holidays suggested I was certainly going to be present for a consider-able time. I scarcely visited lessons from this point on, which also made me more of a colleague and less an intruder. I could share the usual staffroom discussions about problem pupils and I noticed more open discussion in front of me of the teaching problems that are common to all teachers. Finally, I was invited to take part in the staff outing.

This shift to a more complete teacher role did not have any bearing on the second round of interviews, since the pupils had by now left the school and did not see my change of status. Some of them saw me visit their new school or college, but still as a visitor, who on one occasion gave a guest lesson.

Stage 4

A first draft manuscript was written during the summer holidays. It was written in a form which was mainly aimed at outsiders to the minority but there were remarks and tentative recommendations on the language policy. It was written as explicitly as possible, i.e. with less use of "perhaps", "may", "might", "sometimes" etc. than in the final monograph. My original intention had been to write as descriptively as possible. The inclusion of explicit opinions and recommendations was a result of being often involved in staffroom discussions and of discussion with another academic researcher who had made recommendations in the past. The situation seemed to demand an opinion of all those involved. At this stage then I was more participant than observer. The value of this kind of formulation was that I would not find myself accused later of having dissimulated my analysis and viewpoint. And by stating my points starkly I might provoke comment from teachers on any incipient misinterpretations on my part.

The manuscript was shown to the staff for comment. It was presented after a staff meeting. Attendance at the presentation was not compulsory but there was almost complete attendance, despite the late hour. Two copies in English were left in the staffroom for reading. My presentation included some evaluative statements and replies to questions about the language proficiency of the pupils and the effectiveness of the school in preparing pupils for adult life in Danish society. My role clearly changed at this meeting to that of an evaluator. This role was forced upon me by the questioning more than I wished although I had deliberately made evaluative comments in my introductory remarks and the two topics had often been discussed in the staffroom.

In the few days before the fieldwork period ended, a number of teachers read the draft manuscript. Attitudes towards me again changed. Some teachers thought I had been watching them and the school carefully, i.e. they seemed to have forgotten that I was an outsider, until the text reminded them but their reaction was not hostile. I had reminded them, they said, of things they had known and forgotten, or stopped noticing, and one was pleased because he felt that my work confirmed his own views of problems in the minority schools. I had to ask him not to cite my work at this stage as it was still only preliminary.

Stage 5

The formality of leaving the school changed my role temporarily back to that of a colleague on the staff. The same kind of ceremony took place as when another member of staff had left before the summer holidays. My final departure from the field was marked by a discussion with the Schulrat and an interview with *Der Nordschleswiger*. The publication of the article took place immediately after my departure and, referring to my work, clearly put me publicly in the role of an academic.

Stage 6

Six months later I returned to the school for several days. The purpose was to hear responses to the draft manuscript. The manuscript had been circulated and most teachers had read some of it, and some had read all of it. The Headteacher provided detailed comment on a number of points. Other teachers met at a semi-formal meeting in the Headteacher's house and I explained that this meeting was still part of the whole method and research. The manuscript provoked a lot of discussion but no criticisms of it were made. One teacher said that they were willing to accept my criticisms because they knew me well. The Schulrat made the same kind of comment on another occasion. He was impressed, he said, by the feel for the minority expressed in early chapters, and therefore was all the more willing to ask my opinion on problems. He spontaneously contrasted my method with that of academics working with tests and occasional, short visits. He proposed that I write a report in German which I might present to the teachers in all the minority schools.

The pupils who were interviewed had received summaries in German of Chapter 5 and copies of the chapter were circulated. Only one or two saw the complete chapter. About half the pupils came to the school in their own time to discuss the summary. They were in agreement with most of the summary and made some criticisms. The summary did not however do justice to the nuances of the interviews and some of the criticisms were a result of this.

The purpose of this return to the field was not only to check on the accuracy of my interpretation but also for ethical reasons. It would be impossible to disguise the school to anyone in the minority who reads the monograph. It was important therefore that those involved should be given opportunity to comment. The comments themselves provided further insights, and some changes were made. The most significant point however was that the manuscript was accepted with its criticisms because the author was known to the people involved.

Eventually the role of critic was one which I was encouraged to take. In a sense this was an integral part of the participation, since discussion of the problems and advantages of the minority's schools was frequent in the staffroom and in public meetings. However, although I listened to such discussion I contributed as little as possible and then only in private conversation. My views were given no more weight than anyone else's. The "publication" of my manuscript changed my position. I now became a participant with some recognized expertise and the advantage of being a newcomer/outsider. It was thus possible to ask my opinion and to accept criticism because I had been through the earlier stages of acquiring an insider's view — which had been recognized in the manuscript — before making an outsider's comments.

Stage 7

As a result of the Schulrat's request during my first return to the field, I wrote a report and recommendations (Appendix 3). This report extracted from the main text the point concerning the significance of the teachers in the maintenance of the German character of the school. It also stressed the paradoxical nature of the minority's wishing to preserve its group identity and yet provide pupils with adequate linguistic and cultural capital for them to have successful careers in majority institutions. By stressing the signficance of a constant renewal of the teaching force from Schleswig Holstein and the consequent reinforcement of the schools' German character, the importance of the language could, it was suggested, be played down. Where language should be the focus of attention is in respect of the pupils' bilingualism. It was pointed out that bilingualism is largely ignored or treated as a problem in the schools. Rather than this, it should be treated as a positive personal resource for pupils — not so much as a means of finding employment but as a characteristic which can have positive psychological effects if handled in positive ways. Above all, pupils should be encouraged to be aware of and value their own bilingualism.

In the course of this report, the following recommendations were made:
1. with respect to increasing pupils' life chances in majority institutions
   (a) introduction to Danish socio-economic, political and aesthetic culture:
      - that the subject Contemporary Studies focus exclusively on Denmark, be taught in Danish and possibly be combined with the subject Danish
      - that the subject History should lay more emphasis on Danish history and, possibly, be taught in Danish in appropriate parts
   (b) strengthening of standard Danish:
      - that consideration be given to earlier introduction of standard Danish, preferably in the light of a scientific investigation of the linguistic socialization of pupils in the early years.
2. with respect to pupils' own consciousness of their bilingualism and the positive treatment of bilingualism
   (a) that a bilingual language policy be formulated for the schools
   (b) that there be developed in-service courses for teachers on bilingualism in theory and practice
   (c) that methods be developed for teaching pupils about their own bilingualism, encouraging positive attitudes towards it and making them aware of their socio-linguistic position.

This report was completed and sent to the Schulrat about six months after Stage 6. Approximately eight moths later I was invited to address the teachers' association at their annual general meeting, and gave an oral presentation of the report. After this meeting several teachers requested copies and I had to refer them to the Schulrat who then decided to send copies to all the schools in the minority. He then asked my permission to have the report published in the newspaper *Der Nordschleswiger* and this took place within one month, being given front page prominence in the Nordschleswig section. As this book goes to press, I await further developments and responses to this.

Appendix 2

Übersicht und Zusammenfassung auf Deutsch

1 Nordschleswig und die deutsche Minderheit

In diesem einführenden Kapitel wird die Minderheit, ihre geographische Situation, ihre Geschichte und ihr offizieller Vertreter — der Bund deutscher Nordschleswiger — skizzenmäßig beschrieben. Es wird erstens eine idealtypische Bauernfamilie dargestellt, die in ihren drei Generationen die Minderheit auf verschiedene Weise erlebt. Die Familie existiert nicht, soll aber den Kern des Lebens der Minderheit vertreten, ohne daß die bäuerliche Bevölkerung als einziger Typ der Minderheitenmitglieder gesehen wird. Deswegen werden andere Gruppen kurz erwähnt und ihr statistischer Anteil an der Minderheit aufgezeigt. Die Geschichte der Minderheit wird nicht als historische Darstellung behandelt, sondern als erlebte Geschichte von drei Generationen: die "Großelterngeneration", die die Entstehung der Minderheit im Jahre 1920 noch in Erinnerung hat; die "Elterngeneration", die die Niederlage von 1945 und den Rückgang der Minderheit erlebte; und die "Kindergeneration", die nach 1955 geboren, und in einer Atmosphäre der wachsenden Toleranz erzogen worden ist. Die geographische Lage und die ungleichmäßige Verbreitung der Minderheit in Nordschleswig ist Thema des vierten Teils und zuletzt wird der Bund deutscher Nordschleswiger beschrieben. Es wird hier zum ersten Mal das Paradoxon des dänischen Staatsbürgers deutlich, der sein Bekenntnis zum Deutschtum seiner Umgebung gegenüber sichtbar machen soll. Die Lösung des Paradoxons — und insbesondere wie es in der Schule gemeistert wird — ist ein Hauptthema der folgenden Kapitel.

2 Das Schulsystem der Minderheit

Der erste Teil dieses Kapitels behandelt die gesetzliche Basis der deutschen Schulen: ihre Eingliederung in das dänische Privatschulsystem einerseits und ihre Verbindung mit dem deutschen, vor allem schleswig-holsteinischen Schulsystem andererseits. Folgende Merkmale des Schulsystems werden erwähnt: Finanzierung erstens im dänischen Gesetz verankert und zweitens durch Zuschüsse von der Bundesrepublik; eine Lehrerschaft, die hauptsächlich in Schleswig–Holstein ausgebildet wird; Lehrpläne, die aus dänischen und deutschen Quellen zusammengesetzt sind; die offizielle Formulierung der Aufgaben der deutschen Schule, "eine deutsche Schule" und "eine deutsche Schule im dänischen Staat" zu sein.

Der zweite Teil des Kapitels beschäftigt sich mit der Frage, inwiefern die Minderheitenschule eine deutsche Schule ist, mit deutschem Charakter und deutscher Bildungsphilosophie. Diese allgemeine Fragestellung wird im folgenden Kapitel an dem Beispiel einer bestimmten Schule noch weiter erläutert.

3 Beschreibung einer Schule

Die Schule, die hier beschrieben wird, ist die deutsche Schule Tingleff. Die Beschreibung begrenzt sich auf den besonders deutschen Charakter der Schule, und will nicht als volle Beschreibung der Schule aufgefaßt werden. Die Beschreibung wird in sechs Teilen durchgeführt: der Ort Tingleff, die Schule im allgemeinen, die Schüler, die Lehrer, ein typischer Schultag, und die deutschen Merkmale der Schule. Die Beschreibung enthält viele Einzelheiten, die sich nicht kurz zusammenfassen lassen.

Im letzten Teil werden aber folgende wesentliche Punkte eingebracht. Schülern in der 10. Klasse wurde die Frage gestellt, was sie als deutsch an der Schule empfänden. Sie dachten sofort an die deutsche Sprache, aber dann konnten die meisten nur noch das Fach Geschichte nennen, wobei sie empfanden, daß gewisse Schwerpunkte auf die deutsche Geschichte gelegt werden. Für alle war es aber fast unmöglich, die eigene Schule und ihr Schulleben zu analysieren, weil sie keine andere Schule erlebt hatten und weil sie noch zu eng an ihre Erlebnisse gebunden waren. Zweitens folgt eine Beschreibung des Notensystems und des Verhältnisses zu deutschen und dänischen Prüfungen. Dazu kommen die anderen Veranstaltungen, vor allem Sport und die außerschulische, aber von Lehrern unternommene Jugendarbeit. Drittens werden die Lehrpläne analysiert, vor allem die Fächer Deutsch, Dänisch, Geschichte und Gegenwartskunde. Es wird unter anderem festgestellt, daß sowohl Deutsch als Dänisch als "Muttersprache" unterrichtet werden sollen, ohne daß die implizierten Schwierigkeiten dieser Situation genügend behandelt werden. Dieser Frage wird

eine ausführliche Besprechung gewidmet, in der die Verantwortung der
Lehrer angeschnitten wird, der Zweisprachigkeit ihrer Schüler gerecht zu
werden. Es wird abschließend gesagt, daß es viele Faktoren gibt, die die
Schule deutsch machen, obwohl die Sprache am sichtbarsten ist. Ein
Faktor, der andere miteinander verbindet, ist die Herkunft und Ausbildung der Lehrer. Daß viele Lehrer Deutsch als Muttersprache haben, daß
sie oft deutsche Staatsbürger sind, und daß fast alle eine deutsche
Ausbildung haben und deutsche Beamten sind, sind wichtige Einflüsse auf
die Schule.

4   "Sprache und Kultur" in der Schule

In diesem Kapitel werden Themen wieder aufgegriffen und ausführ-
licher behandelt, die im dritten Kapitel schon als wichtige Merkmale der
Schule erschienen. Es handelt sich um den Sprachgebrauch im täglichen
Leben der Schule und in diesem Zusammenhang um die Fächer Deutsch
und Dänisch. Diese werden besonders betont, weil sie den Schülern und
Lehrern bewußt sind — was bei anderen Merkmalen nicht immer der Fall
ist — und weil sie in der offiziellen Erklärung der Aufgaben der Schule
eine Hauptrolle spielen.

Der Sprachgebrauch wird in drei Kategorien beschrieben: die gesprochene Sprache, die Schriftsprache und Sprache als Schulfach. Die
vorherrschend gesprochene Sprache der Schüler ist wider Erwarten Sønderjysk, der dänische Dialekt Nordschleswigs, obwohl die offizielle
Sprache der Schule Deutsch ist. Die Lehrer bestimmen das Gespräch
zwischen Schüler und Lehrer und bestehen auf Deutsch, ohne daß sie
Einfluß auf die dänische Intonation haben. Mit Mitschülern, die zu Hause
Sønderjysk sprechen, spricht man aber hauptsächlich Sønderjysk, obwohl
die Wahl der Sprache teils von dem Gesprächspartner — der mitunter
Deutsch als Hauptsprache hat — und teils von dem Thema abhängig ist.
Zusammenfassend wird festgestellt, daß die Schüler in der Tat weniger
Deutsch im Laufe des Schultags sprechen, als sie selber glauben. Was die
Lehrer betrifft, wird der erwünschten Norm der Schule meistens gefolgt,
und es wird normalerweise aber nicht ausschließlich Deutsch gesprochen.
Wo das Thema und die Gesprächspartner es erlauben, wird auch Sønder-
jysk gesprochen. Im Allgemeinen findet man bei den Lehrern eine
tolerante Einstellung der gesprochenen Sprache gegenüber.

In der Schriftsprache ist man konsequent. Alles, was die Lehrer lesen
sollen, schreiben die Schüler auf Deutsch, vom Fach Dänisch natürlich
abgesehen. Deutsch wird in allen offiziellen Texten gebraucht, sowie

Briefe an Eltern, ausgehängte Bekanntmachungen u.s.w. Andererseits werden sowohl dänische als auch deutsche Unterrichtsbücher verwendet, wo also die dänische Schriftsprache erscheint. Da viele Schüler verhältnismäßig wenig Deutsch sprechen, dürfte die von ihnen gelesene und auch geschriebene deutsche Schriftsprache eine umso wichtigere Rolle im Prozeß des Spracherwerbs spielen.

Es wird dann die Frage der beiden Standardsprachen als Schulfächer behandelt. Nach dem Lehrplan werden Deutsch und Dänisch muttersprachlich unterrichtet. Die Mehrzahl der Schüler spricht Sønderjysk als Muttersprache und für sie ist die Muttersprachendidaktik in Deutsch nicht angebracht. In der Praxis wird der Deutschunterricht folglich mit einigen Techniken der Zweitsprachdidaktik durchgeführt, obgleich die Lehrer keine derartige Ausbildung haben. Auf ähnliche Weise versuchen die Dänischlehrer Interferenzen vom Deutschen zu verhindern, und sie haben auch mit dem Verhältnis Dialekt-Standardsprache zu tun, wie jeder andere Muttersprachlehrer. Die Stellung der dänischen Standardsprache ist problematisch. Für die meisten Schüler ist sie als zukünftige Sprache am Arbeitsplatz und im alltäglichen Leben in Dänemark notwendig. Ihre Stellung in der Schule kann aber kaum die notwendigen Sprachdomänen abdecken. Ihre Stellung kann aber nicht anders werden, weil sie von der Dominanz der offiziellen deutschen Sprache abhängt, die als das wichtigste und vielleicht einzige Merkmal des deutschen Charakters der Schule betrachtet wird. Dieses Problem wird ausführlich behandelt.

Die Fächer Deutsch und Dänisch schließen auch die Literatur ein. Der Literaturbegriff ist aber nicht in beiden Fächern gleich. Grob gesagt wird die Literatur im Fach Deutsch durch Textanalyse und aus einem historisch-biographischen Sichtpunkt behandelt, während die Entwicklung im Fach Dänisch dazu neigt, unter Literatur auch nichtliterarische und nichtsprachliche Texte sowie Bilder und Werbung einzuschliessen, die eher soziologisch als historisch behandelt werden. Auf diese Weise tragen beide Fächer bei, eine gewisse Kultur im erweiterten anthropologischen Sinne zu vermitteln. Die Vermittlung der dänischen und deutschen Kultur ist das Thema des nächsten Abschnitts, wo festgestellt wird, daß die Schule vor allem eine sprachgebundene Kultur vermittelt. Da die Schule Schüler auf ein Leben im dänischen Staat vorbereiten will, muß man sich fragen, ob genügend Kenntnisse der dänischen Kultur im allgemeinen erworben werden. Im großen ganzen zeigt die Analyse, daß es gewisse Lücken gibt. Insofern Schüler auch eine Einführung in die deutsche Kulturwelt erhalten sollen, entsteht die Frage, was unter "deutsch" zu verstehen ist, ob nordschleswig-deutsch oder bundesrepublik-deutsch oder deutsch der deutsch-sprechenden Länder u.s.w. Die vorläufige Schlußfolgerung, die aus der Beschreibung der Schule zu ziehen ist, deutet darauf hin, daß die Schule weder auf ein Leben im dänischen Staat noch auf ein Leben in der Bundesrepublik ganz vorbereitet.

Im letzten Abschnitt dieses Kapitels werden die Äusserungen der Schüler der 10. Klasse über ihre Sprachkenntnisse besprochen. Die Nuancen ihrer Meinungen sind schwer zusammenzufassen, aber für viele darf das folgende Zitat ihre Situation vertreten: "Ich spreche lieber Deutsch als Hochdänisch (Standarddänisch); ich finde, daß Deutsch mehr meine Muttersprache ist als Hochdänisch, aber meine richtige Muttersprache das ist also Sønderjysk".

5 Die Schulabgänger

Der Inhalt dieses Kapitels ist ein Bericht und eine Analyse von Interviews mit ungefähr dreißig Schülern, die den Übergang der Schule zur Arbeit oder zu einer weiterführenden Schule erlebt hatten. Rund zwanzig dieser Gruppe wurden im letzten Monat ihrer Schulzeit und im ersten Monat zu Beginn der Lehre oder der weiterführenden Schule interviewt. Die zehn anderen hatten die Schule ein bis zwei Jahre vorher verlassen. Ein Teil der ganzen Gruppe bestand aus Schülern, die auf das deutsche Gymnasium aufgenommen wurden, und dadurch einen Kontrast bildeten mit anderen, die in die dänischsprechende Welt übergetreten waren. Die Sprache war für beide Gruppen markant, entweder weil sie jetzt die dänische Standardsprache gebrauchen mußten oder aber weil sie unter einem noch stärkeren deutschen Einfluß kamen. Andere Faktoren haben sich aber auch bemerkbar gemacht, und wurden in den Interviews besprochen. Im Zusammenhang mit der Frage, inwieweit die deutsche Schule auf ein Leben in der dänischen oder deutschen Welt vorbereitet, bieten diese Interviews greifbare Erlebnisse und Meinungen in einem wichtigen Augenblick des Übergangs, ohne daß feste Schlußfolgerungen für die ganze Problemstellung nur aus dieser kurzen Anpassungszeit zu entziehen wären. Die Einzelheiten enthüllen aber gewisse Schwierigkeiten und interessante Erfahrungen, die in einer Zusammenfassung verloren gehen.

6 "Sprache und Kultur" in der Minderheit

Der Ausdruck "Sprache und Kultur" ist nicht nur für die Schule bedeutend, sondern wird auch in der Öffentlichkeit als Grundlage der ganzen Minderheit dargestellt. In diesem Kapitel wird also die Bedeutung des Ausdrucks im Leben der Minderheit ausgelegt, um danach die Stellung der Schule noch einmal in dieser Hinsicht zu betrachten.

Im ersten Abschnitt wird das Verhältnis Kultur — Politik besprochen, und die Frage gestellt, ob die Grundlage der Minderheit nicht eher politisch als kulturell ist. Im zweiten Abschnitt wird der Begriff Kultur behandelt, indem kulturelle Aktivitäten skizziert werden. Es wird festgestellt, daß vieles, was innerhalb der Minderheit stattfindet und ihr ein eigenes Leben verleiht, nicht unbedingt als "deutsch" bezeichnet werden kann. Die "deutsche" Natur des kulturellen Lebens kommt daher, daß Kultur aus der Bundesrepublik durch Fernsehen und durch Tournees und Gastvorstellungen eingeführt wird. Es gibt also eine bestimmte Kulturpolitik, die von dem Bund deutscher Nordschleswiger vertreten, und die im dritten Abschnitt untersucht wird. Es wird hier behauptet, daß trotz der ausführlichen Beschäftigung mit Kultur, die Sprache als maßgebend für die Identität der Minderheit von der Minderheit selber betrachtet wird. Die deutsche Sprache bietet eine Verbindung mit anderen deutschsprechenden Völkern und Volksgruppen, und wird gerade deshalb als maßgebend betrachtet, weil andere Merkmale nicht genügend zwischen der Minderheit und der umgebenden Bevölkerung unterscheiden.

Die Sprache wird, wie oben schon gezeigt, von den meisten Minderheitenmitgliedern nicht als Muttersprache gesprochen, was ein Gegensatz zu manchen anderen Minderheiten bildet. Diese Situation wird also im nächsten Abschnitt von einem soziolinguistischen Standpunkt aus besprochen, und als eine Art Diglossie beschrieben. Aus dieser Analyse kommt die Hypothese, daß die Macht innerhalb der Minderheit nur von gewissen Mitgliedern erworben werden kann, die Deutsch als Muttersprache haben. Es werden einige Informantenaussagen und andere Belege gebracht, um diese Hypothese zu unterstützen.

Im letzten Abschnitt werden die Begriffe "Sprache und Kultur" in der Schule und in der ganzen Minderheit verglichen. Im allgemeinen sind die Parallelerscheinungen offen und klar. Es gibt eine Diglossiesituation in der Schule wie in der Minderheit. Die deutsche Kultur und Natur der Schule wird hauptsächlich aus der Bundesrepublik eingeführt. In einer wichtigen Hinsicht ist die Schule aber anders, nämlich dadurch, daß sie sich auch mit der dänischen Sprache und Kultur befassen muß. Die anderen Teile der Minderheit halten sich möglichst fern von allen Kontakten mit der dänischen Sprache und Kultur, obwohl ein gewisser Kontakt unvermeidlich ist. Die Schule muß aber die einzelnen Schüler auf zwei Welten vorbereiten, während die Minderheit an sich nur eine Welt erlebt. Die Mitte dieses Paradoxons, das schon im ersten Kapitel erwähnt wurde, bleibt die Sprachpolitik und die Angst davor, daß eine Verbreitung der dänischen Sprache die Identität der Schule und der Minderheit angreift. Schließlich wird die Möglichkeit einer Lösung des Problems angeschnitten.

7 Ethnizität, Sprache und Schule

In diesem letzten Kapitel werden die Hauptthemen wieder aufgegriffen, um eine Zusammenfassung in theoretischer Hinsicht darzustellen.

Der erste Abschnitt ist jedoch eine Entwicklung der früheren Kapitel, da das Leben in der Minderheit aus der Perspektive des Einzelnen untersucht wird. Hier werden wieder die Aussagen der interviewten jungen Leute gebraucht, um den Nuancen der Situation näher zu kommen. Die Rivalitäten zwischen Minderheit und der übrigen Bevölkerung sind ihnen zweifellos bewußt, sowie die politische und kulturelle Tätigkeit des Bundes deutscher Nordschleswiger. Dagegen zeigen sie eine gewisse Ungeduld den herkömmlichen Einstellungen gegenüber, und es darf nicht vergessen werden, daß sie auch andere Interessen und Vorstellungen haben, als die der Minderheit. Die Frage der Identität wird in den folgenden Worten eines Jugendlichen ausgedrückt: "Wir sind deutsche Nordschleswiger, nein wir sind Nordschleswiger, also (auf) deutsch (ausgedrückt), die anderen sind Sønderjyder". Man sieht hier noch einmal die Bedeutung der Sprache, aber auch daß die Verwandschaft mit dem Deutschtum in weiterem Sinne nicht so sehr unterstrichen wird.

Im zweiten Teil des Kapitels wird die Frage der Identität und Natur der Minderheit als soziale Gruppe erörtert. Die Definition von einer ethnischen Gruppenidentität wird mit Hilfe der anthropologischen Literatur besprochen, und auf die deutsche Minderheit angewandt. Die Identität einer ethnischen Gruppe wird durch Grenzphänomene (*boundary markers*) fixiert, und in Nordschleswig ist die Sprache und durch sie der Schulbesuch maßgebend. Es wird auch kurz erwähnt, daß andere soziale Gruppenbildungen vor allem auf ökonomischer, klassenmäßiger Basis eine Rolle spielen können, und daß es in Nordschleswig einige Zeichen dafür gibt, daß ethnische Identität durch andere politisch-soziale Phänomene ersetzt wird.

Der Beitrag der Schule zur ethnischen Identität wird ausführlich besprochen, indem behauptet wird, daß die von den Eltern bestimmte Wahl der Schule eine Verlängerung der biologischen Grundlage der ethnischen Zugehörigkeit ist. Die bewußte Entscheidung, daß man zu der Gruppe gehört (*self-ascription*), die das zweite Hauptmerkmal der Identi-

tät ist, kommt also erst nachher, etwa in der Pubertät oder sogar noch
später. Diese Identität bringt gewisse Begrenzungen der sozialen Rollen
mit sich, die dem Einzelnen offen sind, da die Tätigkeit der Minderheit
hauptsächlich hinter den Kulissen des sozialen Lebens der dänischen
Gesellschaft stattfinden müssen.

Die deutsche Minderheit wird auch mit anderen europäischen Minderheiten verglichen, in dem eine taxonomische Perspektive übernommen
wird. Damit kann auch die Verwandschaft mit anderen deutschen Minderheiten erklärt werden. Schließlich wird die Zukunft der Minderheit
untersucht: die Vergangenheitsorientierung jeder ethnischen Gruppe ist
besonders ein Problem für die deutsche Minderheit, da heutzutage die
jungen Leute wenig Interesse daran zeigen. Die Rolle der Schule ist dabei
entscheidend.

Im dritten Teil wird die Rolle der Sprache, die in früheren Kapiteln in
Einzelheiten beschrieben wurde, aus theoretischer Sicht besprochen. Es
wird der Unterschied zwischen Sprache als Kommunikation und Sprache
als Symbol in einer Minderheit eingeführt sowie das Problem, daß in der
deutschen Minderheit die Sprache für einige als Symbol für andere als
Kommunikationsmittel dient. Diese ungewöhnlich stabile Situation verur-
sacht die spezifischen Probleme der Sprachpolitik in der Schule, die in
früheren Kapiteln beschrieben worden sind. Es werden hier also die
Ursachen des Problems untersucht, und die offizielle Haltung analysiert.
Dies führt zu einer Zusammenfassung der Rolle der Schule, wo die
Sprache und Kultur der Minderheit und Mehrheit vermitteln werden
sollen. Die Schwierigkeiten dieser Haltung, die schon früher zum Vor-
schein gekommen sind, stammen daher, daß eine muttersprachliche Beherrschung beider Sprachen und Kulturen verlangt wird. Es wird also
diskutiert, ob dies notwendig und realistisch ist. Die Erwartungen der
Mehrheit, in der der Einzelne seine sozial-ökonomische Stellung finden
soll, werden den Erwartungen der Minderheit gegenübergestellt. Muß der
einzelne sowohl bilingual als auch bikulturell sein?

Im fünften Abschnitt werden die Begriffe Bilingualismus und Bikul-
turalismus mit Hilfe der Fachliteratur besprochen. Die Situation in Nordschleswig ist noch komplizierter, weil es dort drei Sprachvarietäten gibt:
Deutsch, Sønderjysk und Standarddänisch. Es wird von dem einzelnen
verlangt, daß er in gewissen Hinsichten aber nicht auf allen Ebenen
bikulturell wird. Das Ziel der Schule wäre also erreichbar, was die
kulturellen Kenntnisse betrifft. Die Existenz der drei Sprachvarietäten
bedeutet aber, daß die Erwartungen auf sprachlicher Ebene nicht genau
dieselben sind, daß die kulturellen und sprachlichen Domänen sich nicht

genau decken. Es wird sprachlich mehr verlangt, und zwar in der dänischen Standardsprache. Das Mitglied der Minderheit müßte also akzeptieren, daß eine gewisse Beherrschung der für ihn mit negativen Assoziationen verbundenen dänischen Standardsprache unvermeidlich ist, wenn ihm alle ökonomischen und sozialen Gelegenheiten offen stehen sollen. Für die Minderheit bleibt also das Problem der Sprachpolitik der Schule die Folge der Aufgabe, die Schüler auf ein Leben zwischen zwei Kulturen vorzubereiten.

Appendix 3

(Report to the Minority's Education Officer (Schulrat) arising from the text *The Minority School and Ethnic Survival*)

Schul – und Sprachpolitik in den deutschen Minderheitenschulen Nordschleswigs

Die Schlußfolgerungen, die aus dem Text *The Minority School and Ethnic Survival* als besonders wichtig für die Schulpolitik zu entziehen sind, beziehen sich auf zwei Themen: erstens die Rolle der Schule in der Identitätsbildung und die Folgen für die Sprach- und Kulturpolitik der Schule; und zweitens die Zweisprachigkeit als Bedingung und auch als Inhalt der Pädagogik.

Schule und Identitätsbildung

Es wird in dem oben genannten Text mit Unterstützung der Fachliteratur berichtet, daß zwei Hauptfaktoren die ethnische Identität des Einzelnen bestimmen. Der erste Faktor, chronologisch gesehen, ist, daß man durch Geburt und Eltern an eine ethnische Gruppe gebunden ist. Der zweite Faktor heißt "self ascription", d.h. eine Entscheidung des Einzelnen, daß er einer bestimmten Gruppe zugehört. Es wird also folglich behauptet, daß die Schule einen entscheidenden Beitrag zu dem ersten Faktor leitet, weil die Wahl der Schule bei den Eltern liegt und deswegen eine Verlängerung des Prozesses der Identifikation des Kindes mit und durch die Eltern darstellt. In diesem Sinne bildet die Schule die Identität des Kindes weiter, auf eine Weise, die der Situation einer Minderheit eigen ist.

Die Schule bildet aber die Identität auch auf eine zweite Weise weiter, die nicht nur bei einer Minderheitenschule zu finden ist. Jede Schule hilft in dem allgemeinen Sozialisationsprozeß, der in der Familie anfängt und während der ganzen Kindheit von anderen Einflüssen weitergetragen wird. Dieser Sozialisationsprozeß beinhaltet sowohl sprachliche als auch kulturelle Teile, die miteinander eng verbunden sind. Der "kulturelle" Teil besteht aber nicht nur aus einer Einführung in die geschaffenen kulturellen Güter der Gesellschaft – Literatur, Musik u.s.w. wie auch gesellschaftlichen Institutionen – sondern auch und noch wichtiger aus einer Erkennung und Internalisierung der auf die ganze Gesellschaft verteilten und akzeptierten Einstellungen und Kenntnisse des alltäglichen Lebens ("shared meanings" nach Taylor). Die Schule trägt auch durch ihre den Lehrern und Schülern oft unbewußten Werte und tägliches Tun zu diesem Prozeß auf eine bedeutende Weise bei. Der "Ethos" der Minderheitenschule wird also "deutsch", weil die Lehrer "Deutsch" sind, erstens durch ihre Ausbildung in Schule und Hochschule und zweitens zum Teil durch ihre Staatsangehörigkeit und durch ihre eigene Sozialisation während der Kindheit in Deutschland. Diese kulturelle Sozialisation bezieht auch die linguistische Sozialisation ein. Die deutsche Sprache ist nur ein Teil des ganzen Prozesses, jedoch wichtig, weil sie ein Mittel der Formulierung und Kommunikation von Werten und Einstellungen ist. Die Sprache dürfte also nicht aus diesem Zusammenhang herausgeholt werden, um sie als einziges und entscheidendes Kriterium des deutschen Charakters der Schule oder des Sozialisationsprozesses darzustellen.

Daß dies trotzdem passiert, ist aber verständlich, wenn man jetzt die Bildung einer ethnischen Identität für die Gruppe betrachtet. Wie die Fachliteratur zeigt, benötigt eine Gruppe ein sichtbares Zeichen ihrer Identität, um sich von anderen Gruppen und besonders der Mehrheitsgruppe abzugrenzen. Die Sprache wird gewöhnlich als ein solches Abgrenzungsphänomen benutzt. Die Wichtigkeit der Sprache in der Identitätsbildung des einzelnen wird also zugunsten der Identitätsabgrenzung der Gruppe übertrieben.

Für die Schule hat diese verständliche Übertreibung wichtige Folgen. Es wird in dem angegebenen Text gezeigt, daß die Schule unter einer gewissen Spannung arbeiten muß. Einerseits ist sie verpflichtet, die Identität der Gruppe – mit dem Ausdruck "deutsche Sprache und Kultur" formuliert – zu unterstützen andererseits hat sie die Pflicht, Schüler auf ein Leben in dem Staat der dänischen Mehrheit vorzubereiten. Bis jetzt wird diese Spannung zum Vorteil der Gruppe gelöst, d.h. eine Gewichtung der deutschen Sprache und Kultur und eine niedrige Priorität für die dänische Sprache und Kultur. Diese Prioritätssetzung spiegelt den Gebrauch der Sprache als Abgrenzungsmerkmal wider und beinhaltet die implizierte und unerklärte Annahme, daß Sprache die Basis aller Kultur ist, daß Kultur und Sprache nicht geteilt werden können, daß Kultur von Sprache abhängig ist. Was die Schule betrifft, ist aber im Text *The Minority School and Ethnic Survival* behauptet worden, daß diese Annahme und diese Prioritätssetzung weder den Sozialisationsprozeß richtig spiegeln noch den Bildungsbedürfnissen des einzelnen genügen.

Wenn diese Bildungsbedürfnisse erfüllt werden sollen, muß der Unterschied festgehalten werden zwischen der Einführung in die allgemeinen, meist aber nicht nur sprachlich formulierten Einstellungen und Kenntnisse – was ich hier als "sozialkulturelles Bewußtsein" bezeichnen möchte – und der Erwerbung von Kenntnissen der kulturellen Güter der Gesellschaft, zu denen, die formelle literarische Hochsprache gehört; das zweite entspricht dem, was in der Minderheit "Sprache und Kultur" genannt wird. Das soziale Wissen wird in der Schule durch den von den Lehrern abhängigen Ethos als unbewußter Prozeß vermittelt, ist aber die Basis der ethnischen Identität des einzelnen. "Kultur und Sprache" wird im Gegenteil als Teil des Curriculums betrachtet, und bietet einen unentbehrlichen, aber nicht grundlegenden Teil der Identitätsbildung des einzelnen, obwohl es für die Gruppe eine wichtige Abgrenzungsrolle der Mehrheit spielt. Die Erkenntnis dieses Unterschieds läßt den Weg dafür offen, andere Prioritäten einzuführen, ohne daß man befürchten müßte, die ethnische Identität des einzelnen zu schwächen. Wenn der Ethos der Schule bestehen bleibt, können andere Prioritäten im Bereich "Sprache und Kultur" eingeführt werden. Die Erkenntnis dieser Möglichkeit setzt aber eine gewisse Offenheit voraus, die Teil des Bildungsprozesses sein dürfte, worauf ich später zurückkommen möchte.

In diesem Falle würde die Möglichkeit bestehen, mehr dänische "Sprache und Kultur" zu unterrichten, d.h. genügend Kenntnisse der geschaffenen kulturellen Güter wie einerseits Literatur, Geschichte, Hochsprache und andererseits die gesellschaftlichen Institutionen des sozio-ökonomischen und politischen Bereiches. Es erhebt sich also jetzt die Frage, welche Kenntnisse nötig sind und was "genügend" heißt. Nach Fishman und Bullivant darf man annehmen; daß gewisse Kenntnisse ethnisch neutral und sozio-ökonomisch nützlich sind. Obwohl diese Begriffe mit Vorsicht zu gebrauchen sind, deuten sie trotzdem darauf hin, daß solche Kenntnisse der ethnischen Identität des einzelnen und der Gruppe nicht angreifen würden. Sie bieten auch einen Anfangspunkt für eine Untersuchung der Bedürfnisse der Schüler in der nachschulischen Welt der Arbeit und des Zusammenlebens in dem dänischen Staat. Der Frage der Hochsprache muß eine weitere Besprechung gewidmet werden. Der Prozeß der Erwerbung von ausreichenden Sprachkenntnissen muß wegen der Natur des Spracherlernens über längere Zeit laufen, aber auch weil der sønderjyske Dialekt eine weitere und komplizierende Dimension der

Sprachenlage bildet. Es wurde festgestellt, daß die Schüler im 10. Schuljahr eine Entfremdung der dänischen Sprache gegenüber empfinden, die ihre sozio-ökonomischen Chancen beeinträchtigen könnte.

Es entstehen die folgenden Empfehlungen: (I) Einführung in dänische sozio-ökonomische, politische und ästhetische Kultur:
– das Fach Gegenwartskunde beschäftige sich ausschließlich mit Dänemark aus dänischem Standpunkt ohne Vergleich mit Deutschland, und sei von einem Lehrer unterrichtet; der den Inhalt völlig beherrscht und auf Standarddänisch unterrichtet; es besteht auch die Möglichkeit dieses Fach mit dem Fach Dänisch zusammenzulegen, da dies auch dem dänischen Kulturbegriff in dänischen Schulen entspricht.
– das Fach Geschichte beschäftige sich mehr mit dänischer Geschichte als bisher. Es sollte auch überlegt werden, ob die dänische Sprache an entsprechenden Stellen als Unterrichtssprache einzusetzen wäre.
(2) Verfestigung der Kenntnisse der Standardsprache: – es sollte überlegt werden, ob eine frühere Einführung der Standardsprache notwendig ist. Diese Überlegung müßte aber in Zusammenhang mit der Frage der sprachlichen Sozialisation in deutscher Sprache gesehen werden, weil eine höhere Effektivität dieses Prozesses in den ersten Schuljahren die Einführung der dänischen Schriftsprache beeinflussen würde. Bis jetzt wird kaum Rücksicht darauf genommen, daß die meisten Schüler zweisprachig sind.

Eine wissenschaftliche Untersuchung des Spracherwerbs in den ersten Kindergarten- und Schuljahren wäre zu erwünschen, die zum Beispiel die Methoden des MOTET-Projekts in Bradford, England, und der verschiedenen Untersuchungen in Kanada anwenden könnte.

Zweisprachigkeit und Pädagogik

Die zwei Hauptziele der Minderheitenschule – auf deutsche und dänische Sprache und Kultur vorzubereiten – enthalten für den einzelnen Schüler eine implizierte Zweisprachigkeit, die genauer beschrieben aus Bilingualismus und "Bikulturellismus", d.h. Sprach- und Kulturkenntnissen, besteht, Trotzdem wird weder theoretisch noch in der Schulpraxis darauf geachtet, daß Schüler zweisprachig sind. Es wurden einige Unterrichtsmethoden beobachtet, die die seit längerer Zeit in Nordschleswig tätigen Lehrer anwenden, um gewisse Schwierigkeiten zuvorzukommen, aber im großen ganzen ist die Einstellung zur Zweisprachigkeit eher negativ. Das bedeutet, daß die Zweisprachigkeit aus pädagogischer Sicht als eine Notwendigkeit akzeptiert, womöglich aber übersehen und sonst als ein Problem behandelt wird. Sowohl Schüler als auch Lehrer betrachten die Zweisprachigkeit als eine nützliche aber nicht ungewöhnliche Fertigkeit, die in der Spedition u.ä. vorteilhaft sein kann. Die meisten Schüler gebrauchen diese Fertigkeit in der Tat nicht, und lassen ihre Berufswahl kaum von ihrer Zweisprachigkeit beeinflussen. Diese negative Einstellung in der Minderheit im allgemeinen ist ganz verständlich, weil die Zweisprachigkeit normalerweise den ersten Schritt zur Assimilation einer Minderheit bedeutet.

Die deutsche Minderheit ist aber bedeutend anders. Weil sie aus einem sønderjysk-sprechenden und einem deutsch-sprechenden Teil besteht, und weil diese Situation durch die vor allem von beamteten Lehrern erhaltene Verbindung mit dem Schulsystem Schleswig-Holsteins verhältnismäßig stabil bleibt, kann es sich die deutsche Minderheit erlauben, die Zweisprachigkeit direkt zu behandeln. Sie kann es sich erlauben, eine aktive und positive Politik der Zweisprachigkeit zu entwickeln, ohne daß sie die Gefahr der Assimilation dadurch vergrößern würde. Die Assimilation kommt eher von anderen Seiten, unter anderem durch eine Ablehnung der Mitglieder, die glauben, ihre Lebenschancen würden durch ihre unterentwickelte Zweisprachigkeit Schaden nehmen.

Eine positive Zweisprachigkeitspolitik würde andere als kommerzielle Vorteile unterstreichen und fördern. Sie würde sich auf die intellektuellen, erzieherischen und moralkulturellen Vorteile beziehen, die die richtigen Bedingungen in der Umgebung der Zweisprachigkeit erzeugen können. Denn die Fachliteratur zeigt, daß die Einstellung zur Zweisprachigkeit mindestens ebenso wichtig ist, wid die Zweisprachigkeit an sich und die pädagogischen Maßnahmen, die sie fördern sollen. Einerseits gibt es "schlechte" Zweisprachigkeit bei den Imigrantenkindern Westeuropas oder Amerikas; andererseits gibt es "gute" Zweisprachigkeit bei den Kindern der "Immersion Programme" in Kanada oder Wales. Die Grundbedingungen in Nordschleswig sind günstig und ließen sich mit denen in Wales vergleichen; die sozio-ökonomischen Umstände sind gut, das Selbstbildnis der Minderheit und ihrer Mitglieder ist sicher und zuversichtlich. Eine positive Zweisprachigkeitspolitik setzt aber gewisse Kenntnisse bei Lehrern und Schülern – und deren Eltern – voraus.

Die Lehrer müßten die soziologisch- und psychologischorientierte. Theorie studieren, die bei einem erweiterten Niveau und mit vergleichenden Aspekten unterrichtet werden müßte, Sie müßten dazu noch die lokale Situation theoretisch beobachten, und auch die praktischen Probleme der Didaktik der Sprachen und aber auch anderer Fächer untersuchen. Die

Basis einer solchen Weiterbildung wäre in der Fachliteratur, unter den Experten anderer Minderheiten und bei den Hochschulen in anderen Ländern wo Erfahrungen schon existieren. Diese Weiterbildung würde auch einen wichtigen Beitrag zum Unterricht in den ersten Kindergarten- und Schuljahren bringen, wie oben erwähnt wurde. Außerdem müßten die Probleme des Unterrichts bewußt analysiert werden, die daraus entstehen, daß es in derselben Klasse gemischte zweitsprachige und muttersprachige Schüler gibt.

Die Schüler brauchen einen anderen Ansetzungspunkt. Ihre Kenntnisse müßten auf Grund ihrer eigenen sprachlichen Situation in allen Hinsichten entwickelt werden. Sie lernen Deutsch, Sønderjysk, Standarddänisch und mindestens eine Fremdsprache. Sie besitzen also einen Reichtum an linguistischer Erfahrung und unbewußten Kenntnissen, die Unterrichtsstoff bieten würden. Auch ihre Kenntnisse sollen aber soziolinguistische und psycholinguistische Aspekte einbeziehen, damit sie z.B. die Stellung der Sprache als ethnisches Abgrenzungsphänomen verständen. Die Grundlage einer Allgemeinsprachdidaktik, die nicht nur von Sprachlehren praktiziert wären, wäre unter anderem bei der neuesten Entwicklung in der englischen Fachdidaktik zu finden. Die Didaktik der "Language Awareness" findet man bis jetzt am besten von E. Hawkins in seinem Buch *Awareness of Language* (1984) zusammengefaßt.

Die folgenden Enpfehlungen entstehen:
1. die Formulierung einer schulischen Zweisprachigkeitspolitik für die Minderheitenschulen;
2. die Entwicklung eine Lehrerfortbildung in der Theorie und Praxis der Zweisprachigkeit;
3. die Entwicklung einer Zweisprachigkeitsdidaktik, die den Schülern bewußte und positive Einstellungen und Kenntnisse ihrer eigenen Fertigkeiten und sozio-linguistischer Situation beibringen würde.

Bibliography

AGAR, M.H., 1980, *The Professional Stranger*. London: Academic Press.

ALCOCK, A.E. *et al.* (eds), 1979, *The Future of Cultural Minorities*. London: Macmillan.

ANDERSON, A.B., 1979, The survival of ethnolinguistic minorities: Canadian and comparative research. In H. GILES & B. SAINT-JACQUES (eds), *Language and Ethnic Relations*. Oxford: Pergamon.

BAETENS-BEARDSMORE, H., 1982, *Bilingualism: Basic Principles*. Clevedon, Avon: Tieto Ltd.

BARTH F., 1969, Introduction. In F. BARTH (ed.), *Ethnic Groups and Boundaries*. London: Allen and Unwin.

BDN 1982, *Grenzland "82"*. Apenrade: Bund deutscher Nordschleswiger.

BIEHL, H. H., 1960, *Minderheitenschulrecht in Nord- und Südschleswig*. Hamburg: Hansischer Gildenverlag.

BRACKER, J., 1972-73, Die dänische Sprachpolitik 1850–1964 und die Bevölkerung Mittelschleswigs. *Zeitschrift der Gesellschaft für Schleswig Holstein Geschichte*, 97, 127–225; 98, 87–213.

BRANDT, O., 1975, *Geschichte Schleswig Holsteins* (7 ed.). Kiel: Muhlau Verlag.

BULLIVANT, B., 1984, *Pluralism: Cultural Maintenance and Evolution*. Clevedon, Avon: Multilingual Matters.

BURGESS, R.G. (ed.) 1984, *The Research Process in Educational Settings: Ten Case Studies*. London: Falmer Press

BYRAM, M.S., 1981, Minority Schools in the former Duchy of Schleswig, *Journal of Multilingual and Multicultural Development*, 2, 3, 175–82.

— 1985, Language choice in a minority school. *International Review of Education*, 31, 323–34.

COHEN, A., 1969, *Custom and Politics in Urban Africa*. London: Routledge and Kegan Paul.

— (ed.) 1974, *Urban Ethnicity*. London: Tavistock Publications.

DEUTSCHER SCHUL- UND SPRACHVEREIN FÜR NORDSCHLESWIG, 1976, *Materialien zur Geschichte Schleswigs*. Apenrade: Deutscher Schul- und Sprachverein.

— 1983, *Jahresbericht 1982/3*. Apenrade: Deutscher Schul- und Sprachverein.

DE VOS, G. & ROMANUCCI-ROSS, L. (1975) *Ethnic Identity*. Palo Alto, Calif.: Mayfield.

DONALDSON, M., 1978, *Children's Minds*. Glasgow: Fontana/Collins.

EDWARDS, J.R., (1977), Ethnic identity and bilingual education. In HOWARD GILES (ed.), *Language, Ethnicity and Intergroup Relations*, 253–82. London: Academic Press.

EGGER, K., 1977, *Zweisprachigkeit in Südtirol*. Bozen: Athesia.

ELKLIT, J. & TØNSGAARD, O., 1979, Nationalt tilhørsforhold i Nordslesvig, *Acta Jutlandica*.

FLINK, T., 1955, *Sønderjylland siden Genforeningen i 1920*. Copenhagen: J. H. Schultz.

— 1964, Den kirkelige Sproggrænse, *Sønderjyske Aarbøger*, 275–85.

FISHMAN, J.A., 1980, Bilingualism and biculturalism as individual and as societal phenomena, *Journal of Multilingual and Multicultural Development*, 1, 1, 3–16.

GILES, H., BOURHIS, R.Y. & TAYLOR, D.M., 1977, Towards a Theory of Language in Ethnic Group Relations. In H. GILES (ed.), *Language, Ethnicity and Intergroup Relations*. London: Academic Press.

GILES, H. & Powesland, P.F , 1975, *Speech Style and Social Evaluation*. London: Academic Press.

GOODENOUGH, W.H., 1964, Cultural Anthropology and Linguistics. In D. HYMES (ed.), *Language in Culture and Society*. New York: Harper.

GRAS, S. & GRAS C., 1982, *La révolte des régions d'Europe occidentale de 1916 à nos jours*. Paris: Presses universitaires de France.

GREGORY, M. & CARROLL, S., 1978, *Language and Situation*. London: Routledge and Kegan Paul.

GULLICK, C., 1979, Ethnic Interaction and Carib Language, *Journal of Belizean Affairs*, 9, 3–20.

HARGREAVES, D.H., 1967, *Social Relations in a Secondary School*. London: Routledge and Kegan Paul.

HAUSER, O., 1959, Die preussische Sprachpolitik in Nordschleswig, *Schleswig Holstein Monatshefte für Heimat und Volkstum*, 11 April.

HENNINGSEN, A., undated, *Aus einem Leben in zwei Kulturen*. Flensburg: Christian Wolff.

HJELHOLT, H., 1923, *Den danske sprogordning og det danske sprogstyre i Slesvig mellem krigene (1850–1864)*. Copenhagen: Aschehoug.

JAPSEN, G., 1968, *Det dansksprogede skolevæsen i Sønderjylland indtil 1814*. Tønder: Historisk Samfund for Sønderjylland.

KARDEL, H. 1971, *Fünf Jahrzehnte in Nordschleswig*. verlag der heimatkundlichen Arbeitsgemeinschaft in Apenrade Heft 22.

KOMJATHY, A. & STOCKWELL, R., 1980, *German Minorities and the Third Reich*. New York: Holmes and Meier.

KRACHT, H. 1984, personal communication.

KREJCI, J. & VELIMSKY, V., 1981, *Ethnic and Political Nations in Europe*. London: Croom Helm.

LACEY, C., 1979, Problems of sociological fieldwork: a review of the methodology of 'Hightown Grammar'. In M. WILSON (ed.), *Social and Educational Research in Action*. London: Longman.

LAMBERT, W.E., 1967, 'A social-psychology of bilingualism, *Journal of Social Issues*, 23, 91–108.

— 1977, Effects of bilingualism on the individual. In P.A. HORNBY (ed.), *Bilingualism: Psychological, Social and Educational Implications*. New York: Academic Press.

— 1978, Cognitive and socio-cultural consequences of bilingualism, *Canadian Modern Language Review*, 34, 3, 537–47.

— 1979, Language as a factor in intergroup relations. In H. GILES & R. ST. CLAIR (eds), *Language and Social Psychology*. Oxford: Blackwell.

LENZING, H., 1973, *Die deutsche Volksgruppe in Dänemark und das nationalsozialistische Deutschland 1933–39*. Bonn: Rheinische Friedrich-Wilhelms Universität.

MARTENSEN, T-J., 1975, Die Sozialstruktur des Bundes Deutscher Nordschleswiger und ihre Bedeutung für die Assimilationsproblematik. In K.D. SIEVERS (ed.), *Beiträge zur Frage der ethnischen Identifikation des Bundes Deutscher Nordschleswiger*. Flensburg: Akademie Sankelmark.

MIDGLEY, M., 1980, *Beast and Man. The Roots of Human Nature*. London: Methuen.

MINISTRY OF EDUCATION, 1977, *Lov om friskoler og private grundskoler*. Copenhagen: Ministry of Education.

— 1978, *Act on folkeskolen*. Copenhagen: Ministry of Education.

MITCHELL, J.C., 1974, Perceptions of ethnicity and ethnic behaviour: an empirical exploration. In A. COHEN (ed.), *Urban Ethnicity*. London: Tavistock Publications.

NELDE, P.H., 1979, *Volkssprache und Kultursprache*. Wiesbaden: Franz Steiner.

NYBERG, M., 1980, Findes der dialektbarrierer i Danmark, *Dansk Folkemaal*, 22, 2, 1–29.

— 1981, Findes der dialektbarrierer i Danmark (2), *Dansk Folkemaal*, 23, 69–130.

PEDERSEN, K.M., 1977, *Dialekt, regionalsprog, rigssprog – en analyse af børns skolesprog*. Aabenraa: Institut for grænseregionsforskning.

RERUP, L., 1982, *Slesvig og Holsten efter 1830*. Copenhagen: Politiken.

ROHWEDER, J., 1976, *Sprache und Nationalität. Nordschleswig und die Anfänge der danischen sprachpolitik in der ersten Hälfte des 19. Jahrhunderts*. Glückstadt: JJ. Augustin.

SALOMON, K. 1980, Konflikt; Groenseland. Sociale og nationale modsoetninger i Sønderjylland 1920–33. Copenhagen: Gyldendal.

SCHULTE-UMBERG, V., 1975, Das Problem der ethnischen Identifikation am Beispiel von Familie und Schulsystem im Bereich des Bundes Nordschleswiger. In K.D. SIEVERS (ed.), *Beiträge zur Frage der ethnischen Identifikation des Bundes Deutscher Nordschleswiger*. Flensburg: Akademie Sankelmark.

SCHÜTT, H.F. & VAAGT, G., 1975, Die Zeit der nationalen Auseinandersetzungen um Schleswig, *Grenzfriedenshefte*, 1, 129–36.

SIEVERS, K.D., 1975, *Beiträge zur Frage der ethnischen Identifikation des Bundes Deutscher Nordschleswiger*. Flensburg: Akademie Sankelmark.

SØNDERGAARD, B., 1980, *Sprogligt deficit*. Aabenraa: Amstcentralen for Undervisningsmidler i Sønderjylland.

— 1981, Tosprogethed med diglossi – højtysk, rigsdansk, sønderjysk i Nordslesvig, *Danske Studier*, 76, 73–90.

— 1983, Öffnung ja – Identitätsverlust nein?, *Grenzfriedenshefte*, 2 (1983), 84–89.

— 1984, *Sprogfordelingen i det bilinguale Curriculum*. Aabenraa: Amtscentralen for Undervisningmidler; Sønderjylland.

SØNDERJYLLANDS AMTSKOMMUNE, 1983, *Skolevæsenet i Sønderjylland 83/84*. Aabenraa: Sønderjyllands Amtskommune.

SPRADLEY, J.P., 1980, *Participant Observation*. New York: Holt, Rinehart and Winston.

STEPHENS, M., 1976, *Linguistic Minorities in Western Europe*. Llandysul: Gomer Press.

STRUWE, K., 1981, *Denmark: Socio-cultural Information*. Dossiers for the intercultural training of teachers. Strasbourg: Council of Europe.

STUBBS, M., 1983, *Language, Schools and Classrooms* (2nd edition). London: Methuen.

SVALASTOGA, K. & WOLF, P., 1963, *En by ved Grænsen*. Copenhagen: Gyldendal.

TAYLOR, C., 1971, Interpretation and the sciences of man, *The Review of Metaphysics*, 25, 1, 3–51.

TOFT, G., 1981, Politische und kulturelle Konflikte in *Nordschleswig 81*. Aabenraa: Bund deutscher Nordschleswiger.

— 1982, *Die bäuerliche Struktur der deutschen Volksgruppe in Nordschleswig*. Flensburg: Institut für regionale Forschung und Information.

VEJLEDNING DANSK, 1976, *Undervisningsvejledning for folkeskolen 1: Dansk*. Copenhagen: Undervisningsministeriet.

WEIGAND, K., 1966, Die Sozialstruktur der deutschen und der dänischen Minderheit im Jahr 1965, *Grenzfriedenshefte*, 4, 237–47.

WHYTE, W.F., 1955, *Street Corner Society* (2nd edition). Chicago: University Press.

WILLKOMMEN, D., 1975, Zur Stellung der Kommunikation bei den Mitgliedern des Bundes Deutscher Nordschleswiger. In K. D. SIEVERS (ed.), *Beiträge zur Frage der ethnischen Identifikation des Bundes Deutscher Nordschleswiger*. Flensburg: Akademie Sankelmark.

ZEH, J., 1982, Die deutsche Sprachgemeinschaft in Nordschleswig, in *Bonner Beiträge zur Soziologie* Band 19. Stuttgart: Ferdinand Enke.

Index

Aabenraa/Apenrade, regional centre
    13–14
– Gymnasium 104–7
– school 31, 40
Accent 76
– Nordschleswig 43, 47, 67, 97
– Schleswig 43
Accommodation, language 67, 71, 111,
    120–1, 128
Agreements, Bonn–Copenhagen 12–13,
    17, 41, 119, 140
Agricultural society, German 6, 32, 103,
    115, 145
Agriculture:
– careers in 40, 90, 103
– importance to region 13–14
Alcock, A. E. *et al*. 147, 160–1
Attitudes, language 76–7, 82 *see also*
    pupils, Tinglev: percpetions of language
Awareness, language 42, 95–6, 108, 123,
    167

Barth, F. 139–140, 143–5, 147
Biculturalism 158–61
Bilingualism xiii, 24, 58, 63–5, 157–63
– as advantage 33–4, 42, 53, 86, 133,
    170–1
– as disadvantage 56, 62, 86–7
    see also interference language
Boundaries, minority 2, 97, 139–140,
    143–4, 150–1
– and school 148, 154–5
Bullivant, B. 156
Bund deutscher Nordschleswiger 4, 6, 8,
    11, 13
– and career options 40
– and membership of minority 8–9,
    14–20, 101, 134
– and politics 19, 147
– and schools 17
    see also culture

Careers available to minority 33–4,
    39–42, 53, 85–6, 141, 165
– in West Germany 95
Change, linguistic 44 & n.
Choice, language 161
Civil servants, numbers in German
    minority 40
Class, social, and ethnicity 141, 148
Code-switching 3, 69, 71, 95–6, 127
Cohen, A. 139, 145
Colloquial language *see* German:
    colloquial
Commerce:
– careers in 40, 42, 86
– training for 104
Competence, cultural 150–1
Competence, language:
– Danish 73, 76–7, 78, 90–1
– German 56, 63–4, 73, 127, 150–1
– Sønderjysk 68
Content of education, and pupil
    responsibility 46
"Continuation school" (efterskole) 31, 33
Correction, language 67, 72, 74
– written language 73
Crafts, German, lack of 117
Culture, Danish 80–1, 111, 129, 137, 150,
    152–3
– need for increased knowledge of 156–7,
    171
– in schools 23
Culture, German 11, 32–3
– and Bund deutscher Nordschleswiger
    15, 19, 117–18, 128
– indigenous 115–17, 148–9
– and individual 137, 147–8, 150, 159, 162
– and language 18, 48, 56, 112–31, 143,
    158–63
– and maintenance of minority 115–16,
    150
– maintenance in schools 9, 23–4, 26–8,

48, 66, 77–8, 80–1, 128–31, 145, 154
– and politics, see politics
– pupils' views 48–51, 111, 136–7
– see also German, use of; literature:
  German; newspaper, German
  language; policy, language
Curriculum 23–4, 50–1, 64–5, 77, 86, 129
– changes in 149
– German influence 62
– hidden 44, 52–5, 163
– official 55–63
– and West German education system
  25–6
– see also content of education; syllabus

Danish (Rigsdansk) language 152–3,
  159–62
– earlier teaching of 153, 171
– insufficient knowledge of 64, 76–7,
  84–5, 98, 103, 150, 152–4
– status of 84–5
– teaching of 46, 48, 57–8, 62–3, 73,
  74–5, 78–81, 82, 98, 103, 129
– in transitional period 90–1, 98, 107–8
– use by children 41, 42, 70, 76–7, 83–5,
  95
– use by teachers 43, 71, 72–3
– see also culture, Danish; mother tongue:
  Danish as; vocabulary
Denmark:
– German minority in, see minority,
  German; Nordschleswig
– minority loyalty to 11, 17–18, 23–4
Deutsche Jugendverband für
  Nordschleswig (German Youth
  Association for North Schleswig) 54
"Deutscher Schul- and Sprach-verein" 14,
  17, 23, 27, 128, 130–1
– and curriculum 25, 55
– and examinations in German 46–7
"Deutschsprechend" (German-speaking)
  pupils 68, 95
De Vos, G. & Romanucci-Ross, L. 141,
  148
Dialect, attitudes to 46, 76–7, 83–4, 90,
  98, 122, 149; see also Sønderjysk dialect
Diglossia 120–1, 158
Distribution, language 66, 67–71

Education, minority:
– higher education 5, 40, 90, 98, 103
– and ideology of minority 17
– and maintenance of minority
  community xiv, 3, 4–5, 9, 11, 14,
  20n., 21–2, 163

– vocational 2, 5, 40, 104, 150
– see also content; Gymnasium; schools,
  German; Social Education;
  socialization
Edwards, J. R. 22, 151
Elections, see politics/political action
Elklit, J. & Tønsgaard, O. 142–3
English, teaching of 42, 63, 82
Ethnicity:
– behavioural 139
– "bi-ethnicity" 159–60
– cognitive 139, 149
– see also minority: as ethnic group;
  schools, German: and ethnic identity
Evaluation of pupils' work 52

Family, and ethnic identity 89, 100; see
  also parents
Finance:
– support for German minorities 19,
  22–3, 26, 112–13, 118
– village schools 4, 39
Fink, T. 138
Finnish language 87
Fishman, J. A. 142, 158
Flensburg, Pädagogische Hochschule 43,
  66, 80, 164
Formality/informality in schools 43–5,
  49–50, 67, 71, 154
"Frie Grundskolers Faellesråd" (Private
  Schools Joint Council) 27

German, use of:
– in adult society 2, 5, 11, 71
– by children 3–4, 37, 40–1, 66–70, 82–6,
  95–7, 128
– colloquial 67, 85–6, 98
– and educational success 41–2, 103
– as home language 40–2, 43, 71, 94–5,
  100–2, 109–10, 120–3
– and maintenance of minority 64, 72,
  103, 113, 140–1, 143–4
– methods of teaching 73–5, 78–80, 108–9
– in school xv, 5, 9, 10, 30, 40–1, 44–6,
  48–51, 56–7, 62, 75, 82, 154
– in sport 54–5
– as symbol of ethnicity 149–54, 170
– in transition period xiii–xiv, 90, 97–8,
  105–7
– see also Hochdeutsch; language, spoken;
  language, written; mother tongue:
  German as; second language, German
  as
Germany, Federal Republic of:
– careers in 95

- contact with, for German minority 21, 85, 97, 101, 116, 118, 133, 144, 154
- Danish minority in xi–xii
Goodenough, W. H. 159
Gymnasium, German 13, 40, 42, 89–92, 104, 111
- German nature of 105–7

Haderslev/Hadersleben, minority in 31
Handbook, see yearbook, school
Handelskole (Danish Commercial College) 90–1, 93, 104, 107–11, 153
"Haussprache" (language of the home) 94–8, 100, 105
Headteacher, role and responsibilities of 45, 131
History, teaching of 51, 55, 58–61, 81, 148–9, 171
Hochdeutsch (standard German) 43, 63, 67, 72–3, 85, 98; see also German, use of

Identity, ethnic, see ethnicity; minority, German
Imperialism, on school syllabus 60–1
Interference, language 56, 63, 67, 69, 77, 96
- in Danish 46, 75, 83, 91, 111
- in German 74
- in Sønderjysk 83, 108
Intolerance, minority experience of 2, 10–12, 99, 138
Intonation, Nordschleswig 67, 85

Kin-culture 147, 154
Kindergärten:
- German 3–4, 6, 31, 33
- use by majority 29, 32
Komjathy, A. & Stockwell, R. 141
Krejci, J. & Velimsky, V. 145–7

Lambert, W. E. 162
Language, minority, see German, use of
Language, spoken:
- of pupils 66–70, 73, 91
- of teachers 71–2
Language, written 72–3, 78, 91, 96, 154; see also literature
Literature:
- Danish 78–81
- German 78–81

Maintenance, language xiii; see also German: and maintenance of minority

Majority, Danish:
- attitudes of 162
- and minority children xiii, 32, 100–1, 150
Marker, boundary, see boundaries, minority
Martensen, T.-J. 40
Materials, teaching:
- Danish 45–6, 51, 53, 61, 62, 73, 75
- German 53, 61, 62, 74, 118
methodology, ethnographic 29, 164–71
methods, teaching 25, 72, 74–5
Midgley, M. 132
minority, German:
- as ethnic group 19, 138–54, 170, see also schools, German
- as ethno-linguistic community 146, 149–54, 163, 165
- history of 61–2, see also Nordschleswig: history of
- identity, ethnic, sense of 21, 82–3, 99–104, 107, 109–11, 113, 118, 134–6, 158–60
- and the individual 19–20, 132–8, 140–4, 147–8, 149, 155–6, 158–9
- and majority society xiii, 1–3, 102, 141–2, 145
- membership of 7–9, 11–12, 14–15, 17–20, 29–30, 64, 87, 89–90, 92–3, 132–8, 140
- numbers 7, 15, 20n., 31, 134
- social institutions of 6–7, 32, 63, 101, 132, 143–5
- see also boundaries, minority; German, use of; Tinglev/Tingleff
Mitchell, J. C. 139
mother tongue:
- Danish as 57–8, 74–5, 152–3, 157
- German as 56–7, 58, 63–4, 65, 72, 73–4, 86, 109, 150, 157
- Sønderjysk as 57, 58, 82, 86
Music, German influence on 51, 62–3, 81

Nationalism:
- Danish 134
- on school syllabus 60
Needs, pupil 129–30, 152, 159
Newspapers, Danish language 6
Newspapers, German language 5–6, 9, 14, 17, 83, 98, 144
- and German culture 115, 119–20, 147
Nissen 113
Nolde, Emil 117
Nordschleswig:
- geography of 1, 13–14

– German minority in   xi–xiii, 1–5, 17–18,
   113
– history of   10–13, 17, 32, 119, 148–9
– see also education

Parents:
– and curriculum   64
– and ethnic identity   142–3, 155–6
– relationship with schools   4, 6, 27
– see also family
People, German, concept of   118–19, 138,
   146; see also Germany, Federal
   Republic of
Performance in German   47
Policy, language:
– and minority culture   117–20, 129–30
– in schools   67, 77, 151–2, 168, 171
Politics/political action:
– and culture   112–13
– and ethnicity   107, 141, 147
– and language   122–7
– political party   6, 9, 15, 19, 118
– in school   50–1, see also Social
   Education
– see also Bund deutscher
   Nordschleswiger; Schleswigsche Partie,
   die
Priest, German   31
Pronunciation   43, 46, 76, 109; see also
   accent
Pupils, Tinglev:
– career choices   39–42, 53
– origins of   39, 165
– perceptions of curriculum   59, 61, 62,
   79–80
– perceptions of identity   134–7
– perceptions of language   70, 76, 82–8,
   95–111
– see also language, spoken

Qualifications, school-leaving, recognition
   in Germany   52–3

Radio, West German   9
Reading, teaching of   58, 75
Referendum, 1920   10, 30–1
Religion   138, 151, 161

Schleswig, history of   10–13, 60–2; see also
   Nordschleswig
Schleswigsche Partie, die (German party)
   31, 118, 135, 145;
– see also politics: political party
Schools, German   20–8, 29–65
– aims of   21–6, 48, 56, 58, 64, 75, 78,

   80–2, 118, 128–9 137, 156–8, 160
– closure of   4–5, 11, 39
– and ethnic identity   3, 154–8, 160, 163
– as focus for community   4, 34, 64–5, 89,
   90, 100, 112, 128, 140–3, 148–51
– German character of   48–51, 58–9, 65,
   75–8, 87–8, 107, 130–1, 132, 149–50,
   170
– and language   123–4
– and links with West German education
   systems   24–8, 34, 43, 52–6, 162
– pupil attitudes to   91–2
– public examinations   13, 23, 46–7, 52,
   55, 75, 79, 152–3
– size   4–5, 39
– see also culture, German; curriculum;
   education, minority; Gymnasium;
   language, spoken; language, written;
   teachers; Tinglev/Tingleff; yearbook,
   school
Schulte-Umberg, V.   21, 100
Second language, German as   57, 64, 74,
   81, 86, 109, 150, 157
Separation, language   46
Shift, language   xiii, 95, 151, 161–2
Sievers, K. D.   15, 121
Social Education   46, 50–1, 53, 55, 58, 72,
   81, 129
– and creation of local identity   149
– and Danish culture   171
Socialization, as aim of minority schools
   xii–xiii, 21, 81–2, 150, 154, 156, 171
Sønderborg/Sonderburg, minority in   31
Søndergaard, B.   71, 146, 164
Sønderjysk dialect   2–3, 4, 10–11, 32,
   75–6, 125, 151–2, 157, 159–61
– as home language   41–2, 57, 58, 70,
   82–3, 95–6, 101, 120–2, 127
– in transitional period   90, 97–8, 104–8,
   111
– use by schoolchildren   36, 37, 44, 46,
   62, 63, 64, 68–70, 84–5, 102, 128, 154
– use by teachers   43, 71, 128
– see also mother tongue
Spelling, interference   56
Sponsorships   118, 144
– and education   26, 34, 39, 53, 112–13
– and sport   53
Sports:
– and links with West Germany   53
– and maintenance of minority   15, 101,
   115, 120, 145
– teacher involvement in   31, 43, 54
Svalastoga, K. & Wolf, P.   xii, 20n., 32,
   40, 142

Syllabus, official (Lehrpläne) 55–63, 74–5, 78, 81; *see also* curriculum

Taxonomic approach to minorities 145–7
Teachers:
– careers in teaching 40, 43
– children of 40–1, 47, 65, 68, 70
– and German character of school 170
– and German language 83, 125–7, 149, 154–5
– and local institutions 31, 43, 114
– residence 39
– and sport 54
– and syllabus 55, 62, 64–5
– teacher-pupil relationships 5, 25, 44–5, 49–50, 66–7, 111
– typical day 45–8
– and West German education system 24–5, 27, 32, 43, 52, 65, 77, 106–7
– *see also* language, spoken; training, teacher
Television:
– Danish 4, 85
– German 3–4, 5, 9, 83, 86, 98, 101, 116, 144
Timetables, fixed 47
Tinglev/Tingleff 30–2
– school 31, 32–65, 82, 128, 131, 165
– social institutions 143
– typical day 45–8
– *see also* pupils
Toft, G. 8, 15, 31, 40, 100, 121, 126, 135

Tolerance, and minority indentity 7, 19
Tønder/Tondern, minority in 31–2, 40, 43
Training, teacher 25–6, 43–4, 61, 74, 80, 130
Transition period, language use xiii–xiv, 165, 167
– for former pupils 89–93
– for recent pupils 94–111
Transport, to school 35–9
Trilingualism 58, 159

Use, language 94–7, 152–3, 166; *see also* Danish, use of; German, use of; Sønderjysk dialect

Varieties, language 66, 75–6, 82, 85–6, 121
Vocabulary, Danish 91, 98
Vocational training, *see* education

Weigand, K. 8
West Germany, *see* Germany, Federal Republic of; schools, German
Whyte, W.F. 164
Willkommen, D. 40–1, 135

Yearbook, school 33–4, 86
Youth clubs, youth work:
– and ethnic identity 101, 103, 120, 128
– teacher involvement 31, 43–4, 54
– *see also* sport

Zeh, J. 135